Alvaro del Portillo
Bishop Prelate of Opus Dei

Alvaro del Portillo
Bishop Prelate of Opus Dei

◆

Salvador Bernal

Little Hills Press ◆ Scepter Publishers

This edition is published by
Little Hills Press Pty. Ltd.
37 Alexander Street
Crows Nest NSW 2065
Australia
Fax +612 9438 5762
Tel +612 9437 6995
email: info@littlehills.com

ISBN 1-86315-134-6 (paperback)
ISBN 1-86315-135-4 (hard cover)

First published in Spanish by Ediciones Rialp as *Recuerdo de
Alvaro del Portillo, Prelado del Opus Dei* in 1996.

©Scriptor, S.A., 1996.
©Spanish edition, Ediciones Rialp, S.A., 1996.
©English edition, Little Hills Press Pty. Ltd., 1999.

Published in the United States of America by
Scepter Publishers, Inc.
P.O. Pox 1270
Princeton, NJ 08542
United States of America
Fax (609) 683-8780
email: general@scepterpub.org

ISBN 1-889334-18-9 (paperback)
ISBN 1-889334-17-0 (hard cover)

Contents

About the author

Salvador Bernal is most widely known as the author of the first published biography of Blessed Josemaría Escrivá de Balaguer, *Apuntes sobre la vida del Fundador del Opus Dei* (published in English as *Profile of Monsignor Josemaría Escrivá*). First appearing in 1976, this book has sold over 100,000 copies in Spain alone, and has been translated into English, French, Italian, Portuguese, German, Dutch, Japanese, and Polish.

From 1976 to 1994, Salvador Bernal had the opportunity to spend many hours with Don Alvaro del Portillo, who in 1975 was elected to succeed Blessed Josemaría as head of Opus Dei. This book is a loving portrait drawn on the basis of his own many personal experiences, as well as an abundance of previously unpublished testimonies from others.

Born in Segovia in 1941, Salvador Bernal has lived mostly in Madrid. He has doctoral degrees in law (Barcelona, 1968) and in journalism (Madrid, 1969). From the late fifties on, he has had many articles and essays published in various newspapers and magazines. Currently he is president and chief editor of the Madrid publishing company Aceprensa.

Introduction

In the early hours of March 23, 1994, Bishop Alvaro del Portillo, the Prelate of Opus Dei, died in Rome. I heard the news a bit after nine in the morning and soon found myself drafting an article which had to be sent to a newspaper in Madrid before five in the afternoon. But despite the pressure, my heart was filled with the same feelings I had had on June 26, 1975, when Monsignor Josemaría Escrivá died. I was even writing similar words, as I found when I reread a column I had written back then, almost twenty years before, entitled "Changing Tears into Prayer."

"We cry when someone dies; we feel sorrow, our heart is grieved, and everything is filled with bitterness," Saint Augustine wrote in his *Confessions*. How well he knew the contradictions of the human heart, and the powerlessness of created things to satisfy its hunger for happiness. There were no better words to describe the pain I felt that morning in March. And it grew even sharper as the realization began to sink in that I would never again see the lovable face of this man who, though worn out by a thousand battles, constantly lavished affection on people and never lost the youthfulness of love.

From 1976 to shortly before his death, I spent many hours at his side. With others, I spent many summers with him, both at work and in times of recreation, far from his usual daily round in Rome; and often I also went there, to the Eternal City, to work on projects he entrusted to me. And so, very soon after his death, I felt I just had to make the affable but strong character of Alvaro del Portillo widely known. Especially since he had always tried his best to hide himself away, even to the point of disappearing behind the founder of Opus Dei. He was indeed "a most faithful son and successor to Blessed Josemaría," to borrow a phrase from the prayer approved by the Vatican for private devotion to him.

In October 1976 my *Profile of Monsignor Josemaría Escrivá* was published, and this book has been widely read. Hence, in presenting now this book about Don Alvaro, I want my readers to understand that I am trying to describe his personality primarily from memory, on the basis of my own experiences, though obviously I will have to mention other events and facts as well. What I have to say is organized around important moments in Don Alvaro's biography, but it is particularly inspired and supported by episodes of which I myself was a witness.

I must give another warning: These pages presuppose a certain knowledge of the history of Opus Dei and its founder. I have only included whatever details might be necessary to form a framework for my own impressions. Later on, if necessary and when possible, this memoir will be supplemented with further testimony—in the form of published books, documents, and so forth—and with the autobiographical details which crop up in the writings of Don Alvaro himself. But the latter, I feel safe in predicting, will be few and far between. If he ever spoke about himself, it was just for the sake of a good laugh, or else because not doing so would have made it more difficult to articulate exactly and faithfully a particular trait of the founder. For there can be no doubt that the human and Christian virtue of fidelity, which in him was both innate and heroic, summed up the life of Alvaro del Portillo.

Furthermore, I have tried to keep in mind an idea I learned from him in August 1976, when he himself was doing historical research. He wanted, he said, to reflect how Monsignor Escrivá had lived the theological and moral virtues *in crescendo,* in the different stages of his life here on earth. To achieve this, he believed, it would of course be very important to narrate actual events. But one would also have to avoid the danger—especially for those who had come to Opus Dei only a short time before, or who had not known the founder personally—of ending up giving just a series of anecdotes and not an overall vision of his profoundly Christian vision and his deep sanctity.

Such care must especially be taken by anyone writing about Alvaro del Portillo, because his life was imbued with that "charism of normality" which characterizes all those humble people who reach the summit of perfection without doing anything out of the ordinary. One night in 1985, at Solavieya, a conference center in the Spanish province of Asturias, I jotted down in my diary these words: "Another day, all very ordinary, with that feeling of serenity—filled with prayer and with work—that you always get when you're near Don Alvaro." He was the very incarnation of the lay spirituality of Opus Dei. So much so, in fact, that in his presence there came to mind these words from Blessed Josemaría about the Blessed Virgin: "Mary sanctifies the ordinary everyday things—what some people wrongly regard as unimportant and insignificant: everyday work, looking after those closest to you, visits to friends and relatives. What a blessed ordinariness, that can be so full of love of God!" (*Christ Is Passing By,* no. 148).

When I think of Don Alvaro, there come to my mind some really paradoxical ideas: supernatural naturalness, everyday heroism, extraordinary normality. But I honestly do believe that his cooperation with the grace of God transformed the most commonplace, nondescript circumstances of everyday life into something holy, or even divine. To borrow the words of Opus Dei's founder, he translated the prose of everyday life into heroic verse. He put beats and accents of eternity on ordinary existence, even on the very smallest things. And he did everything with a deep humility which overflowed into meekness and self-forgetfulness. Once again we are faced with the paradoxical effect that men and women of God have on others. They try to hide themselves away so that only Jesus shines forth (to borrow, again, the words of Blessed Josemaría), and yet their humility speaks so loudly that many souls find the path to God by following the sound of it.

Some time has now elapsed since his death, and among those who knew him the consensus is unanimous: Alvaro del Portillo was fundamentally a man of extraordinary faithfulness, goodness, and affection. Upon receiving the first Polish-language prayer cards for private devotion to Don Alvaro, Monsignor Stanislaw Dziwisz, secretary to Pope John Paul II, made a spontaneous comment that says it all: "How good the Prelate was!"

I shall always remember the peace and tranquillity in which he lived, and which he inspired in others. These were always clear signs of his union with God. But when I saw that he still possessed that same goodness and equanimity, that phenomenal serenity, even in his advanced years, I began to suspect that it was not so much a matter of temperament as it was the result of spiritual struggle. It was a victory of will and intellect—the victory of a will and an intellect which were docile to divine grace—over the natural tendencies of a very energetic personality. This is what I've tried to show throughout these pages: that Don Alvaro was a most faithful man of peace, even in the midst of the most serious difficulties; that he was friendly and firm, loyal and patient, demanding and strong, daring and full of courage, hard on himself and understanding with others. These features formed a very attractive image of an exemplary pastor in the service of the Church.

1

An Unexpected Call from God

On July 6, 1993, I was with Don Alvaro; he had just come from Rome to spend some time in Spain. It was the eve of the fifty-eighth anniversary of the day on which he had asked to be admitted to Opus Dei. When we mentioned this, he responded so quickly that it was obvious he had already been thinking about it. "How many years it has been!" he exclaimed. "What an account I must render to the Lord God! How much you have to help me!"

The next morning, after Mass, we again spoke of that Sunday, July 7, 1935, when he had first taken part in a day of recollection given by Father Josemaría Escrivá. It was in the Ferraz Street residence for university students in Madrid. Don Alvaro did not remember exactly what time it was when he asked to be admitted to Opus Dei, but he did remember that it was after the second morning meditation. (At that time, for these monthly days of recollection, the founder gave three meditations in the morning and two in the afternoon.) And with a twinkle in his eye, he commented that the fellow who asked him whether he would like to join had made a mistake, because Father Josemaría had told him to wait until the afternoon to make that suggestion. But, he said, the founder "gave a meditation about love for God and love for our Lady which left me aglow."

He seldom said much more about that new restlessness which the Holy Spirit had put into his soul. But he did say that it was what caused him to begin his "true" existence. And on one occasion he said that nothing in July 1935, nor in the months before, had given him any inkling that God was about to call him to Opus Dei. He had grown up in a Christian environment, he received Holy Communion almost every day, and he said the rosary daily, but he was not a fellow who leaned towards pious associations or Church groups. He used to summarize the whole process as "the story of the confident and persevering prayer of our founder, who during some four years, without even knowing me—he did this just because one of my aunts had spoken to him about me—prayed that our Lord would grant me this great gift. And it was indeed the greatest gift, after the faith, that God could have given me."

That aunt, Carmen del Portillo, was also his godmother. She lived with her sister Pilar in the same building, on Conde de Aranda Street in Madrid, in which Alvaro's family lived. Both of them single and deeply Catholic, Carmen and Pilar had in their home a private chapel, with nice wood carvings of Saint Joseph and of the Immaculate Conception. They did a lot of charitable work, especially in connection with the Foundation for the Sick, which was run by a religious order called the Apostolic Ladies of the Sacred Heart. And they were very close to a Jesuit priest named José María Rubio, who was closely connected with a foundation started by Luz Rodriguez Casanova, and who in 1985 was beatified. Soon they also became acquainted with Blessed Josemaría Escrivá, who at that time was the chaplain at the Foundation for the Sick, and they spoke to him about their nephew. And from then on, he prayed for him.

But Alvaro was destined to meet the founder of Opus Dei not through his aunts, but through Manuel Pérez Sánchez, a classmate at the civil engineering school in Madrid. Manuel, who was a few years ahead of him, had gotten him involved in the social work carried out by civil engineering and architecture students in the Society of St. Vincent de Paul.

When Alvaro took an interest in this apostolic venture, Manuel gave him a thumbnail sketch of how the Society operated in general, and, in particular, at the parish of San Ramón, which was in a suburb called Puente de Vallecas. That parish had one St. Vincent de Paul group, or "conference," which consisted of several older persons and five or six university students; this conference met in a building called La Acacia. But to step up the pace of the Society's work, there had also been created another conference that was just for young people. One member of that group, Guillermo Gesta de Piquer, recalls that the parish of San Ramón was in a slum district, where people lived in shacks made of sheet metal and cardboard. The Society of St. Vincent de Paul offered various kinds of help, such as cash, food stamps, medicines, and medical care.

After talking with Manuel, Alvaro began to attend the Saturday afternoon meetings at the central house for the conferences, which was on Verónica Street. First they all did some spiritual reading, and then they each reported the results of the visits they had made in the previous week, and mentioned the needs they had observed. Together they considered how best to care for the individuals or families they would be visiting in the following week. They always went in pairs, and often Alvaro and Manuel went together, since they were going to the same school. "Right from the start," Pérez recalls, "I could see Alvaro's wholehearted dedication to that work, and especially his love and compassion for the children."

Others in the group included Angel Vegas, Alfredo Piquer, and Blessed Jesús Gesta de Piquer (Guillermo's brother), who was martyred in 1936. Angel Vegas mentions also Carlos Valdés Ruiz, César Granda, Florencio Caballero, José María and Alfonso Chico de Guzmán (Alfonso was the

Marquis of Campillo), and their cousin Rafael Moreno. These were all university students, working towards different degrees. But this work of theirs took them all to the most distant suburbs of Madrid, to people who lived in subhuman conditions and who often were hostile towards the Church.

Angel Vegas, who became a professor of political science and economics at Universidad Central in Madrid, has very fond memories of that whole group, because it was so full of spiritual and physical energy. But he remembers being particularly surprised by Alvaro del Portillo. "Here was someone with a lot of social and intellectual prestige," he says, "and he was truly exemplary in this work that he did with needy people. I say that he surprised me because he was one of the most outstanding students at the school, but at the same time he was a very friendly and simple fellow. He was very intelligent, cheerful, refined, down-to-earth, and kind, but above all—this is what really got my attention— profoundly humble. His extraordinary humility made deep impressions on others—impressions of affection, of goodness, of love for God."

The times, of course, were hardly idyllic. As a witness to that, there is Mercedes Santamaría. I made her acquaintance in La Granja (in Segovia) in the fifties, at which time her hair was quite white and her bearing regal. But she had worked in the del Portillo household in Madrid for many years, and she was the mother of Carmen Fernández, who had at one time been a student of my mother's—my mother taught school in La Granja. And Carmen had worked in my parents' home till she got married. Anyway, some years later, when Mercedes learned that I was a member of Opus Dei, she spoke to me with great affection about Don Alvaro. "Now he is working in Rome, next to the Pope," she kept saying, as she proudly showed me a photograph of him with Pope John XXIII and Monsignor Escrivá.

Mercedes had very clear memories of what Don Alvaro

was like in the thirties. One of her most vivid memories was of a Sunday when he came home with a ghastly head wound, and with his jacket soaked in blood. This happened— I learned this from someone else—on February 4, 1934. His parents had gone out for the evening, and so, not wanting to frighten his little brothers and sisters, he just said he had taken a fall. And that didn't seem to her at all unlikely, since it was snowing in Madrid that day. But when she saw how deep the cut was, she insisted on going with him to a clinic, on Claudio Coello Street.

The cure was worse than the disease, as Mercedes immediately suspected it would be, because the doctor's assistant directly applied to the wound the contents of a tube which he had been carrying, already open, in his pocket. The wound became infected, and Alvaro came down with a high fever. For quite a while he had to go to a doctor every day for treatment. It must have been painful, but he never complained.

Alvaro continued to be not very forthcoming about what had happened. But finally his family found out that he, together with some of his friends, had been attacked while on their way to San Ramón, to teach catechism. That Sunday, a group of about fifteen was lying in wait for them, to beat them up. Obviously it had all been set up well ahead of time, because people were leaning over their balconies, ready for the fun. Alvaro took a heavy blow on the neck with a monkey wrench. One of the other fellows nearly had his ear torn off. "But it could have been worse," Don Alvaro offhandedly told us one day in 1987, in Manila. "We happened to be near an entrance to the subway. We took refuge in there as soon as the next train arrived; we got on the train, closed the doors, and got out of there."

God made use of Alvaro's generosity towards the poor in those slums of Madrid to guide him towards Opus Dei. One day in 1935 he noticed that three or four of his friends were having what seemed to be a very interesting chat about something. It piqued his curiosity, so he asked them what they were talking about. "Father Josemaría Escrivá," they said, "and the apostolic work he's doing." So he asked them to introduce him to Father Josemaría. Many years later, Manuel Pérez Sánchez can still describe the scene down to the last detail. They were, he says, on their way to Arroyo del Abronigal; they were going there to visit a poor family. They were walking through some fields of wheat and barley, in what is now the district of La Estrella. It was there that he first spoke with Alvaro about the founder of Opus Dei— "the Father," as they used to call him—and invited him to meet him.

Up till then, though he was leading a full Christian life, Alvaro had seldom had much to do with priests, nor had he noticed any sign that he might have some special call from God. But his very first conversation with Blessed Josemaría made a deep impression on him. This is what he said one day in 1975, in Rome: "He asked me right away, 'What is your name? Are you that nephew of Carmen del Portillo?' She was my godmother, and she was my father's sister, and she had died at a ripe old age after having helped the Father a lot when he was visiting the sick in the poorest areas of Madrid. And since she was my godmother and also my aunt, she had told the Father that she had a very bright nephew. So the Father remembered me—and even remembered something else she had told him about me. When I was little, she said, I liked bananas (*plátanos*) very much, but I couldn't say the word quite right; I would say 'bamamas' (*palátanos*). So the Father added, 'Then you're the fellow who likes bamamas so much?'"

That little anecdote notwithstanding, Alvaro sensed from this brief interchange—this conversation that couldn't have lasted for more than five minutes—that the founder of Opus Dei took him seriously and had a great affection for him. The founder very graciously suggested that they get together for a longer conversation, he took out his appointment book, and they made an appointment for four or five days later.

But when Alvaro arrived, Father Josemaría was not there. "He stood me up," he said years later, with a twinkle in his eye. "It seems that he had suddenly been called to tend to someone who was dying, and he couldn't reach me because I hadn't given him my phone number."

Nonetheless, the young priest had made a deep impression on Alvaro. So some time later, when the 1934–35 school year had already ended, he decided to look him up and say good-bye to him before taking off for vacation. Father Josemaría, he said, "let me come in, and we had a nice, leisurely talk about many things. And afterwards he said, 'Tomorrow we'll be having a day of recollection'—it was Saturday when he was saying this—'so why don't you stick around and make it with us before leaving for your vacation?' I didn't dare say no, but I wasn't very enthusiastic about it, since I didn't know what it was all about."

It was during that day of recollection in the Ferraz Street residence that he suddenly and clearly perceived a divine call—one that he had not at all foreseen—and decided to commit his life to Opus Dei. The founder told him to write a few lines to that effect. This was, I'm sure, his first time to address Blessed Josemaría as "Dear Father," but all he told us years later was this: "I wrote four lines in true engineer style. I started off by saying, 'I know the spirit of the Work, and I want to ask admission'—something like that."

Three months before, on March 11, Alvaro had celebrated his twenty-first birthday.

The Father, despite the exhausting schedule he already had at that time in 1935, devoted many hours to teaching Alvaro the fundamentals of the spirit of Opus Dei. Since by then the classes he was giving for young people were well under way, the Father put together a course just for him, so that he could learn the basics of this plan right away.

For his part, Alvaro postponed his summer vacation. In August he visited his family in La Granja, while the founder remained in Madrid. He stayed in La Granja for some time, much of which he spent doing apostolate with his friends. To one of them he explained the vast panorama of Christian life in ordinary things that is opened up by the spirit of Opus Dei. One or two of them then decided also to join Opus Dei. In the September issue of *Noticias* (a few mimeographed pages sent out as ongoing support to those who had received their formation at the Ferraz Street residence), we read that Alvaro "successfully dedicated himself in La Granja to the famous fishing of which Saint Mark speaks in the first chapter of his gospel."

Starting from July 7, 1935, the life story of Alvaro del Portillo can be summed up in a single phrase: fidelity to his Christian vocation in Opus Dei. From the very first moment, he was well aware that his "yes" to God in this matter meant for him a lifelong commitment. In August 1991, in Barcelona, I heard him exclaim, "Lord, how good you are! How good you are for choosing me—me, out of so many people, when I'd done nothing to deserve it!"

Like that initial decision, his perseverance was profoundly free, but it could and eventually would coexist with an absence of feelings or natural enthusiasm. Just before the fiftieth anniversary of his having joined Opus Dei, Don Alvaro confessed in all simplicity that he had learned this lesson early on. "As usually happens with beginners," he said, "our Lord gave me at the start not only a deep spiritual joy, but also a great feeling of enthusiasm for the vocation which I had received. As the months went by, this human component began to fade away, leaving only that supernatural enthusiasm which must always be at the root of our perseverance. I told our Father about this, and he understood perfectly. In fact, he used this confidence of mine as the basis of one of the considerations he wrote to help all his children." He was referring to point 994 of *The Way:* "'My enthusiasm is gone,' you wrote me. Yours has to be a work not of enthusiasm, but of Love, conscious of duty—which means self-denial."

Don Alvaro then summed up in these few sentences the deep significance of a divine call and of the person's response to it: "A vocation is not a state of mind. Nor does it depend on your health, or on the professional or family situation in which you find yourself. Far above the ocean tide of life, with its ups and downs, its sorrows and joys, our divine vocation always shines like a bright star in the night, pointing out unmistakably the route of our journey towards God. This is what matters, my daughters and sons. This is what is definitive. Anything else that can happen to us is transitory. Never forget it!"

He incarnated, in fact, the teaching of Blessed Josemaría Escrivá that any right response to the divine will is nothing short of a commitment of love. Like every other man in love, he filled his days with loving gestures, sparing himself no sacrifice or hardship, never derailing himself with excuses or evasions. Well he knew that a soul in love, however happy it may be, is never satisfied with its dedication to its beloved—and still less when the beloved in question is God himself.

2

A Christian Home

One day in July 1977, at the beginning of lunch, while serving himself, Don Alvaro was deep in conversation and inadvertently took some potatoes along with the vegetables he usually took. When he realized what he had done, he passed the potatoes to Fathers Florencio Sánchez Bella and Joaquín Alonso, who were sitting next to him, and he thought of something his mother had said to him when he was a little boy. Back then, he told us, he had to eat his lunch very quickly to get back to school on time. As he was leaving, he would often swipe something from his mother's dessert plate, and she would say to him, "From your mouth your children will one day take things away!" And Don Alvaro added that in times past, whenever he remembered this, he'd thought his mother had been mistaken; but no...

His mother's maiden name, Diez de Sollano, comes from a city council: the council of the city of Sollano, in the Zalla district, which is in the Vizcaya region of Spain. At one time, according to the history books, Sollano was run by ten brothers who were so much alike that it was said they each signed their name as "One of the Ten of Sollano."

Clementina Diez de Sollano Portillo was a beautiful and distinguished woman and a good Catholic. Born in the

Mexican city of Cuernavaca, she lived there until the outbreak of the Mexican Civil War in 1910, at which time her parents decided to return to Spain. But she always kept her Mexican citizenship and her soft, gentle Mexican accent. She did part of her studies in London, at a school run by Servants of the Sacred Heart. Besides English (which she could speak quite well), she may also have learned there something else: how to live a thoroughly Christian life with flexibility, without sentimentality, with common sense and a supernatural outlook. A woman of great culture, she loved to read books, and her favorites were biographies and spiritual works. She always kept close at hand a copy of *The Imitation of Christ,* and she went to Mass every day.

Her son Alvaro inherited some of her natural characteristics, such as her friendliness, her delicacy in dealing with people, the smile with which she made even the most difficult decisions, the totally understanding spirit which made it impossible for her to criticize or speak ill of anyone. And also something less lofty: the capacity to eat the hottest European meals with no problem at all. Never were they as spicy and tasty for him as good old Mexican *chile chipotle.*

In the family home he acquired a great devotion to the Blessed Virgin, mostly by way of praying the rosary. Also he learned from the lips of his mother a simple, popular prayer to Mary which he recited every day:

Sweet Mother, never go away.
Keep watch on me both night and day.
Come with me wherever I go,
And never, ever, leave me alone.
Since you most truly are my mother,
Please protect me like no other.
Get me the blessings I need most
From the Father, the Son, and the Holy Ghost.

When Don Alvaro went to Mexico in 1983, he felt very much at home—"even though," he joked, "I now talk like this, very gruffly, whereas when I was a child I spoke softly, like you." And with obvious amusement he added that his grandmother had sung to him, for a lullaby, nothing less than the national anthem of the Mexican Republic.

Another time that he recalled his Mexican heritage was in August 1977, in Asturias, when he heard the diminutive "Santina" (little holy one) used to describe the image of our Lady which represents her as the patroness of that region. That sign of affection, of confidence, of love, reminded him of how he used to call his mother "Mamacita" when he was little. He also confided to us that he had learned from Monsignor Escrivá to invoke the Blessed Virgin as "Madre! Madrecita!"

A few weeks earlier, in that same summer of 1977, he told us—I don't remember in what context—one heroic detail of his mother's deeply Christian life. Though she had too much delicacy of soul ever to speak of this, her son found out that she used to rise very early (I think it was about four in the morning), take a cold bath as a mortification, and then do an hour of prayer. Don Alvaro thought that she did this out of concern about the faith of someone close to her, someone she loved very much.

Her husband, Ramón del Portillo Pardo, was born in Madrid and studied law at Madrid's Universidad Central. He worked for an insurance company called Plus Ultra. Orderly and hard-working, he was very much a family man. His daughter Pilar remembers him as "neat and correct about everything, very educated and elegant, extremely punctual and very meticulous." What stood out most in his character was his preciseness, his exactness, his seriousness. "But he was not severe," says his son Carlos. "I can't remember one time when he was ever harsh or unfeeling or cold."

That really quite amiable and down-to-earth man loved to go to bullfights and also loved to read. But when he got older he began to lose his sight. Actually, that problem must have run in the family, judging from a story Don Alvaro once told about his grandfather. It seems that one day he told his wife, as they were eating, that he was very upset because some sanctimonious old woman, not looking where she was going, had pushed ahead of him into the church. And she replied, "So it was you who almost knocked me over?"

Clementina and Ramón had eight children: Ramón, Paco, Alvaro, Pilar, Pepe, Angel, Tere, and Carlos. Alvaro was born in their second home, which was at 75 Alcalá Street. Almost right in front of it was El Sotanillo, a chocolate shop which played a role in the apostolic activities of the founder of Opus Dei in the thirties. Later on they moved to another place not far away; it was at 16 Conde de Aranda Street.

Alvaro was born on March 11, 1914, and was baptized six days later at the parish of San José (on Alcalá Street). His godparents were an aunt and an uncle: María del Carmen del Portillo and Jorge Diez de Sollano. His full given name was Alvaro José María Eulogio. (In Spain it is customary to include the name of the saint on whose feast day the baby is born. March 11 is the feast day of Saint Eulogius.) On December 28, 1916, Alvaro received the sacrament of Confirmation at the hands of the bishop of Sigüenza, Bishop Eustaquio Nieto y Martín, at the church of La Concepción. His sponsors were the Count of Las Almenas and the Duchess of La Victoria. (At that time in Spain, it was customary to administer Confirmation to little children.)

On his seventy-fifth birthday, in 1989, Don Alvaro celebrated Mass in the prelatic church of Our Lady of Peace in Rome. In his homily he reviewed with gratitude some of the many blessings which he had received from our Lord throughout his life, starting with the fact of having been born in the warmth of a Christian family in which he could learn true piety. His mother, he said, "instilled in me a special devotion to the Sacred Heart and to the Holy Spirit, and a particular veneration for the Blessed Virgin under the title of Our Lady of Mount Carmel." And then he added, "Our Lord God arranged for me to be friends with my father, which obviously helped keep me from getting into bad friendships."

Mercedes Santamaría told me that Alvaro was exceptionally sociable even as a small child. Whenever she took him out walking in a nearby park, people kept staring at him; something about him held their attention. More than once, she said, someone felt moved to say something to him, and he would reply with great naturalness, which encouraged them to continue the conversation. But I wonder if, perhaps, her obvious affection for him has played tricks on her memory. Don Alvaro told people on several occasions that as a child he had been very shy. That was how he explained, for example, why he had not become a lawyer, like his father, and why he blushed so easily. However, I think it's also possible that he interpreted as timidity what was really a sense of modesty, since he always brought this up while he was addressing with obvious confidence thousands of people.

As a child he had some rather serious illnesses. When he was just two or three years old, for instance, he suffered attacks of rheumatism. At that time, after supper, his two older brothers were given a big glass of milk with an egg yolk beaten in, while he, instead, had to take his medicine. He used to envy them and say, using a Mexican expression ("Qué *suertasa* tenéis"), "You're so lucky—you get egg yolks, and I get Sanatogen." Sanatogen was an evil-smelling concoction, a benzene derivative often prescribed for rheumatism. Actually, he must have had some congenital predisposition to this ailment, for he suffered another attack of it when he was about twenty. And after all these years, his sister Pilar still recalls what his doctor, Gregorio Marañón, prescribed for him, perhaps because it was so unusual: a few drops of minced garlic soaked in alcohol.

Alvaro was prone to the normal transgressions and mischief of all children, and sometimes his father felt obliged to punish him. But often he would give him the slip: when his father came up behind him to get hold of him, he would escape by running as fast as he could and hiding under the big dining room table.

Even when he was very little, his father used to take him to Sunday-morning Mass with his brothers and sisters. They would walk from their home on Conde de Aranda Street to the nearby church of San Manuel y San Benito. After Mass they would cross Alcalá Street and take a walk in Retiro Park, where Don Ramón would treat them all to potato chips and lemonade. According to Pilar, who was younger than Alvaro, he was an even-tempered, cheerful, easygoing child, a bit on the chubby side, always with a friendly smile on his face. She cannot remember him ever telling a lie. But she does remember a few childish infractions and many more or less funny practical jokes. His piety showed itself in the ways one would expect in a Christian family of that time and place. Pilar thinks, in fact, that the most outstanding thing about Alvaro was how little he changed over the years. She is sure that "in the depths of his soul he always kept that same innocence, simplicity, and sincere searching for God that he had when he was little."

3

Childhood

Alvaro completed his elementary education, both secular and religious, at Our Lady of the Pillar, a school run by the Marianists. (This school was at 46 Castelló Street, in Madrid.) On the basis of what specific character trait, I do not know, but his teachers generally regarded him as a rather spirited child. On one of his report cards, for instance, the teacher wrote, "His drawings of himself are a bit rough." And his father's comment was, "What do you mean, drawings? He's sculpting himself!" So well did he know his son's strength of character!

One time Alvaro must have done something really bad at the school, because his teacher, Don Genaro, grabbed him by the feet, turned him upside down, brought him to a window, and said gently (for he was a kind man), "If you do that again, I'll throw you out this window."

Always when I heard Don Alvaro speak of his school days, he expressed his gratitude toward the many teachers who had contributed to his intellectual growth and to his practice of the faith which he had received at baptism. But the only one whose name I can recall was his handwriting teacher, Eduardo Cotelo. He was the author of several textbooks that were widely used during the first few decades of the twentieth century. In fact, years later, Don Alvaro was happy to learn that the founder of Opus Dei had also used in his school days some of Cotelo's books.

Old friends of his still remember, after all these years, the Alvaro with whom they shared so many experiences in the classrooms and on the playground of Our Lady of the Pillar, which was both an elementary school and a secondary school. Some of them find it hard to understand why they have not forgotten him—they realize this is somewhat surprising, since they knew him only during their years at school. They think the main reason must have been that his integrity, his authentic goodness, made such a strong impression on them.

Among those former classmates is Alberto Ullastres, an economics professor who became Secretary of Commerce in 1957. Later, in Brussels, he did even more far-reaching diplomatic work as Spain's ambassador to the European Community. He remembers Alvaro del Portillo, even though Alvaro was a year or two behind him. Usually it happens only the other way around: the younger students notice the older ones. Anyway, for quite a while the schedules of Alberto and Alvaro were such that they had recess at the same time. Alberto almost always played soccer on one side of the school yard. On the opposite side, others played handball. And on the sidelines, more or less in the center, there were the "intellectuals," who—though this term did not imply any disdain for sports—preferred to spend their free time talking... Ullastres believes that there were about ninety students in Alvaro's class, but he has forgotten almost all the others. I spoke with him on February 6, 1995, and this is what he said: "All of this was more than sixty-five years ago, so you'll have to excuse me for not being able to give you more details. But for some reason that I can't explain, I still have in my mind a very clear picture of Alvaro chatting with the others, with great composure and tranquillity, while I'm out on the field kicking the ball."

Another schoolmate vividly remembers the day that he and Alvaro first met each other. It was in October of 1922; he had just arrived at Our Lady of the Pillar, and had never been to school before. "They put me in the most elementary class (the one before first year), and I sat down timidly in the row closest to the window—in the second to last desk, I think. To my left was a fellow about eight years old, like myself. He was somewhat chubby, he was smiling, he seemed nice and friendly. His name was Alvaro del Portillo.

"I was given a reader, but I didn't know what I was supposed to do with it. I hesitantly opened it up and then looked over my shoulder at Alvaro to see what he was reading. It was a description of a lion, by the famous French naturalist Buffon. Since this was my first day in school and I didn't know how things were run there, I thought I was obliged to read this, so I launched into these detailed descriptions by the famous naturalist. Well, they were far too detailed to appeal to the average child; within a few minutes I was bored out of my skull. But, no matter what, I continued to follow the example of my neighbor, who was a 'veteran' in the school, and I kept on reading."

Deep friendships were forged. Many remember Alvaro's smile, and describe him as a good fellow who liked to help others. But it was all very normal. One teacher jotted down on Alvaro's report card, "A clown." Though no one knows what he did to earn this epithet, the consensus seems to be that it was some childish prank which one of the stricA Christian Hometer teachers did not appreciate. Alvaro, according to one of these old friends, "was a happy, affectionate, friendly boy who could be a bit naughty and clownish, like all boys." But "those of us who knew him in school," wrote José María Hernández de Garnica (another student who was a year or two ahead of him), "remember him as a wonderful fellow with a great nobility of character and great courage."

Alvaro had a natural aptitude for languages, so his father hired tutors who came daily to their home. Many years later, Don Alvaro made mention of his English teacher (Mrs. Hodges), his French teacher (Mlle. Anne), and his German teacher. (Bishop Javier Echevarría, the present Prelate of Opus Dei, gave me the names of the first two, but I haven't been able to find out the name of the German teacher.)

From an early age, as his sister Pilar recalls, it was obvious that Alvaro had a very good mind. But he did not call attention to any of his talents. For instance, she says, "he could draw very well, but he didn't brag about it. On the contrary, he was extraordinarily simple and humble."

He earned good grades; he spent many afternoon hours studying, usually in the room he shared with his brothers Pepe and Angel. He began secondary school in 1924 and finished in 1931.

All who knew him as a youngster agree on three aspects of his character: he was normal, he was friendly, and he basically stayed the same throughout his life. In fact, as regards his outward behavior, those who later came into contact with Alvaro the engineer, the priest, the monsignor, the bishop, and so forth, all say they found in him the same naturalness, the same open and frank look, the same interest in them that he had shown so long ago.

The look of his blue eyes, scarcely hidden behind the transparent lenses of his glasses, was deep and welcoming. Even as he grew older, we could all see this. Sometimes while we were talking in a family-style get-together, he would momentarily raise his eyes toward the skies, as if he were silently communicating with our Lord his feelings about what we were saying, or as if he were praying for the people, or for the success of the apostolic works, that we were talking about. But then he would pass his hand over his face, and once again we would see in it that wonderful warmth. When it came time for prayer, whether his private prayer or his celebrating of Mass, the light in his eyes seemed to turn inward, but it never went out; rather, it took on a special glow, as of a fire burning serenely.

Alvaro was not only intelligent but also very orderly. He did not like to do things on the spur of the moment. Or at least he always came across as very thoughtful and prudent. A cousin of his on his father's side, Isabel Carles Pardo, says that he never made up his mind on the spot. If he was asked for something or about something which he couldn't take care of right away, he would say, "Well, I'll think it over."

But this was not an attempt to excuse himself, nor was it a sign of indecisiveness or simply a way to buy some time. It indicated, rather, a capacity for reflection and a serene activity. He didn't forget about the matter; sooner or later he did act on it, but with great peace of mind. As soon as he saw clearly what needed to be done—and sometimes he did see this immediately—he got going with it. But always he did this very calmly and with a smile on his face, in such a peaceful way that it gave peace to all those around him.

He was transparently friendly, warm, and personable. The current archbishop of Madrid, Cardinal Angel Suquía, met him in 1938 and remembers him as "a young university student who was very elegant and pleasant, an obviously good young man who spoke from the heart. He impressed me as being at the same time very prudent, very courageous, and very cheerful. Come to think of it, I don't remember one visit with him when I didn't feel more cheerful at the end of it than I did at the beginning."

Alvaro received his first Holy Communion on May 12, 1921, while he was a student at Our Lady of the Pillar. But the ceremony took place not in the school chapel, but in the nearby church of La Concepción, on Goya Street. That day one hundred and ten boys and two girls received

Holy Communion for the first time.

From then on, Alvaro received our Lord in the Blessed Sacrament quite often, despite the hardships involved in keeping the strict Eucharistic fast of those days. He had to take off for school without having eaten anything. Only after Mass would he eat breakfast—having wrapped it up in a piece of paper and carried it in his pocket. It should be noted that although Mass was celebrated daily at Our Lady of the Pillar, no one was obliged to go; the only ones who did were those who wanted to.

As, then, one would naturally expect, Alvaro also actively participated in the other devotional services held at the school. And he never forgot, even in his later years, the hymns they used to sing during the Stations of the Cross. "For the last station," he once told us, "for the burial of our Lord, we sang lines which were very bad as verse, but they touched my heart—and they still do. 'The Lord of all things / Lies behind a great stone / But with joy the world rings / For salvation has shone.' How true this is. God dies, so that we might live. He is buried, so that we might go everywhere. Therefore the earth sings the joy of salvation."

On his summer vacations during the twenties, he also went to weekday Mass in La Granja, but he did not join any Church group. He never even became an altar boy. He preferred to attend Mass as just one more person sitting in the pews. Nor did he stick to one location, as was the custom at the time. Sometimes he went to Mass at the school, sometimes at the convent of the Poor Clares, sometimes at one parish or another, and sometimes at a hermitage called Los Dolores. He would remember with particular affection the Poor Clares. The memory was tinged with some sorrow, for they ended up having to leave that convent in La Granja. But in the summer of 1935, just a few weeks after he had answered his call from God, he had gone to ask prayers from them for Opus Dei.

I learned some of these details one afternoon in July 1978, after praying the rosary with Don Alvaro in his home parish. To get there, we had taken the road that goes from Soria to Segovia, through Torrecaballeros. He told me in passing that it was on this very road—between La Granja and Torrecaballeros—that he had one summer, as a little boy, first learned to ride a bicycle. He also thought of the evening visits that he had made to the Blessed Sacrament when he was a teenager, on his way home from taking a stroll with his friends.

During many of those summers, he lived at 11 Reina Street. Possibly this was the same house his paternal grandparents were staying in, for they also spent their summers in La Granja.

Many years later, when talking about the Eucharist, Don Alvaro would often mention those Castilian sunsets. Undoubtedly it was during those summer vacations that the sight of them first made such an impression on him, but he also relived this experience much later, when he went with the founder of Opus Dei to Molinoviejo, which is also in the vicinity of the Sierra, not far from Segovia. "On that immense plain," he would say, "you can really see the sun go down in the distance. And just when it seems to touch the earth, it seems to blaze out, and the whole sky turns red, and the sun takes on a thousand colors. Now, this is really nothing more than an optical illusion, since the sun, of course, does not actually touch the earth... However, when in the Eucharist we receive our Lord, who is much more than the sun—he is the Sun of suns!—and he touches our body and our soul, what marvels ought to happen within us! By coming into contact with Christ, how ablaze our soul should become! What a transformation this grace should make in it!"

During one of those summers, he went to a place in the province of Asturias called La Isla. There he struck up a friendship with the family of José María González Barredo, who was born in nearby Colunga. (From a casual comment Don Alvaro made in July 1976, and also from the fact that José María asked admission to Opus Dei in about 1932, I gather that this happened sometime during the thirties.) This acquaintance with González's father, who was also named Alvaro, would prove to be of great importance to Don Alvaro. For as we shall see, it was only with his help that Don Alvaro was able to get back in touch with Father Josemaría Escrivá during the Spanish Civil War.

La Isla is a little village with a wonderful view of the Bay of Biscay. When I went there myself, I understood much better a certain comment I had heard from Don Alvaro. He had said that one summer, in the thirties, he had spent many a long time contemplating nature and—without even realizing that he was praying—speaking with God, thanking him for having created such beauty in nature. "And it was at that time," he said, "that our Lord began to enter my heart."

An important event of his youth happened in La Isla. One day, having planned to go with some friends on a motorboat excursion to Ribadesella, Alvaro decided at the last minute not to go—for what reason, he could not remember. Well, it so happened that a gale suddenly blew in from the Bay of Biscay, and before the little boat could reach port, it sank, and all but one of those friends drowned. This one, the youngest, managed to cling to the gunwale despite the force of the waves. While he was struggling with the sea, he promised our Lord that if his life was saved, he would consecrate it to him. Shortly thereafter, he entered Valdediós Seminary.

One thing Don Alvaro would always remember in connection with that event was an unusual application of the word "guapa" (lovely), an adjective often used in Asturias. After the emotionally draining burial of those ten or twelve friends, he heard one of the women from that village say,

"What a very lovely funeral that was!"

Another tragedy had occurred a few years before, in Madrid. When Don Alvaro told us about it, I thought that those two tragedies showed a certain protection of him by divine providence—through, of course, entirely ordinary means. He told us that one Sunday at the end of summer vacation, when the whole family was in Madrid, his eldest brother wanted to take him to the Novedades Theater, where a musical comedy was playing. In the end they did not go— for what reason, as in the case of that fatal motorboat excursion, he could not remember. And on that day, September 23, 1928, this famous nine-hundred-seat theater, which had been opened by Queen Isabel II in 1857, was gutted by a terrible fire. The musical comedy was *La mejor del puerto*—the music was by Francisco Alonso, and the lyrics by Fernández Sevilla y Carreño—so the house was packed. The fire spread so rapidly and created such a panic that rescue was nearly impossible. The best the firemen could do was to keep the fire from spreading to the adjacent buildings. It was a really spectacular fire; according to the newspaper accounts, the flames could be seen all the way from the towns of Villecas, Getafe, and Pinto. Sixty-four people died, and hundreds more were injured. However, most of those sixty-four died not in the flames, but at the exits; they were crushed to death.

I don't know whether Don Alvaro would have agreed with this saying attributed to Oscar Wilde, that "my fatherland was my childhood." But I do know that he always harbored a deep affection for the city of his birth. He had a special sparkle whenever he was back in Madrid. As universal a man as he was, he especially loved being in Madrid; he saw himself as a true *madrileño*. During his visits there, his language became even warmer than usual. Sometimes his affection for Madrid showed itself simply in his imparting to us a bit of local history, as, for instance, when he told us that the old Plaza de Manuel Becerra, then called Plaza de Roma, was for many years popularly known as Plaza de la Alegría (Plaza of Joy), because funeral processions headed for the cemetery of Almudena broke up there. Only the closest family members went on to the cemetery, while the others turned around, put on a happy smile again, and headed home.

Don Alvaro's distinctively *madrileño* good humor showed itself also in the rapidity and ease with which he could give words an original twist. In 1990, for example, I heard him jokingly say to Umberto Farri, who was leaving Rome to go to Chile, "Tell them that I have a great wish to go see them, but that I have to stay back here with that wish."

A while later, in July 1991, he went to an Opus Dei center in the town of Iza, in the province of Navarre. His doctors had insistently recommended that he do some walking; they'd told him that some physical exercise would really be good for him. So one evening someone suggested the handball court on the property as a good place to walk while saying the rosary. "It will be good and cool," said this man, "and it's quite level." And Don Alvaro said with a smile, "What would really be *good* would be a handball court on a slope!"

During his first stay in Madrid after being elected as the successor of the founder, he received many gifts: paintings, books, flowers, many touching gestures of affection—and sometimes money as well. He decided that these monetary gifts should be directed to whatever apostolic undertakings in Spain the directors thought appropriate. One of them, Juan Francisco Montuenga, thanked him publicly "for the universal outlook which you have given us." Don Alvaro replied, "So you call *cash* a universal outlook?" From then on he would ask Juan from time to time how his universal outlook was doing—that was his way of asking if they were having any financial problems, major or minor.

With due discretion, Don Alvaro would absorb the basic style of humor and the stock jokes of each place he stayed in. And of course, since he lived in Rome from 1946 on, it's quite understandable that he leaned especially toward more or less typical Italian humor. To stress, for example, the importance of being completely sincere with one's spiritual director, he used to say, "We must not deceive ourselves like the fellow they tell about in Italy who used to eat pasta with his eyes closed because his doctor had told him, 'Don't even look at pasta!'"

Never, though, did he lose his accent. Yes, it was to South American ears a bit less strong than that of most Spaniards (as Enrique Chirinos mentioned in an article in the 3/22/94 issue of Lima's *El Comercio,* on the occasion of Don Alvaro's eightieth birthday). However, true *madrileño* that he was, he spoke very quickly and, taking things for granted, left off the endings of some phrases—all of which made simultaneous translation difficult for interpreters who did not speak Castilian Spanish. During a get-together in Miami in 1988, Don Alvaro himself told us with great amusement about one time when it was suggested that he speak more slowly. "At the close of the last Synod of Bishops," he said, "when everyone was supposed to say something in his own native tongue, I was allotted barely three minutes. So, since I had a lot that I wanted to say, I started talking very fast. And right away a sign lit up with a message from those doing the simultaneous translation: they wanted me to slow down. I apologized to them in Latin. I said, 'Habeatis me excusatum, sum hispanus' (You'll have to excuse me, I'm Spanish). There was a bit of laughter, and then I continued speaking—more slowly."

Even on his deathbed Don Alvaro showed this wonderful *madrileño* sense of humor. Early on the morning of March 23, 1994, he called up Don Javier Echevarría because he was having a hard time breathing and his heart was beating wildly. Don Javier came over immediately and called the doctor. This doctor, José María Araquistáin, got there very quickly, because he also lived right there at Villa Tevere and had accompanied Don Alvaro on the pilgrimage he had just made to the Holy Land. Realizing how serious the situation was, he went out to get a bottle of oxygen. But as he was walking out the door, Don Alvaro noticed that he was still in his bathrobe. So he asked him, "My son, what are you wearing? A caftan?" "No, Father, it's a kimono!" José María calmly replied. With that gentle little joke, Don Alvaro had helped José María go from being very tense to being very serene, though still quite conscious of the extreme seriousness of Don Alvaro's condition.

4

Some Interests

Around the time when he graduated from high school, as one can see in the family photo album, Alvaro had a look of sober distinction mixed with a down-to-earth sociability. In these pictures he is wearing nicely tailored suits with the starched collars then in fashion, and elegant, classic ties. His red moustache plays counterpoint to a penetrating and appealing sparkle in his blue eyes. A good-looking young man reflecting in every way his upbringing in a well-to-do family, he is exactly what one would expect from a future man of the world. He looks like what he was: a young man with quite normal, natural, spontaneous interests.

From very early on, Alvaro loved to read. Surely, in fact, it was from all the reading he did, and not just from his teachers, that he acquired the ease and grace with which he used the pen. He also had the expert reader's amazing knack for assessing a new book at a glance. I often saw him do this—open a book and very quickly page through the whole thing, including the table of contents, the preface, the footnotes, and the bibliography—a mark of a true intellectual.

His school, Our Lady of the Pillar, concerned itself not just with academic instruction, but also with the cultural development of its students. In 1924, for example, Juan de la

Cierva Codorniú, a famous former student, came in to describe his invention: the autogiro, an early version of the helicopter. There were frequent outings and trips. In 1929 Alvaro and the other students went to Barcelona for a World Expo.

Even as a small child, Alvaro read books of lasting interest. During a 1987 trip to Dublin, he made a reference to Robert Louis Stevenson's famous children's book *Treasure Island*. Ireland, he said, was another treasure island, an "isle of saints."

I was very impressed by a reply he gave someone during a get-together in 1989 with young people in Barcelona. Among other songs, they sang one in Catalan, a song called "La Gavina," and this person offered him a translation. "My child," he said, "that's not necessary, because I understand Catalan. When I was fourteen, I read Ramon Llull's *Blanquerna*."

After all that time he still remembered verses and phrases from classic poets and authors, and often he would spontaneously cite them during family-style get-togethers or in his preaching. Sometimes he used verses from the well-known poet Jorge Manrique to spur people on in the struggle to live Christian virtues in the midst of the world, and thus to put or keep them on the road to heaven. When talking about apostolate, he used to say that like Lazarus in his tomb, people were waiting to hear the voice of Jesus tell them to arise and come forth. And on at least one occasion he quoted these lines from a poem by Gustavo Adolfo Bécquer, "Del salón en el ángulo oscuro," about a harp that lay silent and forgotten in a dusty corner:

> *How many notes slept in those strings*
> *Like birds slumbering in trees*
> *Awaiting the awakening snow!*
> *Ah! and I thought of a voice which sings*
> *To the genius drowsing in our soul's ease:*
> *"Lazarus! Arise, and come forth now!"*

Often he would make use of passages from Cervantes, Quevedo, or Calderón de la Barca to get across the importance of having humility, or of spurning as mere daydreams ideals which have no influence on our behavior. At times he would say, "¡Todos a una!" (All together!)— referring to the unanimous reaction of the populace of Fuenteovejuna in the classic play by Lope de Vega, from Spain's Golden Age—to stress the need for people to help one another in a resolute struggle to achieve Christian sanctity. His focus, of course, was always on just the spiritual and apostolic content of that profound cohesion. This was the first thing I heard from him upon his return from Nairobi, in April 1989: he was happy to have learned that the concept of "all together" was quite familiar to the people of Kenya. As a matter of fact, he said, they often used an equivalent term, "harambee," to call for unity in certain situations, such as when the fishermen pull their boats toward the shore.

Finally, I should not neglect to say, he quoted some more or less witty verses or phrases from famous writers just to make get-togethers livelier, with no intent to teach or preach. Sometimes it was purely and simply for fun, as when he quoted Quevedo's whimsical sayings or poems.

In his youth he was also, as befitted that strong character of his, quite a sportsman. As Don Javier Echevarría said to Pilar Urbano in an interview published in the 5/2/94 issue of the Madrid magazine *Epoca*, "He went in very much for swimming, hockey, cross-country racing, tennis, horseback riding, and soccer." Now, for those who first met him in his later years, this was not easy to picture. He was so focused on the big issues at hand, and on the interests of those around him, that even those who lived and worked with him on a daily basis found it hard to tell what his own interests were. One got the impression that he had renounced all of that in order to be more at the disposal of God's will and at the

service of the Church. Day-to-day life with the founder of
Opus Dei led him to set aside his natural inclinations. For
many years, if he ever did any physical exercise, it was just
taking a walk or playing a game of lawn bowling with
Monsignor Escrivá. But back when he was going to school
at Our Lady of the Pillar in Madrid, says José María
Hernández de Garnica, "he was an excellent defense player
on his soccer team—one greatly feared by the opposing
forwards." And soldiers who served with him in 1939
remember how much he liked horseback riding.

He loved the sea. I remember one time—this was on
some feast day, sometime during the seventies—we went for
an early morning walk in the port town of Avilés, and he
playfully leapt onto the deck of an apparently abandoned
cargo boat. I'm sure that if we had suggested going to an out-
of-the-way spot to do this, he would cheerfully have jumped
back off for a swim in the cool, fresh waters of the Bay of
Biscay. Don Javier Echevarría, in that same interview with
Pilar Urbano, commented that in 1968, when taking off with
Monsignor Escrivá for a boat trip from Naples to Cádiz,
"Don Alvaro was very much looking forward to it, because,
as he put it, 'being on the high seas is so relaxing.'"

The first time I saw him with a tennis racket in hand
was in 1976, and right away I was impressed by the good
form with which he held the racket and served and placed
the ball. He was, of course, out of practice after such a long
time, but he was still a good sportsman. Certainly, as the
years went by, it became more difficult for him to do the
walking and other activities recommended by his doctors.
But I was impressed to see how hard he struggled to do this
physical exercise well, even when he did not at all feel like it.
He overcame his inertia with a sporting spirit, offered to
God all the pain and effort involved, and through it all kept
joking with those around him.

I saw him do this even during his last summer, in 1993.

I remember in particular one overcast and chilly day—by midmorning it was only sixty degrees. Following afternoon tea, Don Alvaro asked whether there would be an evening walk. Don Javier, who had just given him eyedrops (because of a recent cataract operation), answered, "Whatever the Father wishes." Don Alvaro right away replied, "Good, then we can stay here chatting." Don Javier then said, "It would be good for the Father to take a walk." And Don Alvaro replied, in the tone of voice of one who knows he's been defeated, "Ah, well, that is another thing altogether."

On other occasions during that same summer, he instinctively tried to defend himself when Don Javier or Don Joaquín Alonso would matter-of-factly remind him that it was time to change clothes and go for a walk. "Don't put yourself out for me," he would say. Or, "It's all right with me if you want to skip it this time." And whenever someone suggested that it might be good to ask the doctor about such matters, he would respond with a military-sounding expression: "Whoever asks must stay in formation!"

All joking aside, Don Alvaro did heed the advice he received, and did take care of his physical health, inasmuch as this was necessary for serving others. But deep in his heart he could not help but feel a certain antipathy towards the obsession with sports and with physical health in general— the virtual worship of physical well-being—which characterizes our era. Sometimes he joked about this, especially with Don Joaquín and especially when they were jogging together—it was as if he wanted to put some distance between himself and Don Joaquín's youthful vitality. One day I told them I had just read in the paper about a doctor who had had a heart attack while taking an early morning run on a beach in San Sebastián. "You hear that, Joaquín?" said Don Alvaro. Don Joaquín replied, "But he could have had a heart attack anywhere—while running to catch a bus, for instance." "Right, Joaquín," he said, "but still, running..."

Carlos del Portillo tells us that during the thirties, his brother was quite interested in photography. He says that one day Alvaro took several photos of him, putting him in different positions and insisting that he not move. The result, to his surprise, was a print in which he appears to be shaking his own hand. I had never known about this interest of his, but once I found out about it, I understood much better the great enjoyment he took in looking over the pictures he received—shots, for example, of the ordination of some members of Opus Dei to the priesthood—and the detailed comments he made about the ones that didn't come out so well.

One thing I did already know was that from his youth he loved to go to bullfights. This was, in fact, a family tradition. I remember hearing him tell in vivid detail how as a little boy he would go with his father to buy tickets on Victoria Street, near Madrid's Puerta de Sol. Sometimes, in a café on that street or on the next one (Pasaje Matheu), they would afterwards each get a *pepito:* a then-new treat created by the owner of one of those two cafés. His name was Pepe, and he served those fried-veal sandwiches that came to be known by his nickname, Pepito. They became popular all over Spain, and still are to this day.

Before he joined Opus Dei, Alvaro occasionally rented a small bullring with some friends, to bullfight with some calves. Even in his last years, he could still remember quite well the most famous bullfighters of those days. And he often used in his everyday conversation some bullfighting language, as people typically do in Spain.

In June 1976, for instance, I heard him make this wonderful off-the-cuff remark about Monsignor Escrivá. Even though, he said, the founder in his humility regarded himself as a leg of the desk upon which God was writing, the truth was that our Lord "se recreó en la suerte" (enjoyed that stage of the bullfight) of forming his personality. For

another example, Don Alvaro shared with the founder of
the Work the hope—through the mercy of God and the
prayer of his children—of being able to skip over purgatory
"a la torera" (just as a bull jumps over the ring) when God
summoned him to his presence. From Blessed Josemaría
Escrivá he had also learned how to stir up the free initiative
of the faithful of Opus Dei in the immense apostolic
panorama of the contemporary world. He encouraged each
and every one of them to move on in, and not sit forever in
a corner. No one, he said, should just "ver los toros desde la
barrera" (watch the bulls from behind the fence). Rather,
they should "lanzarse al ruedo, bajar a la arena" (jump into
the ring, go down into the arena); they should be involved
in the most diverse human tasks and organizations, whether
public or private.

They should not, of course, shrink from their apostolic
responsibilities for fear or human respect, since a Christian
"se pone el mundo por montera." (This expression, which
literally means "wears the world like a bullfighter's hat,"
figuratively means "doesn't care what people say.") For those
in love with God, there are no obstacles or difficulties; they
leap over all these, too, "a la torera." Furthermore, all Opus
Dei members could always count on intercessory help from
Blessed Josemaría Escrivá; from heaven, as he always did on
earth, "echaría un capote" (he would lend a helping hand)
with understanding and affection. (A *capote* is a bullfighter's
cape.) They especially would need to ask for it when they
were "pinchaba en hueso" (cut to the bone). Certainly they
should confront all their problems "ir derechos al toro"
(heading straight for the bull), without seeking refuge in
either excuses or euphemisms; they should "agarrar el toro
por los cuernos" (take the bull by the horns). Nevertheless,
there would be plenty of situations calling for a "larga
cambiada" (big turnaround).

In May 1983, Don Alvaro held a huge number of get-togethers in Mexico. He asked the regional vicar, Father Rafael Fiol, to help him keep track of the time so that he would stay on schedule. But when the vicar did so, Don Alvaro would say (using a bullfighting term as familiar to Mexicans as to Spaniards), "I told him to give me three signals. At the third, *¡al corral!* (into the ring!). But I've still got one left."

Well knowing the interests and, above all, the daily battles of this son of his, Monsignor Escrivá in about 1949 autographed for him a copy of *The Way* with these words: "For my son Alvaro, who in God's service has had to fight so many bulls."

5

The Engineer

When asked what he wanted to be when he grew up, little Alvaro used to answer, "A bullfighter or a bishop," because he wanted to wear colorful clothes. But according to Professor Manuel Guerra, as reported in the 3/25/94 edition of the Burgos newspaper (*Diario de Burgos*), the scales became definitely tilted one day in the bullfighter direction, right there in that Castilian city. As a child, Alvaro spent some of his summer vacations in Burgos, in the home of one of his aunts. Well, this one day (it was years later that he confided this to Professor Guerra), "I saw from a window the body of the archbishop of Burgos being carried with a military escort. And so, when I saw that bishops also die, my dilemma was resolved: I would be a bullfighter."

But with the passage of time, of course, those ideas changed. At the age of eleven or twelve he toyed with the idea of becoming either an Engineer of Roads, Canals, and Ports (a civil engineer) or a Licentiate in Philosophy and Letters (a doctor of liberal arts). His childish imagination was captivated by the grandiloquent sound of these titles. Sometimes he thought of becoming a lawyer, like his father, but then he thought he would never have the nerve to speak in public with ease and assurance.

When the moment of decision came, he had to be realistic. In 1931, when he finished high school, his family was not doing well financially. And so, even though he at first was planning to enroll in both the civil engineering and the mining engineering programs, he decided for the time being to just take a shorter course of studies and become an assistant civil engineer. He enrolled in this program in 1932, finished it in three years, and thus quickly started making some money.

His interest in and skill at drawing certainly made the course easier for him. Mercedes Santamaría recalls that he spent many hours drawing and also helping less artistically gifted classmates. And Carlos del Portillo has a related childhood memory. A rather rambunctious child, he played one day amidst the plans which Alvaro had been working on all year. He ruined them almost completely by knocking over an inkwell, or something similar. Their mother was very upset that so many hours of Alvaro's work had been wasted, and Carlos awaited his return with real fear. But when Alvaro came home and saw what had happened, he called Carlos over, sat him on his knee, and gave him a talking-to about being more responsible. Carlos was astonished. "Instead of hitting me," he said, "what he did was just explain to me how important that work was, so that from then on I would learn to be more careful!"

At that time, passing the entrance exams for any upper-level engineering program normally called for several years of intense preparation. Alvaro passed the entrance exam for civil engineering in 1933, but he could not begin the program until the following year because the university would not allow him to do this and study for the public works degree at the same time—at least not with an overlap of more than one year. He decided to give the priority to that intermediate program in which he was already enrolled, and to wait the one more year to begin the civil engineering program. So in

1936, when the Spanish Civil War broke out, he had finished only two years of his civil engineering program (1934–35 and 1935–36).

His first job as an assistant civil engineer was with the bridges and building unit of the Department of Public Works—specifically, the hydraulics and hydrography section of it. But he worked the second shift and thus was able to continue his schooling while earning a wage.

Every morning he would walk from home to school through a park, and in total tranquillity pray the rosary along the way. When classes were over, he would walk home with some friends. Well, sometimes he would stop by some old secondhand bookstores—it was a good chance to browse and then maybe buy something interesting. But other times he would walk straight home, back through the park, and take advantage of that opportunity to chat with some friends. Among them was a fellow by the name of Francisco José. Don Alvaro mentioned to us in 1990 that he used to talk at length with Francisco José about religion, because although he was a very good fellow, he professed to be an agnostic. But back then he did not get anywhere with this friend. "And it cut me to the bone," he said. However, even from Rome he never quit corresponding with Francisco José, and in his letters he would always include a "Pray for me." Well, in the last letters which he sent to Don Alvaro, his friend said, "Not to worry—we do indeed pray for you in this house." And he died well, after receiving the sacraments.

After the tragic interlude of the Spanish Civil War, Don Alvaro took up his studies with a renewed intensity. In accord with the special timetable in force in those postwar years, he squeezed the third and fourth years of the program into the single academic year of 1939–40, though this meant, of course, taking a heavy load of courses each semester. In 1941, after graduation, he went to work for the roads, canals, and ports unit of the Department of Public Works. He was assigned to an office in the basin of the Segura River.

All of this required enormous effort, because his tasks kept piling up. Sometimes he did not even have time to attend all his classes, in which case he had to learn the material on his own. One of his classmates, Fernando Valenciano, tells about an extremely demanding professor of theirs. This man would not allow students with three unexcused absences to take the final exam; he failed them automatically. Alvaro found himself in this situation. He, in fact, missed class far more than three times, because he had to help the founder of Opus Dei complete some urgent tasks. However, he went to the professor and, much to the surprise of his classmates, managed to talk him into allowing him to take the exam. Some thought that he would not pass it, but he did, because he had a good grasp of the material. Fernando heard him tell this story only on one or two occasions, but he remembers that Don Alvaro finished it by saying, "Now, this does not mean that you need not go to class. The only reason I didn't go was because I couldn't."

During those years, the founder himself would often tell the fellows who were living in the Jenner Street center, "Don't bother Alvaro now, because he has an exam coming up." Alvaro studied for many hours each day, and when he took his exams, he consistently got good grades.

In 1975, in a professional civil engineering journal, Vicente Mortes shared a memory that sheds some light on this situation. Mortes was present at a gathering of friends in October 1967, in Madrid, at which Don Alvaro was to receive an award: the Great Cross of Saint Raymond of Penyafort. Antonio Inglés, the one in charge of the proceedings, delivered a few very touching words, and Don Alvaro felt that he had to give some kind of address in response. Well, among other things he said this: "When I was in engineering school, my classmates were often surprised because on Mondays I was so tired that I dozed off in class.

This was because at that time I often had to leave on Saturday to run around all over Spain—I worked Saturday and all day Sunday and traveled both nights so that I could return sometime on Monday. There was no telling at what time I would get back—which, by the way, was very annoying to Don Bernardo de Granda."

In 1989 he mentioned in passing, but with great affection, another of his teachers at the engineering school: Professor Mendizábal. This man had a habit of using a triad of adjectives to describe just about anything. He would speak, for instance, of a "strong, robust, and graceful rivet." So when Don Alvaro and Don José Luis Múzquiz were ordained, they were not surprised to receive from him a letter which began, "My dear friends, former students, and priests..."

Alvaro made good friends with his classmates. One of them, Roberto Gomá Pujada, points out that even during the tense years just after the war, "he stood out by virtue of his serenity. I always saw him as a likable and well-balanced fellow." When he got out of school, he made it a point to keep up a lifelong correspondence with those friends. Whenever possible, he also got together with them. He stayed interested in them all, no matter how many years it had been since he had last seen them.

Ricardo Castelo has described the last time he saw him, which was in January 1994. Ricardo was then a patient in the hospital at the University of Navarre, which Don Alvaro was visiting in his capacity as Grand Chancellor; he was there to preside over the conferring of honorary doctorates. Ricardo watched the ceremony from his hospital bed, on closed-circuit TV, and a little afterwards he told his doctor that he wished he could have a talk with Don Alvaro. "And the doctor," he said, "told me that he would mention this to Don Alvaro. Well, I thought that within a few days I might get a note of apology from him—this was the most I could reasonably hope for, since he had so much to do and there were so many people wanting to see him." But that very same day, in the middle of the afternoon, Don Alvaro came to the hospital to see him. "I was touched that he came so quickly, on such a busy day, when he must have been so tired, just to chat with an old friend." They had a very nice conversation. Don Alvaro also asked him about other classmates at the engineering school whom he had not seen for a long time. At the end of the visit, Ricardo kissed his friend's episcopal ring and Don Alvaro gave him kisses on both cheeks, saying, "You say good-bye like a Spaniard; I'll do it like an Italian."

Don Alvaro's civil engineering education was a good one, and he was professionally ambitious. True, he renounced that ambition when his responsiveness to the grace of God carried him in other directions. But he always kept his love for his secular profession. And when the laws governing Spanish universities were reformed and doctoral programs in technical fields were introduced, and transitional provisions were made for older engineers, Don Alvaro—from Rome, in 1965—presented a project on the modernizing of metal bridges in order to obtain his doctorate in engineering.

Many years before, his status as an engineer had put him in a position which no one would have thought possible. (Cesare Cavalleri, publisher of the Milanese review *Studi Cattolici,* told about this in the 3/24/94 issue of the newspaper *Avvenire.*) Alvaro went to Rome in 1943 on a mission from the founder of Opus Dei, to seek from the Holy See a suitable framework in canon law for the new institution. He was then twenty-nine years old. He went to his audience with Pope Pius XII decked out in the resplendent uniform of the Spanish civil engineer: a navy blue outfit with gold buttons and a purple sash. This show of respect for the Roman pontiff was also intended to help disguise Alvaro's youthfulness and to show clearly the fully lay character of the Work.

Well, during his ride on the streetcar, he overheard a conversation between two women who evidently did not recognize his uniform, because one of them said to the other, "It seems impossible—so young, and already an admiral!" Actually, he did look considerably like an admiral; the reason for this was the military origin of the corps of engineers that was now in Spain's civil service. So when he entered the Vatican through the Bronze Doors, the officer of the Swiss Guard dutifully called his men to attention, approached this military authority who had just arrived, saluted him, and gave him the change-of-command signal. Alvaro, who never lost his sense of humor even under the most stressful of circumstances, did not blink an eye. He returned the salute, reviewed the guard, and went right along as if it were the most natural thing in the world. From time to time he would tell this story, and always with a chuckle.

Over the course of the years, though the work he was involved in was so far removed from it, his engineering background would at times show through—when, for example, he used examples having to do with dams and other public works, or when he joked about "safety margins," or when he referred to specific aspects of his profession. His basic training clearly showed itself in the order and precision of his thinking and expression, in those intellectual habits so deeply rooted in Western culture. These he would soon cultivate also through his studies in liberal arts, and in the attaining of a doctorate in history. As Alejandro Llano, rector of the University of Navarre, said in 1994, "He was a living synthesis of two cultures: that of the humanities and that of technology. He was a great intellectual and university man."

6

The Spanish Civil War

At lunch on September 1, 1976, at the Solavieya Conference Center in Asturias, shortly before he was to return to Rome, Don Alvaro was served a bottle of Cigales wine, a gift from someone in Valladolid. Normally he did not drink wine, but he took some on this occasion in memory of his stay in Cigales in January 1939, towards the end of the Spanish Civil War, when he was stationed there by the army.

When the war broke out, in July 1936, Alvaro moved back in with his family. His brothers Ramón, Pepe, and Paco soon took refuge in various places in Madrid. But Alvaro stayed on at home, since it was at Father Josemaría's insistence that he had returned there from the Ferraz Street residence on the afternoon of July 19. He took all the precautions dictated by prudence, but was able, nevertheless, to lead a fairly normal life because of his serene and courageous temperament. Except when it became impossible, he kept in touch with the founder and with other Opus Dei members who were still in Spain's capital.

Next to the family home, which was a downstairs apartment at 16 Conde de Aranda Street, there was a school which had been turned into a barracks. One day Alvaro arrived home late and could not open the door to the entranceway. He strode into the barracks, asked for some assistance, and the sentries helped him get in. It was in June 1976 that I heard him tell this story, but he did not specify the date on which it happened. It may have been some time later on in the war, after he had been drafted and had become, in the eyes of the law, a deserter.

I do know that he stayed in the family home until August 13. On that day, early in the morning, soldiers entered the home of the del Portillos' upstairs neighbor, Cristino Bermúdez de Castro, who was the son of a well-known general. His wife fled down the interior staircase to the del Portillo home, hoping to hide some valuables there. But the soldiers arrived at nearly the same time and searched the place. When they entered Alvaro's room, he put something in his mouth and started chewing. His sister Pilar thinks it was probably a list of his friends' names, addresses, and phone numbers. The soldiers shouted at him, "Hey, you, what are you chewing?" Alvaro calmly answered, "Some paper."

No one in the family was allowed to move until it was time to eat. The presence of the soldiers made it impossible for them to warn Bermúdez de Castro, so he was arrested. He was, in fact, shot that very night, after a kangaroo court trial. And on that same day, the soldiers arrested Don Ramón del Portillo and took him to an unknown destination.

In that situation Alvaro had no choice but to look for a hiding place. Soon afterwards, with his brother Pepe, he moved into a chalet tucked far back on the left side of Serrano Street (coming from the direction of Alcalá Street); the house belonged to friends of the family. The owners had posted on it a picture of the flag of Argentina in the hope that this would fend off searches, although the house was not in fact protected by Argentina.

After a few weeks, Alvaro was curious to know whether

he was still on the payroll of the Department of Public Works, where he was working when the war began. He discovered that he had not been fired; in fact, he was able to pick up his pay for all the time that he had been out. Then he thought of doing something he had never done before: celebrate his good fortune at La Mezquita, a nearby bar located at a major intersection. "My mind was so confused," he recalled many years later, "that I didn't even have the sense to go inside. Without a care in the world I sat down at a table near the sidewalk. It never crossed my mind that at any time I could have been asked for my papers, in which case I would have been jailed immediately."

But it was all providential. There he met Alvaro González, the father of José María González Barredo, one of the first members of Opus Dei. Alvaro González told him that Father Josemaría was staying at his house, which was very close by, on Caracas Street. Father Josemaría was there to get some much-needed rest. But it would not be possible to hide him there for long, because the doorkeeper could not be trusted. "So without thinking twice," recalled Don Alvaro, "I said, 'Then let him come with me!'"

And so it was that Pepe and Alvaro del Portillo were reunited with Father Josemaría in the chalet on Serrano Street. Later they were joined by Juan Jiménez Vargas, another member of Opus Dei. But after barely three weeks they realized that the place was not safe, so they immediately set about finding another refuge. A few days later, the founder went to the home of Professor Eugenio Sellés, at 11 Maestro Chapí Street; Alvaro accompanied him and spent three days there.

Eventually Alvaro moved into the Finnish embassy. He stayed there until early in December 1936, when the embassy was raided by the militia. He and the other refugees were then jailed in what used to be Saint Anthony School. When his mother heard of this, she went to visit him and even brought in some food, which was not an easy thing to do. As a matter of fact, it never reached him. He went very hungry much of the time and suffered innumerable humiliations. But his sister Pilar says that he told them about this "with great peacefulness, with no anger or resentment, just with sorrow for those who had been so carried away by hatred." When his mother and sister managed to see him, he insisted that they should not worry. "He lived through it," says Pilar, "with a great serenity, with that interior peace which was so characteristic of him."

Don Alvaro spoke about that period of his life only on rare occasions. One such occasion took place in the Filipino city of Cebu, at the end of January 1987. He was trying to get across how necessary it is to love and to foster peace, and this brought to his mind the persecution against the Church which had been unleashed in Spain during the civil war. "I had never been involved in any political activity," he said, "and I was not a priest, or a religious, or even a seminarian; I was just an engineering student. I got thrown in jail just because I came from a Catholic family. By then I was already wearing glasses, and one day one of the guards came up to me—his name was Petrof, it's a Russian name—and he put a pistol to my temple and said, 'You're wearing glasses—you must be a priest.' He could have killed me at any moment. I think the only reason he didn't was because God thought I still had a lot of fighting to do against the devil, or because I was not worthy of heaven. It was terrifying."

In January 1992 he was at an Opus Dei get-together in Vienna, and in the group there happened to be a Croatian and a Slovene. At that time the smoke was still rising from a terrible conflict in the former Yugoslavia in which many people had been killed and many Catholic churches had been destroyed. Don Alvaro spoke to the group about the importance of forgiveness. In this context he related another incident from his time at Saint Anthony. "There was a chapel," he said, "in which about four hundred of us were incarcerated. One day a Communist soldier stomped up to the altar, on which there was a picture of a saint, and he put a cigarette butt on the saint's lips. One of the fellows with me went up there and took the butt away. He was killed on the spot for doing that. There was an incredible hatred of religion. But we have to know how to forgive."

Alvaro remained imprisoned until January 29, 1937; he was freed the day after his trial. He could not get into the Mexican embassy, where his parents were staying with his younger brothers and sisters, so he looked for another refuge. He was to find one in the Honduran embassy, as did also the founder and some other members of Opus Dei.

There is no need to mention all the privations and hardships involved in that confinement. Suffice it to say that they coexisted with an atmosphere of peace, a good use of time (it was there that Don Alvaro began to study both Japanese and German), and a supernatural spirit which filled that small room. These scenes have already been sketched in the biographies of Monsignor Escrivá, partly by way of some expressive drawings by Don Alvaro himself which show in detail the layout of the room during the day and how their sleeping mats were arranged at night.

One of the hardest times for Alvaro was when his father died. Don Ramón had, as I mentioned, been arrested in August 1936, but not until the beginning of 1937 was his family informed that he was in the Saint Anthony jail. Not even Alvaro knew it. So many people were imprisoned there, and kept so isolated, that father and son spent all that time in that same building without ever seeing each other. Anyway, when Doña Clementina found out where her husband was, she appealed to the embassy of her native country, Mexico, and thus got him released. He then took refuge with her in the Mexican embassy, but he arrived in very precarious health. A Dr. Calderín diagnosed tuberculosis of the larynx.

Despite treatment, his illness grew worse. So, at the beginning of September 1937, Doña Clementina told Tere and Carlos to get the word to Alvaro, who was still in hiding at the Honduran embassy. He, in turn, told Father Josemaría, who by that time had left the embassy and was moving around Madrid with relative freedom, although his papers did not afford him total safety.

The founder of Opus Dei went immediately to lend his services as a priest to Don Ramón. He gave him the Anointing of the Sick and Viaticum before leaving Madrid at the beginning of October. Pilar recalls that he was dressed in something like a lab coat, such as a doctor or a shopkeeper might wear. To cover up what was happening, they called out when they opened the door, "The doctor's here!" Father Josemaría brought the holy oils in a syringe, and the Blessed Sacrament in tiny corporals inside a woman's cigarette case, the cover of which was decorated with the flag of Honduras. Don Ramón was greatly comforted.

Naturally, Alvaro wished with all his heart to visit his father, whom he had not seen since August 1936. But the founder strongly counseled against doing this. It would not be prudent, he said, for Alvaro to venture out of his hiding place without having his papers in order. Alvaro accepted this, and although it cost him, he offered up to God the sacrifice of not being able to be with his father in his last illness and at his death.

Don Ramón died on October 14, by which time Father Josemaría was far gone from Madrid. As Pilar says, this must have been very hard for Alvaro. "But," she adds, "anyone could have betrayed us. The cook at the Mexican embassy, for example, was politically very extremist and radical. She had a daughter named Mantequilla (Butter). We always told the little ones never to repeat anything from our conversations when they played with her, because of the danger that she might tell her mother and her mother might turn us in."

When Don Ramón died, the del Portillo family—with a lot of hard work—managed to leave Madrid and move to Burgos (on the Nationalist side). As for Alvaro, he remained for a while in the Honduran embassy. Together with Vicente Rodríguez Casado (who until recently had been hiding in the Norwegian embassy) and Eduardo Alastrué, he was planning to leave the capital if they could get passports by presenting birth certificates belonging to people of other nationalities. They managed to get Cuban birth certificates, and they presented them at the Cuban embassy, but the embassy did not accept them.

All along, they kept in good touch with Isidoro Zorzano, who had stayed in Madrid as the director when the founder left. They informed him, in fact, of everything they were doing. And when they mentioned to him the possibility of their leaving the embassy, he at first said no. But then one day in 1938, while praying with his eyes fixed on a crucifix which he kept in his office together with the Blessed Sacrament, he saw that they would cross the front lines on October 12. When Isidoro received this special communication from God, he went to the Honduran embassy and gave them permission to leave as soon as certain matters were taken care of.

Vicente, Eduardo, and Alvaro enlisted in the militia on different days and under false names. "The natural thing," Don Alvaro later recalled, "would have been for us to end up in different places, but they sent all three of us to the same regiment, the same battalion, the same company, and the same platoon. It was incredible. Two of us were corporals and the other was a private. They asked me, 'Can you read?' I said, 'A little.' So they wrote down, 'Semiliterate.' And they made me a corporal! I had no idea what I was supposed to do, since I had not yet done anything at all by way of

military service. And the very day that we arrived at the
front lines, we went across to the other side!"

Alvaro used the names "Pepe Portillo," "Alvaro
Rostillo," and "Juan Alvaro Cortillo." Together with Vicente
and Eduardo, he was assigned to a company of the Twenty-
first Brigade, which left Madrid for the front on August 24.
From then until October 12, their life was full of adventures.
Alvaro recorded these in a handwritten account entitled
"From Madrid to Burgos through Guadalajara." And where
he wrote down his vivid memories of leaving Madrid, there
are a few sentences which very well capture his attitude at
that time: "Throughout the trip, people are making a
thousand guesses about where we are going. To Levante?
Extremadura? Guadalajara? But the three of us say hardly
anything. We haven't a care in the world, because we know
that wherever they take us, that will be precisely the best
point on the whole front for us to cross over."

They went to Anchuelo, near Alcalá de Henares, and to
Fontanar, about six miles from Guadalajara. From there, on
October 9, they began a march to the front lines, crossing
Razbona and Tamajón and then deploying near a village called
Roblelacasa. On the morning of the eleventh, Alvaro, Vicente,
and Eduardo slipped away at a point near Campillo de las
Ranas. They made their way to the top of Ocejón Hill and
followed the Sonsaz River. Then they crossed the bed of the
Sorbe River and spent the night in a cave. The next morning,
they climbed another hill. From the top they could see a town
with a very prominent church tower, and soon they heard a
peal of bells for a nine o'clock Mass; it was the feast of Our
Lady of the Pillar. The town was Cantalojas—it was in the
Nationalist zone. So, after so much time in hiding, they
attended a high Mass. Afterwards they reported to the military
authorities, and thanks to Vicente's father, who was an army
colonel, they reached Burgos on the evening of the fourteenth.

Meanwhile, the founder of Opus Dei continued to work

in and from Burgos. On August 1, he sent a letter to Isidoro Zorzano. Using cryptic wording to elude the censor, he wrote, "My dear friend: I just received a letter from my son Iñasi [Isidoro Zorzano], dated July 15. I hasten to let you know my great joy upon hearing that my grandchildren [Vicente, Eduardo, and Alvaro] are coming to spend some time with me here, since my return to our beloved country has been delayed."

A few weeks later he found out by some supernatural communication that they would cross the front lines on October 12, the feast of Our Lady of the Pillar, and he immediately informed Doña Clementina. Both Pedro Casciaro and Francisco Botella recall that on the twelfth and thirteenth, the founder was very calm, content, and confident, and that on the fourteenth he told them again, "I'll get the word to you in the barracks when they arrive." They received the phone call at about eight o'clock that night.

Alvaro spent the last two weeks of October and the first day of November together with the founder of Opus Dei, while awaiting an army posting. On November 10 he entered an engineering academy for non-career military officers; this was at Fuentes Blancas, a few miles from Burgos. He spent Christmas there that year.

Circumstances did not, of course, make it easy for him to go to Mass, but he always went when he could. Right after signing up for a course at the academy, he asked the colonel for permission to go each morning to the Carthusian monastery of Miraflores. The request must have been an unusual one, for the colonel gave his permission only unofficially. If, he said, the military police ever questioned him, or if he ever had to explain himself to officers in other units, he wouldn't know anything about it.

Besides the considerable distance between the academy and the monastery, Alvaro also had to contend with the early-morning rigors of the Burgos winter, for he returned shortly before reveille sounded. There was also some danger of rabid dogs, and he carried a pistol with him just in case. But his good example did not go unnoticed, nor did his apostolic efforts fail to bear fruit. A few weeks later, when the course ended, he was not going to Mass by himself—about thirty other fellows were going with him.

Early in January 1939, as I mentioned earlier, he was sent to Cigales, near Valladolid. His regiment's assignment was to restore bridges destroyed during the fighting. Vicente Rodríguez Casado was also stationed in Cigales. Father Josemaría went to this small town in Castile a few times to visit them. The first time, on January 13, he made the round trip in a single day. On other occasions Alvaro rode on horseback to Valladolid to be with the founder.

At that lunch in Asturias on September 1, 1976, Don Alvaro recounted an incident which must have taken place on a Saturday afternoon in March 1939—either the eleventh or the eighteenth—when the founder of Opus Dei was with them in Cigales. They were staying in the home of Manuel Alcalde, an elderly, well-to-do gentleman who owned a wine shop, and a younger relative there wanted to show them some good Castilian hospitality. This man's name was Enrique. Don Alvaro did not remember exactly how he was related— he may have been a brother or a brother-in-law—but he did remember him as a very good man, very eager to please, who described his trade as "cirugía menor" (minor surgery): he was a barber. Anyway, Enrique insisted on taking them to the wine shop, where they could have a bit of ham with some good wine. He had, of course, no way of knowing that this young priest practiced austere corporal mortifications which included fasting on Saturdays, especially during Lent. (At that time, the Church required fasting on Wednesdays, Fridays, and Saturdays in Lent. However, in wartime there was a general dispensation.) Father Josemaría made it clear that everyone else could have a snack with a clear conscience, but he refused to dispense himself from the fast, though they strongly urged him to. Alvaro and Vicente, mindful of how hungry he was and how thin he had become, kept insisting that he eat something, and he kept flatly refusing. Enrique finally interrupted, in an attempt to end this in a tactful way. "Don't insist," he told Alvaro and Vicente. "I am quite familiar with people of his stock, and when they say no, they mean no."

His military duties did not prevent Alvaro from continuing his studies in engineering and languages. From Burgos, people sent him magazines in German and English and tried to get him books that would help him with his Japanese. At the suggestion of Father Josemaría, he wrote to the Japanese ambassador, who was then residing in San Sebastián. On January 25 he received an answer, along with several pamphlets. The people at the embassy promised to send him a dictionary later on, if and when they could find one. He also received a letter from a Dominican missionary, the author of a dictionary, with information on how to obtain it.

To the extent allowed by his military duties, Alvaro tried to stay in close touch with the founder, who arrived in Madrid on March 28, 1939. As a matter of fact, Alvaro managed to get together with him on the very next day. That afternoon, his officer's uniform facilitated the task of ejecting a soldier who was illegally occupying the rectory at the Santa Isabel Foundation.

When the war ended, Alvaro remained in the army, as did many others. He was sent to Figueras and then to Olot, near the French border. His regiment's assignment was still road repairs. In Catalonia alone, more than a thousand bridges had been bombed during the war.

In Olot he was able to fulfill his military duties without neglecting either his practices of piety or his cultivating of friendship with his comrades in arms. In his free times he often went with friends to visit sick people in hospitals.

Whenever he had a furlough, he would look up Father Josemaría, in whatever city he might be. The hours of travel time meant little to him, despite all the difficulties and discomfort of the postwar period.

Thus, for example, early in June 1939, thanks to leave granted him by a good friend, Fernando Delapuente (who, not long after, asked admission to Opus Dei), he was able to go to Valencia to see Father Josemaría, who was giving a retreat to university students. The retreat was held in a student residence, Blessed Juan de Ribera Hall, in Burjasot. Well, Alvaro had gone two or three days with practically no sleep at all, but he decided, nevertheless, to do his monthly day of recollection. And even though he sat in the first row, and even though the chapel benches had no backrests, he was fast asleep within ten minutes. The founder related this many years later and concluded, "I was really delighted, because I knew that the sleep of that son of mine, on that particular occasion, was a prayer most pleasing to God."

One day that year, our Lord made it known to Father Josemaría that a son of his was experiencing some kind of personal difficulty, albeit of an external rather than internal nature. (This happened not long after the Jenner Street residence had been set up, so it could not have been before the second half of July.) He was with others, at a family-style get-together, so he called for everyone's attention and asked them all to pray very intensely Saint Bernard's prayer to the Blessed Virgin, the Memorare, for someone in great need of help. This event was the basis of point 472 of *Furrow*: "The Communion of Saints: that young engineer understood it well when he told me, 'Father, on such a day, at such a time, you were praying for me.' This is and will always be the first and most fundamental help that we can provide for souls: prayer." And thus arose the custom in Opus Dei of praying this prayer every day, as many times as one can, for the member of the Work who at that time most needs it.

When Don Alvaro was asked how this custom came about, his answers were usually brief and even evasive. But that is understandable—for this "young engineer" was almost certainly himself. Furthermore, even if for no other reason, he would have spoken of such an event in the third person just to keep the spotlight on the supernatural gifts of the founder, who had "seen" situations which were happening far away.

This is the way he told it to Cesare Cavalleri, as recorded in the book *Immersed in God* (1996, 184): "Around that same time, it also happened that some girls were making an attempt to seduce a member of the Work. We later found out that on the very day they were going to try to put him in a compromising situation, our founder was with some of his sons and suddenly exclaimed, 'At this moment one of your brothers is in great need of help! Let's say a Memorare for him.' I should add that the brother in question had not had time to inform the Father about what was going on. Well, the danger instantly vanished."

I have not been able to determine precisely what the danger was. As I heard it from Fernando Delapuente, who is now deceased, all the other men in Alvaro's unit were lodged in a former convent in Olot, but the officers were living in private homes. Alvaro was assigned to the home of an older woman with an unmarried daughter. But—this is all he said to Fernando—he intended to leave as soon as possible, because he did not like the situation. Every night when he would come home, already worn out, he would find them waiting for him, expecting him to carry on with them a lively chat over cups of hot chocolate. At the end of his leave, he moved to the house that Eduardo Alastrué and Vicente Rodríguez Casado were living in.

Not long after, Alvaro moved to Madrid on a permanent basis, so that he could throw himself into helping the founder while finishing the work for his engineering degree.

7

In Madrid and from Madrid

As soon as he was discharged from the army, Alvaro became the right-hand man of the founder of Opus Dei. But this was especially so after 1940, when he was named Secretary General of Opus Dei.

While he was finishing his studies in civil engineering, which had been interrupted by the civil war, Alvaro was also helping to direct and move forward many apostolic activities in Madrid and other Spanish cities. He played an important role in the formation of the growing number of people who were joining the Work. Furthermore, among the many who were students, he was one of the few who were able to earn money and thus help supply the funds necessary for any apostolic undertaking. To top it all off, a fierce campaign of calumny was soon to be unleashed against Opus Dei and its founder, making it even more urgent to find an appropriate canonical setting for the Work. In those stressful years, Father Josemaría found in Alvaro unfailing support. He was a hewn stone, a rock—in Latin, "saxum."

This was clearly God's doing. Initially it was not Alvaro but another fellow whom the founder had thought of asking to serve in this capacity. But, as the founder would sometimes say when Don Alvaro was not present, he "was discovered."

And with his constantly supportive, affirmative attitude, with that full accord of both mind and heart that he had with Blessed Josemaría, he soon proved himself to be the person who could best help him understand, grapple with, and solve the most delicate and difficult problems.

Father Josemaría, in fact, actually called him "Saxum." The nickname appears already in a letter sent from Burgos on March 23, 1939—fifty-five years, to the day, before Don Alvaro's death. "May Jesus take care of you for me, Saxum," he says. "For yes, that is exactly what you are. I see that the Lord is giving you strength and making operative in you this word of mine, "saxum." Thank him for this and remain faithful to him, despite . . . so many things. . . . If only you could see how great is my longing to be a saint, and to make saints of all of you!"

In a letter dated May 18, 1939, the founder wrote these beautiful, poetic words: "Saxum! How white in my eyes is the long, long way which lies ahead of you! White and full, like a field ready for the harvest. Blessed fruitfulness of an apostle, more beautiful than all the beauties of the earth! Saxum!" Alvaro was then only twenty-five years old.

Not long before, on February 10, Father Josemaría was in Cigales, giving a day of recollection. We have a handwritten outline of a meditation that he gave on that day, and this is its first point: "Tu es Petrus... saxum. You are a rock, a stone! And the reason you are is because that is what God wants. In spite of the enemies who surround us, and in spite of yourself, and in spite of myself—in spite of everyone and everything that you may be up against. Rock, foundation, support, strength—fatherhood!"

Don Alvaro was a highly qualified right-hand man, a true rock, a firm foundation supporting the founder both in day-to-day life and at crucial points along the theological and juridical path of Opus Dei. Monsignor Escrivá stressed this on several occasions when Don Alvaro was not present.

He would say, "He knows how to make, with a smile, a sacrifice of everything personal. Many times he has been heroic—many times—and with a heroism which seems something quite ordinary." At a gathering in La Lloma (near Valencia) on November 14, 1972, he literally said this: "Don Alvaro is a most faithful son. . . . Many times he has offered his own back to spare me the lashes, and has taken the blows and insults with a smile—even recently."

In 1994 Don Javier Echevarría, in the previously mentioned interview with Pilar Urbano, summed it up thus: "I always saw Don Alvaro making himself unobtrusive, staying in the background but close enough to the founder to be able to see, hear, and attend to him. You could see even in his body language his constant attitude of wanting to learn from him. Considering the extraordinary talents of Bishop Alvaro—which, by the way, he used for the benefit of ordinary people—this showed a great faith and humility. In all truthfulness, I must say that Alvaro del Portillo was gifted with outstanding natural and supernatural qualities. Because of his exceptional intelligence, his cultural refinement, his excellent education, his highly developed social skills, the loftiness of his thinking, the depth of his interior life, and a long list of moral virtues which he lived to a heroic degree, he was in my eyes a giant. I am not exaggerating. And yet I saw him always waiting on the founder, seconding him in everything, putting all his talents into helping him establish and develop Opus Dei. He deliberately chose to be a faithful executor of the founder's wishes."

His lifelong identification with Monsignor Escrivá became evident early on, probably as far back as the time they spent together in the Honduran embassy during the Spanish Civil War. It seems to have been from the very beginning something basically intuitive. A gesture or just half a word from the founder was enough for Alvaro to know what needed to be done. And always he did it with great confidence and respect, tact and good will. He never hid his deep conviction that his sole mission in life was to help the one whom God had chosen to found Opus Dei.

In January 1948 he accompanied the founder on his first trip to the shrine of Loreto. After the two of them prayed for a while in the holy house where Jesus is said to have been born, Monsignor Escrivá asked him, "What did you say to our Lady?" Don Alvaro answered in a teasing tone of voice, "You want me to tell you?" Monsignor Escrivá said, "Oh, yes, I insist." So he told him this: "Well, I said what I always say, but I said it as if for the very first time. I told her, 'I ask of you whatever the Father is asking of you.'"

In the forties, in Madrid, as Secretary General of Opus Dei, he was in charge whenever the founder was away. It was up to him to move along many things relating to the development of the apostolate. But he also had to bear the brunt of responsibility in times of sorrow—for example, when the founder's mother died. The death of Doña Dolores Albás took place on April 22, 1941, when the founder was in the town of Lérida, giving a retreat for priests. It was Don Alvaro who had to communicate the painful news and take care of matters until the Father arrived the next day, at two in the morning.

Many years later, I was deeply impressed by the humility with which Don Alvaro related some of the circumstances of this difficult time. On the day of the death, he had just gotten through doing something quite unusual. He had stayed up almost the whole night before, working in an apartment which was being used as an Opus Dei center—this was on Martínez Campos Street, in Madrid. There was a job he wanted to have finished and ready for the founder upon his return. It was the typing up, on good paper, of the Work's by-laws, which had just received diocesan approval. Alvaro was dictating these to Ricardo Fernández Vallespín, who was living in the center. (Ricardo was an architect, but also a

very good typist.) This was a task which required great
concentration, because mistakes could not be erased on that
kind of paper; a single error meant that the whole page had
to be retyped. When they finished, not long before dawn,
Don Alvaro caught a couple of hours of sleep, at Ricardo's
suggestion. Then he did his morning prayer and went to
Mass. When he arrived at the Diego de León Street center
(part of which was Doña Dolores' residence), the woman
they all called "the Grandmother" had already died.

Don Alvaro used to tell this story as confirmation of
the fact that her illness had not seemed serious, which was
why Father Josemaría had gone on to Lérida. Also, if the
situation had seemed at all alarming, then Don Alvaro, who
was in charge of Opus Dei in Madrid during the founder's
absence, would have stayed at Diego de León to do his work,
for he too was living there.

Don Alvaro's memories of the Grandmother
overflowed with affection and gratitude. His serenity did
not keep him from feeling things deeply, and he was never
one to hide his feelings. As a matter of fact, this trait of his
was particularly appealing to the Grandmother. When she
saw his cheeks redden, she would say with a twinkle in her
eye, "You are high quality; you could be a son of mine!" She
herself had a fine, fair complexion, not pale—her skin
naturally had good color, though she did enhance it with
cosmetics—and she blushed easily. That was what she meant
by "high quality."

During the forties, Alvaro's apostolic activity was
intense. I don't want to detail the expansion of Opus Dei in
Spain after the end of the civil war, but I would like to give
some idea of how many trips Alvaro took on roads and
railway lines which had been badly damaged during the war.
Early in June 1939, he went to Valencia. On December 28
he traveled to Saragossa, and from there to Barcelona and
then Valencia. In 1940 he was in Saragossa on February 18,

February 25, March 3, and March 29. On the last of these trips he then proceeded, with the founder, to Barcelona and Valencia. He did the same on May 12, and on May 14 he went again to Saragossa. (On his first trip to Barcelona, he looked up Rafael Termes, who had taken with him that minicourse for non-career military officers in Burgos, and he had a long talk with Alfonso Balcells, whom he had met a few months before in Burjasot. Both of these fellows would later ask to be admitted to Opus Dei.) On June 29 he arrived once again in Barcelona, with José Luis Múzquiz. By this time the tiny rented apartment known as "El Palau" (The Palace) was being used as an Opus Dei center—the first in Barcelona.

In the accounts that I have read, these fellows talk most about the profound impact made on them by Blessed Josemaría, as is to be expected. Alvaro, along with the other early members of the Work, remains in the background. But Teodoro Ruiz, who spoke with the founder for the first time in January 1940, in Valladolid, also talks about the impact that Don Alvaro made on him. "I went out," he says, "to look for one of my friends, and when I came back with him, Don Alvaro was speaking in great detail about the life of piety fostered in this apostolic undertaking. He stressed unity with God through prayer and the sacraments—an intense spiritual life without anything strange, unusual, or ostentatious, a solid piety that did not call attention to itself. For a priest to say this—even that was a novelty. But for just a regular, ordinary fellow to say it—and especially one of those pursuing a career in highway engineering, who in the Spain of that time were the elite of the university—this was cause for no end of surprise." They were, of course, moved by the teaching and example they had received from Father Josemaría, but they were also struck by the depth to which Alvaro had assimilated it.

Teodoro Ruiz relates another anecdote which illustrates

the mettle of Alvaro del Portillo. This happened during one
of those trips to Valladolid at the beginning of the forties.
One day the founder and a group of students were going to
the cathedral for Mass—a Mass to be celebrated by the
founder. Suddenly, to everyone's surprise, Alvaro said,
"Father, if you don't mind, I'll go to Mass on my own, at
another church." Teodoro did not understand this until
Father Josemaría explained it. Alvaro, he said, had done this
as a way of ensuring that no one would feel compelled to go
in a group to Mass.

Alvaro's dedication in those years also showed itself in
the trips he made with the founder to visit the bishops of
Spain, to inform them about the apostolate of the Work.
These trips really took it out of them. They had to travel,
without a break, in a bad car over bad roads with enormous
potholes caused by the war. Later on, after Father Josemaría
was diagnosed with diabetes, they did get at least one break:
they had to stop wherever they happened to be when it was
time for his insulin injection, and ask someone the favor of
letting them come in or of helping them find some suitable
place.

These trips cemented the well-documented friendship
of Monsignor Escrivá with the Spanish episcopate. That Don
Alvaro also shared in this cordial relationship was especially
obvious in the case of the bishop of Madrid-Alcalá, Bishop
Leopoldo Eijo y Garay. Certainly he expressed great
admiration for the founder of Opus Dei. But he liked Alvaro
every bit as much. And Carlos del Portillo remembers the
day that Bishop Eijo told their mother, Doña Clementina,
that she'd better hold on to her memories of her son Alvaro,
because one day they would be seeing him on the altar.

Bishop Eijo's esteem and even admiration for Alvaro
was very great indeed. Only this can explain the tone of a
letter in which he asks Alvaro's pardon—something nearly
inconceivable at that time for a man in the exalted position

of bishop of Madrid-Alcalá. This letter, dated January 27, 1943, begins as follows: "Dearest Alvaro: Better late than never. Long before now I should have sent you a receipt for the thousand pesetas which on February 2, 1942, you sent me for the outlying districts, at the Father's request." (Yes, even Bishop Eijo referred to the founder of Opus Dei as "the Father.") "This will surely be of use to you in the keeping of your accounts. Apologies for such a delay."

Their relationship was full of warmth and good humor. Bishop Eijo, for instance, used to tease Don Alvaro about his smoking. This was a habit he had taken up at the suggestion of the founder of Opus Dei, who thought that at least one of those first three priests of the Work should be a smoker. The general attitude with regard to smoking was different then, and the founder wanted to ensure that future priests of the Work would feel free to smoke. However, Don Alvaro's lack of practice was all too evident during his frequent visits to Bishop Eijo, who was a heavy smoker. After rolling the cigarettes, the bishop would offer a light to Don Alvaro, who, instead of inhaling, would often exhale, extinguishing the match or lighter. Then the bishop, who was known for his sense of humor, would say, "Well, now, Alvaro, are you smoking, or are you just blowing hot air?"

Juan Antonio González Lobato relates another incident which is very expressive of that friendship. This happened sometime between 1946 and 1948, at the Villanueva Street center in Madrid. Don Alvaro had just come there from Rome and had fallen ill—so ill that he had to keep to his bed. A phone call for him from the bishop's secretary was taken by Juan Antonio, who lived at that center. He told the secretary that Don Alvaro could not come to the phone because he was sick in bed. Well, when Don Alvaro found out, he immediately requested some help in tidying up his room, because he suspected that Bishop Eijo would be coming to see him. And sure enough, that's what happened.

The bishop showed up at the center, went straight to Don Alvaro's room, shut the door, and spent a long time talking with him, while Juan Antonio and someone else kept the secretary company.

In those intense years following the civil war, God did not keep Alvaro from ever getting sick, as he did at so many other times in his life. Hardly had he moved to the Jenner Street residence when he came down with some kind of liver disease. I remember him commenting about how affectionately the founder's mother treated him. "She once made me a very rich punch," he said, "with milk, egg yolk, sherry, and sugar. It was wonderful, but neither of us realized that it would knock my liver out. I drank it and right away threw it up. I said to the Grandmother, 'What a pity, Grandmother—it was so good!'"

Not long afterwards, his face became inflamed. The doctor advised him to apply compresses soaked in very hot water. Carmen Escrivá prepared them with boiling water. Teodoro Ruiz remembers being astonished when he saw Don Alvaro applying those steaming cloths with no hesitation or complaint.

I have not been able to determine whether it was these or some other pains that the founder was referring to, but at the end of the letter that he wrote to Alvaro from La Granja on September 25, 1941, he asks, "How is Isidoro? Did they give him the injection? And have they brought medicines for you?"

In the midst of so many different activities, Alvaro behaved with a great naturalness which radiated a constant consciousness of God's presence, ongoing prayer, a unity of life in all circumstances, spiritual maturity. In his first conversation with him, Teodoro Ruiz was surprised by the ease, assurance, and spontaneity with which an engineering student talked about prayer and the sacraments. He was surprised by the total lack of either glibness or unctuousness.

Alvaro's words, he said, were very persuasive, appealing, and novel. Above all, they obviously came from personal experience, not just theory. "You could see," he said, "that this was a man with a solid and practical faith—a faith nourished with a sturdy piety that was based on much prayer, frequent recourse to the sacraments, and a tender devotion to the Blessed Virgin."

8

Hard Times

In the difficult years following the Spanish Civil War, Alvaro soon tasted the bitterness of the opposition faced by the founder of Opus Dei. And he had to cope with some family problems as well.

Don Ramón del Portillo had died without fully understanding or approving of his son's commitment to Opus Dei. Doña Clementina, on the other hand, immediately understood the extent of his commitment and was always very happy with the path that he had chosen. In Burgos, during the war, she came to know the founder very well, and she very much admired him. She saw him as a zealous priest who was a great friend of her son and of the whole family. She trusted him completely, and found it relatively easy to understand and appreciate the novelty of Opus Dei.

Shortly after the war ended—possibly as early as October 1939, when he returned from his assignment in Olot—Alvaro told her that he was going to live in the university residence run by Father Josemaría Escrivá on Jenner Street, in Madrid. There they could take up again the cultural and apostolic works they had begun in the Ferraz Street residence, which had been destroyed in the war.

Doña Clementina made not the slightest objection. But this separation from her son was hard on her. Things were not easy for her family, especially financially. Also, this was a time in which she, a relatively young widow, had to make a new life for herself in Madrid. Her oldest son, Ramón, had moved out. Paco and Pilar were about to get married. Angel and Pepe were in the army and stationed far away. Tere and Carlos were still small children. She had been counting on Alvaro for help. And besides, she felt a special affection for him. As Carlos explained it, "He was so good, so affectionate and helpful to everyone, and especially us little ones!"

Then anonymous letters began to arrive, all with one message in common: that Alvaro had been hoodwinked by an unorthodox priest and was in serious danger of eternal damnation. Doña Clementina was even visited by a religious—from a teaching order!—who warned her about this great danger hovering over her son. He was astonished, he said, that a fellow of Alvaro's caliber could allow himself to be influenced by such people. It was the beginning of what Monsignor Escrivá would call, using words inspired by the Gospel, "the opposition of good people."

Doña Clementina told this religious that she knew quite well both her son and the priest in question, and with that she bade him farewell. But the gossip continued. And she could never understand why. Sometimes, says Pilar, Alvaro would give their mother a hug and tell her over and over that someday she would understand.

Meanwhile, Alvaro was very concerned about the family problems, financial and otherwise. One great worry for his mother was that her youngest son, Carlos, was showing no interest in school. During the war he had gotten out of the habit of studying, and now he couldn't seem to get back into it. One day—this must have been sometime in 1941—Father Josemaría and Alvaro suggested to her that it might be a good idea for Carlos to board for a while at a good school, and said that the Work would cover whatever it cost. It too was in great financial need, but both Father Josemaría and Alvaro saw this as a clear obligation of charity. So Carlos continued his secondary education at a highly regarded school run by Capuchins—Our Lady of Lecároz, in the province of Navarre—and became a good student.

It was there that he heard, in 1944, the news that his brother Alvaro would soon be ordained. And it was then that he suddenly understood a change which had taken place in his mother's routine in recent months. She had, for the first time in her life, taken up embroidery, and her explanations to Tere and Carlos had not been very convincing. "It's just that... I'm trying to keep alive some traditional Mexican arts! I'm trying to relearn what I was taught as a girl." Now they discovered that she was embroidering an alb for Alvaro, for his ordination.

Doña Clementina had been delighted to hear the news. It was one of the great dreams of her life to have one of her sons become a priest, and now this dream was coming true. She was always very happy about this, even though, not long afterwards, the growth of the apostolate of Opus Dei made it necessary for Alvaro to leave Madrid for good.

As for Alvaro, he could deal with any problem patiently and gently, because he trusted always and completely in the grace of God. Without losing his almost proverbial calm, he acted courageously, even daringly; he was a man who grew in the face of obstacles. His was the peaceful demeanor of a natural-born fighter—respectful and not aggressive, but gifted with deeply rooted and persevering strength. To his life could easily be applied a metaphor often used by Monsignor Escrivá to illustrate the struggle for sanctity, a metaphor expressed by Don Alvaro in these words: "The work of the farmer requires effort, tenacity, patience. One must plough the earth, fertilize it, and water it. One must protect the

Alvaro at the age of about three.

With his family in 1925. Alvaro is the first on the left.

Dressed in the uniform of a Spanish civil engineer in 1944.

The ordination of Don Alvaro by Archbishop Leopoldo Eijo y Garay of Madrid in 1944. With him are José Maria Hernández de Garnica and José Luis Múzquiz (Father Joseph Muzquiz).

plants from frost, or from too much exposure to the sun, and fight off pests. One must live a life of hard work, of silent struggle, in the cold and in the heat, in rain or in drought, before harvesting the crop."

Encarnación Ortega tells this story from her years as Central Secretary of Opus Dei. One day Cardinal Tedeschini told her that he had just introduced two monsignors to Don Alvaro, and that as soon as Don Alvaro left the room, they commented that his mere presence radiated peace. And he, though of course he agreed with them, had felt obliged to add this clarification: "But when it comes to defending the Church or the Work, he defends it with the strength of a lion!"

Don Alvaro gave abundant evidence of his human and supernatural strength throughout those many years with the founder of Opus Dei when problems were so abundant. Monsignor Escrivá once said to Pilar, "How many difficulties your brother Alvaro has had to overcome! How much misunderstanding! How much fatigue! How many financial problems!"

From the time he was named Secretary General of Opus Dei in 1940, Don Alvaro was the main support for the founder also in connection with that "opposition of good people." This can be seen in the letter which Father Josemaría wrote to him from La Granja (near Segovia) on September 25, 1941. That morning, the founder had offered his Mass for the pope. "And after the Consecration," he said, "I felt an inner impulse (though I feel very sure that the Work will be greatly loved by the Holy Father) to do something that cost me tears. With tears that burned my eyes, as I gazed upon the Eucharistic Jesus there on the corporals, with all my heart I actually told him this: 'Lord, if it is what you want, I accept the *injustice*.' I'm sure you can guess what I meant by 'the injustice'—the destruction of this whole *work of God*. I know I pleased him by saying this and really meaning it. But how could I have refused to make this act of union with his will, if he was asking me for it? There was another time, in 1933 or 1934, and only God knows how much it cost me, when I did much the same."

In the heart of Don Alvaro was engraved from the very beginning, in letters of fire, that bottom-line prayer of Blessed Josemaría: "If Opus Dei is not of service to the Church, then let it be destroyed, let it disappear." Hence he did everything possible to make his entire life an ongoing crescendo of love and service to the Church and to the Work. From that radical perspective he carried out countless assignments from the founder relating to Spanish bishops, even when he was a layman, and won them over with his friendship and affection. José María Hernández de Garnica once asked him if jobs like these weighed heavy on him. Wasn't it hard on him, he asked, to have to relay messages from the founder to these high-ranking ecclesiastics? How did he get the courage to do it? Alvaro replied, "I just keep in mind the miraculous catch and the words of Saint Peter, 'At your word I will let down the net.' I think about what the Father has told me, and I know that in obeying him, I am obeying God."

It is a well-documented fact that the intervention of Dom Aurelio M. Escarré, the abbot of the Benedictine monastery of Montserrat, put a stop to the oppositions which Opus Dei began to suffer in Barcelona soon after the civil war. In the interests of promoting Church unity and of learning more about this new foundation, Abbot Escarré invited Alvaro del Portillo to spend Holy Week of 1943 as a guest of the monastery, along with several notables from Barcelona. Don Alvaro's presence as Secretary General of Opus Dei was one among several public demonstrations of recognition and esteem by the Benedictines of Montserrat, who were so influential in Catalonia.

At the very same time that the Work and its founder

were being persecuted, they were gaining prestige in ecclesiastical circles. In fact, many diocesan bishops invited Father Josemaría to preach retreats for their priests or seminarians. Some of them—Bishop Marcelino Olaechea, for example—left written records of their enthusiasm and gratitude for the great good which he had brought to their dioceses. Alvaro, with characteristic astuteness, compiled a dossier of comments by prelates and religious superiors about these retreats, well realizing what excellent material they would make for defending the founder against unjust accusations. As it turned out, they never were needed for that purpose. Nevertheless, as Don Alvaro himself pointed out, they have great historical value "as testimonies that are chronologically very close to the facts being described. Especially in view of the circumstances, these words have extra value in that they are so heartfelt and spontaneous."

Although he never failed to take the measures dictated by prudence, Don Alvaro was convinced early on that "difficulties exist to test our fidelity to the Lord—a fidelity which must be total, absolute, beyond question." He warned against relying on first impressions. But he also constantly warned people against the most dangerous thing of all: namely, pride, or inordinate self-love. He encouraged everyone to work hard at practicing humility and not making or looking for excuses. He was convinced that for each and every one of us, the help of God is always proportionate to the need of our soul in the particular circumstances of any given moment.

In those most difficult years, he seemed inoculated against discouragement. And for the rest of his life he continued to set forth the shining example of the founder, who in the thirties had overcome adversities much greater than any which were later encountered. In this context he liked to use a mathematical metaphor. "I always give you," he would say, "the same equation: The greater the difficulty, the more grace from God. The unknown in the equation is our good will. This, indeed, we must give him—completely."

Actually, Don Alvaro rarely spoke of those terrible "oppositions of good people," notwithstanding the heroism displayed by Blessed Josemaría. Back in 1976, he did ask me to think about the fact that members of Opus Dei have a right, and even an obligation, to know what happened, because it was part and parcel of the life of the founder. But from the very beginning of the "oppositions," Monsignor Escrivá had said that the members of the Work should not talk even among themselves about those machinations, so as not to offend against charity in the slightest. And Don Alvaro, of course, respected his wishes. I should note, however, that for him this did not mean that in the future those events should be examined with nothing but the cold detachment of a historian who has no personal stake in them.

He knew how to live with both an energetic spirit and a gentle heart, as Bishop Leopoldo Eijo y Garay expressed it on the day that he was ordained. Bishop Eijo was very happy that day. Incidentally, he on that same day described all that opposition as "a sign of divine predilection which the Lord has allowed for the purpose of bringing forth from it great good." And in this context he has also told of a conversation he had had with Don Alvaro some time before. Some difficult and delicate matter had come up—something that easily could have provoked feelings of anger or bitterness—and the founder was away from Madrid. When Alvaro phoned him to tell him about it, he told him to speak with Bishop Eijo and do whatever he suggested. According to the bishop, Alvaro set out the matter very calmly, objectively, with no hint of hard feelings. And when the bishop expressed a fear that some of the younger fellows in the Work might react in a much less supernatural manner—that they might, in fact, lash out in anger that was not at all edifying—Alvaro immediately put him at ease. "Don't worry," he said. "We can all see, Your Excellency, that God is allowing this to happen so that by means of this sacrifice that he is asking of us, we will become better persons. And that makes us very happy. When a good surgeon wants to do a good job, he chooses a good instrument. In the case of this opposition, our Lord has chosen to use a scalpel made of platinum."

"I must admit," Bishop Eijo told us, "that I was very impressed with this answer of his. Here I was supposed to be the one giving encouragement and comfort, and I ended up being the one who learned a lesson and was comforted."

When Alvaro explained that the metaphor was not really his, that he had heard it used many times by the founder, the bishop praised him all the more. "So much the better!" he said. "For it's obvious that you have assimilated very well the spirit of the Father. A good son, you know, does follow the instructions and guidelines given him by his own father. You're a chip off the old block!"

All of this happened more than a year after that day— February 14, 1943—when the Lord showed the founder the juridical framework which would make possible the ordination of members of Opus Dei. On May 25, at the height of World War II, Alvaro went to Rome to present to the Holy See—with the supporting documentation, and in accordance with the founder's instructions—a request for a *nihil obstat* for the juridical establishment of what would become, on December 8 of that year, the Priestly Society of the Holy Cross. The plane that he took to Rome crossed paths with some warplanes, and he actually saw them bomb a ship. The trip was frightening, but Alvaro basically remained unperturbed. "I was sure," he told us in 1976, "that nothing would happen, since I had my papers. It never once crossed my mind that the plane could have been shot down."

He stayed in Rome until June 21. On June 4 he was granted an audience with Pope Pius XII, in which he explained to him in detail what Opus Dei was all about.

Around that time he also discussed this and established good relations with many key members of the Roman Curia: with, for example, Cardinals Maglione (the Vatican Secretary of State), Tedeschini, La Puma, Vidal y Barraquer, Marchetti-Selvaggiani, and Pizzardo, and with several monsignors, such as Montini, Ruffini, and Ottaviani, who would one day play outstanding roles in the history of the Church. Many of these cardinals and monsignors already knew something about the Work from Salvador Canals and José Orlandis, who had arrived in Rome in November 1942 to do postgraduate work toward their law degrees and, at the same time, to take theology at the Angelicum.

In his book *Wartime Memories of Rome,* José Orlandis says that he accompanied Alvaro in many of those visits and meetings, and that it certainly seemed to him that "those men of the Roman Curia, every one of whom had a lifetime of experience in the service of the Church, all listened to Alvaro del Portillo with respect and profound interest." And this, he says, was "precisely because their long experience had enabled them to perceive immediately the extraordinary human and supernatural qualities of the speaker, as well as the importance that this 'new thing' that he was explaining to them would have for the future of the Church and of the world."

According to reports received by José Orlandis from various sources, Pope Pius XII was very favorably impressed by Alvaro. Says Orlandis, "On June 28, when I was already back in Spain, Cardinal Tedeschini told me that Pope Pius had talked with him quite a bit about that visit. And half a year later, on December 27, Monsignor Montini mentioned that the Holy Father still remembered very well that conversation he had had with Alvaro del Portillo."

9

The Priesthood

In 1940, at the request of the founder of Opus Dei, Alvaro del Portillo, José María Hernández de Garnica, and José Luis Múzquiz started studying for the priesthood, without giving up their professional jobs or apostolic activities. Years later, Don Alvaro explained it thus: "It was all very simple! There is nothing complicated about the Work. Our Father just knew perfectly well that he could rely on us. We responded freely, without any kind of pressure."

I thought of those words when I heard this story told by Encarnación Ortega. When Bishop Leopoldo Eijo y Garay found out that Alvaro was going to become a priest, he asked him, "Alvaro, do you realize that this means you are going to lose your personality? Now you're a prestigious engineer, but afterwards you'll be just one more priest!" He was very impressed with the answer he received: "Your Excellency, I gave up my personality to Jesus Christ a long time ago."

In accord with the permissions granted by this bishop, the bishop of Madrid-Alcalá, the future priests received a flexible but in-depth preparation, thanks to the quality of their teachers and to the intellectual caliber of the students themselves, as is related in great detail in so many of the books about the founder. Their pastoral formation was taken care of by Father Josemaría himself; he was even the one who gave them their pre-ordination retreat. This took place May 13–20, 1944, in the monastery of El Escorial, in an area set aside for guests. On May 20, at the end of the retreat, they received the tonsure (in accordance with the law of the Church at that time) in the chapel of the bishop's palace. On May 21 and 23, they received the minor orders. On May 28, the bishop of Pamplona, Bishop Marcelino Olaechea, conferred on them the order of subdeacon in the oratory of the Diego de León Street center. On June 3, in the chapel of the seminary of Madrid, they received the order of deacon at the hands of the auxiliary bishop of Madrid-Alcalá, Bishop Casimiro Morcillo. Finally, on June 25, Bishop Eijo y Garay ordained them priests, in the chapel of the bishop's palace.

Years later the altarpiece of this chapel was transferred to La Santísima Virgen de Almudena, the new cathedral of Madrid, to be the setting for a carving of our Lady in this guise under which she is the patroness of the diocese. This image has an interesting connection with Don Alvaro. From Rome he gave Bishop Eijo valuable help in obtaining permission for its official coronation, which took place on November 10, 1948. On the following day, the bishop dictated a heartfelt letter of thanks to Don Alvaro. "Thanks a million," he said, "for immediately cabling to me the Holy See's authorization for the official coronation of La Santísima Virgen de la Almudena. . . . I have prayed hard that our Lord will reward you for this great favor you've done for me and for all of us. Had it not been for you, the appointed day would have arrived and the coronation would not have taken place. And how much gratitude we owe to Cardinal Tedeschini, for taking care of everything so quickly once you had spoken with him!"

Don Alvaro celebrated his first solemn Mass on June

28, 1944, in the chapel of Our Lady of the Pillar School. He was assisted by a Dominican priest, Father José Manuel de Aguilar, and by the principal of the school, Father Florentino Fernández. His sister Pilar recalls a curious detail, the like of which had happened to the founder of Opus Dei at his own ordination. Don Alvaro's mother did not get to be the first person to receive Communion from his hands, because his aunt Carmen (who was also his godmother) slipped in ahead of her.

From that day forward, his family and friends would always be impressed by the simplicity and piety with which Don Alvaro celebrated the Eucharistic sacrifice. Carlos del Portillo relates a good case in point. Don Alvaro went one day to say Mass in the private chapel of his aunts Pilar and Carmen, and the doorkeeper of the house, Elvira, asked if she might attend as well. Afterwards she told them, "That young fellow Alvaro—he says Mass so perfectly!"

I myself often had the privilege of participating in Masses celebrated by Don Alvaro. He said Mass slowly and attentively, obviously savoring the infinite value of the Eucharistic sacrifice—"the ineffable miracle which the omnipotence of God renews each day," as he used to put it. He never hurried, not even when he had to say Mass early because he was going on a long trip. He paid loving attention to all the details. He put his whole self into the four dimensions of the Mass: adoration, thanksgiving, atonement, and petition. And he fully entered into the liturgical texts. Often, in fact, he would allude later on to the readings or prayers of the day, to passages that he found particularly striking.

Above all, I was impressed by his intensity at the moment of Consecration. He said the words slowly and carefully, in a way that was both natural and solemn. When he elevated the Body and Blood, he kept his eyes fixed upon the Eucharistic species and lifted his arms as high as he could.

It made me feel as though heaven and earth almost physically came together at that moment. And then he made the slow, prolonged genuflection that Blessed Josemaría always recommended.

When he gave the final blessing, I was always very moved by the expansiveness of it. His right hand moved very high and then very low, far to the right and then far to the left—a gesture making it very clear that he was blessing the whole world and not just the people at that Mass.

His capacity for becoming absorbed in the liturgy was also evident at more solemn ceremonies with many people present, such as nuptial Masses, First Communions, ordinations, and Masses celebrated for the faculty and students of the University of Navarre. Well beforehand, he would go over what had to be done, and he would encourage the master of ceremonies to keep giving him directions, clearly and with no hesitation, so that by simply following those directions he could stay focused on the presence of God. Although, by the way, he had no ear for music, he did like liturgical singing. He liked both Gregorian chant, for its austere sobriety, and also many popular devotional hymns.

Don Alvaro's words were normally measured and simple, but he waxed quite eloquent when it came to the Eucharist. As an example, here is an excerpt from a speech he gave at the University of Montreal in 1988: "God is infinitely powerful and infinitely beautiful. We cannot begin to imagine how wonderful he is. The sweetest music, the most marvelous symphony, the most incredibly beautiful colors—the whole world, the entire universe, is nothing at all in comparison with him. And that God of infinite greatness, infinite power, infinite beauty, hides himself under the appearance of bread, so that we can approach him with confidence!"

Don Javier Echevarría accompanied him on the pilgrimage to the Holy Land which was the last big event of his life, and in a talk given on January 28, 1995, in the main lecture hall of the University of Navarre, he told us this: "I remember vividly the deep emotion that Don Alvaro clearly felt as he approached the places where Jesus walked. I remember the devotion with which he touched and kissed that holy ground. I remember, too, the deep recollection with which he made his private prayer and meditation, and with which he prepared himself for the Eucharistic sacrifice. And I remember especially his last Mass. He was so immersed in God, so united with Christ, that he seemed to feel himself to be Christ himself before that altar on which he, as a priest, was making present the sacrifice of Christ on the cross. I will never forget this as long as I live. Those images of him celebrating Mass in the Church of the Cenacle, close to the place where Jesus, surrounded by his apostles, instituted the Eucharist, are forever engraved in my memory."

After his ordination, Don Alvaro became an even firmer support, so to speak, for the founder of Opus Dei. The overwhelming avalanche of supernatural gifts which God was pouring out on Father Josemaría made it necessary for him to have at his side an intelligent and humble priest who was truly close to him. The founder had a responsibility to discern and to get confirmation of the paths which the Holy Spirit was opening in his ardent and vibrant soul, and to distinguish, when necessary, between what had to do with his interior life and what had to do with the foundation. And the reality is that he only went ahead with complete peace of mind when he began to open his heart and soul to Don Alvaro not only as his closest associate, but as his confessor as well.

Despite the openness and ease that characterized their relationship, that first confession was one of the few times in his whole life when Don Alvaro became noticeably nervous. Monsignor Escrivá on several occasions told this story in public. The confession took place on June 26, 1944—

the very day after Don Alvaro's ordination. The two of them were at the Villanueva Street center, in Madrid. Father Josemaría asked Don Alvaro if he'd heard any confessions yet, and when he said no, the founder said that he would like to make a general confession to him. Well, the confession had hardly started when Don Alvaro began to worry that he might forget the words of absolution. He knew the prayer by heart, but, as he himself had just said, he had not as yet given anybody sacramental absolution. This was so much on his mind that as soon as Father Josemaría got finished confessing his sins, Don Alvaro started saying the prayer of absolution. The founder had to interrupt him. "My son," he said, "I can understand it if you don't want to give me any advice, but you do need to at least give me a penance!" So Don Alvaro gave him one, but then when he started the prayer of absolution again, he forgot how it went. He had to repeat it after the founder!

From that day forward, the priestly soul of Don Alvaro would express itself also in his passion for the sacrament of Penance. He often compared the human soul to a blank page, or to an open book. We need to fill up our souls, he said, with love of God, not leaving any space for discouragement, even when we feel the weight of many personal limitations. "A good goal for this year," he advised people in Rome on New Year's Day in 1980, "will be to fill up this blank book, this book which opens today, with the elegance and delicacy with which people in the Middle Ages illuminated precious manuscripts—with a perfect calligraphy, with no blotches. But since there will be blotches—since we all have a fallen nature and are full of wretchedness—let us not lack the courage to recognize these blotches for what they are, so that we can get rid of them. And how will we get rid of them? By humbly availing ourselves of the sacrament of Penance."

On Holy Thursday of 1982, in a talk on the importance

of being humble and sincere in our confessions, he said, "When I was little, I often saw how shepherds would get their sheep to cross streams. They would first take across a small goat with a cowbell attached to him. With the racket he made, the sheep were easily brought across; they just followed him, with no fear. Well, that's the way it is with confession. If we say first of all the thing that is hardest for us to say, then everything else comes out quite easily."

Following here, too, the example of Blessed Josemaría, Don Alvaro expected the faithful of Opus Dei to bring many souls to confession. For this reason he was very touched when he heard about a remark that Pope John Paul II spontaneously made on November 4, 1980. The Pope was having breakfast with Cardinal Wyszynski and a Polish bishop, and when Opus Dei came up in the conversation, he said that the members of the Work have "the charism of confession." Don Alvaro used to tell this story to move his children to action, because, as he put it, "God gives charisms to be used—and not just for oneself, but also to help others." His conclusion was always this: "We must take many people to the sacrament of Penance. But to do this, my children, the first thing we must do is make a good confession ourselves."

I often heard Don Alvaro stress the importance of cultural, doctrinal, and spiritual formation for the members of Opus Dei, and especially for the priests. He wanted them to achieve a depth of theological and pastoral knowledge equivalent to the knowledge they had as professionals in their secular fields, but he also wanted them to avoid all unnecessary delays in completing their study programs. One point he insisted on was the importance of doing the doctoral dissertation without delay. That was what he himself had done, as directed by the founder.

Monsignor Escrivá established as a general rule that every priest of Opus Dei should have, prior to ordination, a doctorate in a secular field as well as a doctorate in an ecclesiastical discipline. But as it happened, the first three priests were all engineers, and at the time that they were ordained, even the highest-level technical schools in Spain did not grant doctorates. So Alvaro, because he could not get a doctorate in engineering, signed up for the Philosophy and Literature program at Universidad Central, in Madrid.

He was, however, exempted from class attendance. And so, having done the course work on his own, he obtained his licentiate on April 24, 1943, and his doctorate a year later, on May 12, 1944. His dissertation (directed by Dr. Cayetano Alcázar Molina, the head of the department) was titled "The First Spanish Expeditions to California." He had to do the research bit by bit (mainly in the Archivo Histórico Nacional in Madrid and the Archivo de Indias in Seville) and had to steal time from his sleep; the only days he could work on this full-time were a few that he spent in a country house near Piedralaves, close to Avila, in the spring. Nevertheless, his presentation won first prize for a doctoral dissertation in the field of Philosophy and Literature in Madrid. Later it was published as a book—a quite lengthy one!—under the title *Discoveries and Explorations on the Coasts of California.*

A couple of years later, when they were both permanently settled in Rome, Monsignor Escrivá decided the time had come for Don Alvaro to start working toward a doctorate in a Church-related field. He went to the Pontifical University of St. Thomas (also called the Angelicum) and in 1948 was awarded a doctorate in canon law.

Apart from spiritual considerations, I believe that the quality of that history dissertation which Don Alvaro did in 1944 and the speed with which he did it are clear evidence of his intelligence, his talent for writing, and his exceptional memory. Don Alvaro's memory was, of course, a natural gift, but it grew on account of his affection for other people— I saw this for myself on innumerable occasions. And I have to admit that my rather plain style of writing in Spanish benefited considerably from his help. I was always amazed that he stayed so fluent in Spanish, when he had lived outside of Spain ever since 1946.

In his day-to-day work he often consulted dictionaries, mainly to find synonyms and thus avoid tiresome repetition. However, his aim was not to cultivate a sophisticated style. Rather, both because of his intellectual background and for pastoral reasons, he sought a kind of "gift of tongues": a way of speaking and writing which was precise, accessible, and pleasant, which would make it easy for people to understand his spiritual and apostolic messages.

I think the conciseness of his writing style also had to do with his knowledge of Latin. In high school he earned good grades in Latin, and afterwards he continued to work at it, especially during the forties. He was very fluent in Church Latin, both in speaking and in writing; he used it in the work of governing Opus Dei and also in the great amount of work he did in the different dicasteries of the Roman Curia. In the 3/27/94 issue of the Italian newspaper *Avvenire,* Monsignor Francesco di Muzio mentioned Don Alvaro's "keen interest in Latin inscriptions and Roman art."

Upon ordination, Don Alvaro gave up his professional work and dedicated himself exclusively to carrying out his priestly ministry. Of course, this did not mean that he stopped working on behalf of Opus Dei. On the contrary, his priesthood only added to that workload.

Throughout his priestly life, his preaching was a permanent echo, as it were, of the teachings of Blessed Josemaría. But he had a style of his own, even if it was less original. Perhaps because of his reflective nature, Don Alvaro was a more brilliant writer than speaker. Nevertheless, his spoken words went straight to the bottom of people's hearts, largely because the look on his face and the gentle tone of his deep voice conveyed not only the great affection that he felt for his listeners, but also an almost tangible humility.

On countless occasions he would begin his talk with these
words: "The important thing is not what I say. The important
thing is what the Holy Spirit suggests in the soul of each
one of you—and in mine as well."

As far as possible, he avoided the use of technical or
highly specialized terms. But when he had to use them, he
explained them clearly. He felt that clarity was a duty, and
he achieved it even if it meant throwing out the rest of his
planned speech in order to give more precise explanations
or additional information. Whenever he explained
something, he went right to the heart of the matter, to a
depth of meaning which did not admit of complications.
He was like a good teacher—full of common sense and
theological rigor, desirous of awakening a reflective
understanding and of not leaving any loose ends—rather than
like a leader, more or less charismatic, who just wants to
impose his own convictions. His talks could be somewhat
lengthy, but they were always clear and very pleasant to listen
to.

He spoke with vigor and simplicity. He did not need to
use many arguments to win the agreement of his listeners.
He won them over with the depth of his faith, and with the
authentically and consistently Christian life which practically
poured out of his pores. Maybe his words alone would not
have convinced everyone, but the way he said them—his tone
of voice, his facial expressions, his gestures—carried so much
conviction that it was nearly impossible not to agree with
him. In 1945 Ramona Sanjurjo attended a retreat which Don
Alvaro preached in the city of Vigo. She was already a good
Catholic, but she says, "Never had I heard anyone speak like
that about the love of God. It was for me a great discovery."

He spoke with tenderness and exactness, without any
rhetorical intent. His only concern was to help people
improve in their relations with God, in fulfilling the demands
of charity, and in their apostolic effectiveness. What he said

In London during the summer of 1958, with Blessed Josemaría and Jesús Gazapo.

In an audience with Pope John XXIII in 1960.

In Guatemala on 19 February 1975, his name day.

In an audience with Pope Paul VI in 1976.

was always based first of all on Sacred Scripture. After that, his most immediate source was Monsignor Escrivá: his writings, his teachings, his heroic example, and so forth. Don Alvaro, as extensive as was his doctrinal and theological background, did not confine himself to making theoretical propositions, because his heart was set on incarnating the Gospel and the specific spirit of the Work.

From Monsignor Escrivá he learned very well that giving a meditation means doing one's personal prayer out loud. And he did not mind letting people know this. Case in point: on October 2, 1983, the fifty-fifth anniversary of the founding of Opus Dei, when Andrés Rueda thanked him for what he had said to him and the other fellows, Don Alvaro replied, "For what I said to *you?* I was talking to God!"

In his preaching he was warm, understanding, and affable, but also very demanding. Often he often used the adverb "more" (*más*) to communicate the urgency that is inherent in any real love for God. Gently he helped each person to face up to his or her responsibility to love God and souls. This was always his main concern. No matter what he was talking about, everything he said was linked to this one theme: that because the plenitude of Christian life is rooted in charity, love is of the utmost urgency.

Don Alvaro faithfully incarnated the priestly ideal proposed by the founder of Opus Dei: he was one hundred percent a priest, in accordance with the radical self-giving of our great high priest, Christ. On the day that Don Alvaro would have celebrated his golden jubilee as a priest, Don Javier Echevarría expressed it thus: "His human and spiritual gifts were a kind of compendium of the qualities which we want to find in a priest, a minister of Christ, a servant of souls: a humble intelligence, a simple piety, a full dedication to others, a compassionate caring for the weak and the needy, the strength of a father, a contagious peace. These qualities are summed up in a phrase from Saint Augustine: 'The

dwelling place of charity is humility."' (The phrase is from
De sancta virginitate, 51.)

His great heart led him so to venerate the priesthood
and religious life that he felt a deep fraternity with all his
fellow priests. I was particularly touched by something he
said one day to Luis de Moya, a priest of the Prelature who
in a car accident in April 1991 had become a quadriplegic.
Don Alvaro had already visited him at the University of
Navarre on a number of occasions—first in the hospital, and
later in Aralar Hall—and had shown him great affection in
all kinds of little ways. But he was especially thrilled when
Father Luis, after a tracheotomy, became able to speak fairly
well—because, he said, all that a priest really needs in order
to exercise his priestly ministry is a voice and the intention.
More than once I saw how it consoled him to kiss the rigid
hands of Father Luis. "You cannot move them," he said, "but
they still have the divine power to forgive sins. Even if you
do not move them, they open the gates of heaven."

In such scenes one can clearly see the special love that
Don Alvaro had for his fellow priests. It was, quite obviously,
a love based on his faith in the sacramental order and in the
priest's irreplaceable mission of mediating between God and
human beings. Don Alvaro devoted a lot of time to priests,
both in his work of governing and in his writing and
preaching. He loved them as brothers and admired their
heroic virtue. When speaking to them, he often used an
expression borrowed from Monsignor Escrivá: he said it was
like "selling honey to the beekeeper." (In 1987, when he was
with priests in Manila, he jokingly altered this to "selling
coconuts in the Philippines.") He never ceased to stress the
importance of fraternity among priests, and to visit the most
isolated ones in order to boost their spirits and joyfully serve
them.

He was also very concerned, right up to the end of his
life, about the increasing shortage of vocations to the

priesthood. He spoke about this to everyone, including lay people. In September 1983, for example, he said to tens of thousands of people in Madrid, "Pray hard for the seminaries. The shortage of priests is not someone else's problem. No one can afford not to care about it. It is the obligation of every Catholic to do something about it." But he did, of course, remind priests of the concern that they in particular ought to have to perpetuate their ministry. In February 1988, for instance, he said to a group of priests and seminarians in Chicago, "When the time comes to render up our accounts to God, it will be good for each one of us to have left at least one successor in the priestly ministry." And then he added the rest of this piece of advice that the founder of Opus Dei used to give to his brothers in the diocesan priesthood: "Since one successor might fall by the wayside, it's better for us to look for two—or, even better, three."

One practical manifestation of that spirit was the setting up of an international ecclesiastical formation center near the University of Navarre. (Another such center was later set up in Rome, when the Pontifical Athenaeum of the Holy Cross was established.) When the University of Navarre initiated a Bachelor of Arts theology program, just after the promulgation in 1979 of the apostolic constitution *Sapientia Christiana (On Christian Wisdom)*, bishops from different countries began to send some of their seminarians there. After studying the matter with the archbishop of that diocese, Don Alvaro started working towards the setting up of a formation center for all seminarians attending the University of Navarre. And thus it was that in 1988 the Holy See erected the Bidasoa Formation Center.

In April 1990 Don Alvaro went to Bidasoa to spend some time with its residents—about one hundred seminarians from about twenty countries and fifty dioceses. I went with him, and for me it was an incredible experience. This is what he said to them first: "My sons, a priest who does not make a constant effort to be holy does great damage to the Church. A lukewarm, careless, negligent priest does much harm to souls. So you should ask our Lord to give you—and always to keep giving you—a very, *very* great feeling for the priesthood. But for that to happen, you will have to take the necessary means: that is, live each and every day in a great awareness of the presence of God." I remember, too, the fatherly tone of voice in which he spoke to them about love for the Blessed Virgin, about "paying court" to our Lord in the tabernacle, about piety and study, about a spirit of service, about docility towards their diocesan superiors, about developing a spirit of fraternity by learning how to understand and forgive... He spoke on all kinds of subjects and answered the young men's questions. It all added up to a very attractive synthesis of priestly spirituality.

Don Alvaro's veneration for the priesthood was, of course, inseparable from his love for members of religious orders, even though Opus Dei is not any kind of religious order. His affection for those consecrated souls grew greater and greater after he met and became friends with many religious who were friends of the founder. Some of them, in fact, were among the professors who prepared Don Alvaro for ordination. But I don't think it's necessary to repeat names and facts which appear in the biographies of Monsignor Escrivá. I will only mention that when Don Alvaro died, many cardinals, bishops, priests, monks, and nuns sent letters saying how much they had loved him, how grateful they were to him, and how much they admired him, simply as a person and also as a priest and bishop. He had helped them solve pastoral problems or juridical difficulties; he had given them retreats or talks; he had given his priestly help to many consecrated souls who went to him for advice.

For Don Alvaro, having a priestly soul included meeting the demands of justice. Many times I heard him stress how necessary justice is for peace. He was not referring only to issues related to the social teachings of the Church. His intense desire for a just peace was linked more directly with the central message of Christ, who, as he put it, "came to bring to the world not hatred or the class struggle, but love." For Don Alvaro, the most effective means towards that end was the personal struggle to sanctify one's own work by filling it with ethical content and with a spirit of serving each person and all of society. From this would arise an immense number of initiatives which would directly foster a more humane and dignified standard of living among disadvantaged individuals and societies all over the world. (I will have occasion to say more about these initiatives later on.)

Don Alvaro recommended that one first use the supernatural means of prayer and mortification, and only then start talking. And when talking, he said, one should try not only to make oneself clearly understood by the others, but also to really understand them. He liked to call to mind this vivid image used by the founder: that so often, in these matters, what looks convex to one person looks concave to another. He said that one generally can and should compromise, search for common ground, listen to and consider the reasonings of the others. Sometimes he alluded to the proverbial capacity of Italians to reach an understanding. One could not, of course, compromise on matters of Catholic dogma, or where human rights or the inviolable rights of the Church were at stake. But on other matters there was always room for compromise. To take this as a solid principle constituted the best safeguard of freedom.

To those who worked in politics, Don Alvaro used to pass along a piece of advice that Blessed Josemaría had given to priests: that they should "live the plus sign"—not clash with others, not shove others aside, not look for what separates, but, instead, always look for what unites—especially since the plus sign is the sign of the cross, which is a summons to mortification, sacrifice, and patience.

Love for freedom was a basic feature of Don Alvaro's personality and of his priestly soul. He was thrilled at the thought of human free will, that wonderful gift from God, that human privilege so closely connected with all the mysteries of faith, although he was fully aware of the shadows it can cast. He was not oblivious to the wretched clamorings of humankind for its tragic slaveries. He directed Opus Dei with prudent pastoral norms. But he was never pessimistic or doubtful about the value of human freedom. On the contrary, he always showed a great enthusiasm for personal spontaneity. He was convinced that understanding and confidence are the foundation for a coexistence that is harmonious, rightly pluralistic, full of liberties. In 1980, in answer to a question about the difficulties of establishing schools in an already developed country, Don Alvaro said, "The devil has two great allies. One is ignorance, and the other is lack of freedom."

10

In Rome

Don Alvaro's identification with the founder was no less evident than his desire to pass unnoticed. He helped the founder both energetically and tactfully, with exquisite finesse. So, despite his desire to remain in the background, he was often asked by the founder to take the first steps in carrying out certain tasks, or to assume a great share of the responsibility in matters of great importance to the Work—especially after his first visit to Rome, in 1943.

The broad outlines of this part of the story are well known. In February 1946 Don Alvaro was again sent to Rome by the founder. He moved into an apartment rented by Salvador Canals in the Corso del Rinascimento area; its balcony faced Piazza Navona. For the next four months he worked intensely, following step by step the instructions he had received from Father Josemaría. He did battle armed with his gift for relating to people, and this he did with all his might. And when he had done all he could do, humanly speaking, and it became clear that the founder would have to come in person to the Eternal City, he told him so in no uncertain terms.

Father Josemaría Escrivá landed in Genoa on June 22, just before midnight. Don Alvaro, together with Salvador

Canals, traveled from Rome to meet him there. Thus began another period of prayer, work, and discussion which would culminate in the granting of the *Decretum laudis* on February 24, 1947, and of the definitive approval on June 16, 1950.

In 1946 Don Alvaro was still Secretary General of Opus Dei; now that he was in Rome, his participation in the governing of the Work would not come to an end until the day he died. From 1947 to 1956 he was Procurator General. During that time, he also served as Italy's regional vicar (from 1947 to 1951) and as rector of the Roman College of the Holy Cross (from 1948 to 1953). He was then Secretary General again from 1956 until the death of Monsignor Escrivá in 1975, at which time he succeeded him as head of Opus Dei, in which capacity he served until God called him to himself.

Don Alvaro was, in short, always wherever the founder needed him to be, doing whatever would most help the founder to move the Work forward. But back in those earlier days he was hardly noticed, even by Opus Dei members who saw him almost every day. All eyes were always fixed on Monsignor Escrivá. During the family-style get-togethers, Don Alvaro might sit in a corner or even remain standing if there were not enough seats. However, he was always on the alert for when the founder might need something. He would answer with amazing promptness when he was asked for a name, a date, the confirmation of some fact, or details concerning some event. "Do you remember, Alvaro? Why don't you tell them?" the founder would ask. And Don Alvaro would instantly do so.

Monsignor Escrivá had, of course, complete confidence in Don Alvaro, and sometimes he communicated this in very down-to-earth and humorous ways. Once he gave him a photo with this psalm verse written on it: "Man and beast thou savest, O Lord" (Ps 36:6). Then he said, punning on Don Alvaro's surname, "This opens up a small door (*portillo*) to hope."

Carmen Escrivá, who also had a good sense of humor, used to contradict her brother when he would claim that he loved all his sons and daughters equally. "No, no," she would say, "you love Alvaro more." And then, seeing that her brother was getting upset, she would add, "Don't worry—our Lord also had three apostles whom he loved more." "Don't be silly," he would reply.

One day in July 1977, at the insistence of those who were with him, Don Alvaro told the story of what happened right after his appendectomy in 1950. (They did have to twist his arm to get him to tell this story.) The operation, he said, was complicated and took longer than expected, because his appendix was not in the normal position, so he had to be given an extra amount of anesthetic. Well, when the operation was over, the doctors could not revive him. But Monsignor Escrivá came up to him and just whispered, "Alvaro," and he got an immediate response: "Yes, Father." Long afterwards he found out that this had made the founder very happy. He had told someone, "He even obeys when he's asleep!"

In describing his relations with Monsignor Escrivá, Don Alvaro liked to use a military phrase: "according to regulations." He applied this principle even to the smallest details of everyday life—although the founder would remind him that it was Jesus Christ, and not him, that he should be imitating. At the same time, though, in his own unobtrusive way, he did take initiative in his practicing and promoting of faithfulness to the founder.

A good example of this took place also in 1950, when Monsignor Escrivá was about to celebrate his silver jubilee as a priest. Don Alvaro suggested that, in accord with Roman custom, a commemorative plaque be set up in Villa Tevere. The founder adamantly rejected that idea—until, that is, Don Alvaro deployed the following argument. "Father," he said, "we are in Rome, and in Rome they set up plaques to commemorate great events. If we don't do this, then those

who come after us will say that either we were stupid or else
we didn't love you. And both of those things would be most
unfair. Do we love you? Of course we do! Are we stupid?
Well, maybe—but not so stupid as that!" Then and there,
Monsignor Escrivá gave in. "All right," he said, "do what
you like, but on one condition—that above that plaque you
place a donkey!"

Don Alvaro drafted the text of the inscription, and the
plaque was mounted—with a donkey above it—in a gallery of
Villa Tevere. He had exploited, if you will, the founder's deep
sense of justice. Years later he would use the same argument to
secure the founder's consent to the filming and videotaping
of much of his preaching in many countries. This was, to tell
the simple truth, an initiative for which future generations
will never be thankful enough to Don Alvaro.

He also kept himself in the background whenever he
spoke of the work involved in acquiring and adapting Villa
Tevere for use as the central headquarters of Opus Dei,
although in this he had played a major role. He would
mention things like the advice which Monsignor Montini
(the future Pope Paul VI) had given to the founder, or the
gigantic faith of Monsignor Escrivá despite the lack of means,
or the constant and confident prayer of the members of the
Work. But it was, in fact, Don Alvaro who made possible
the wonderful solution to the problem. He did this, in the
first place, by winning the confidence of Princess Virginia
Sforza Cesarini when he accompanied Monsignor Escrivá
in the first negotiations. Then he won over a friend of hers
whom she introduced to them: Count Gori Mazzoleni. With
Count Mazzoleni, Don Alvaro and Salvador Canals
conducted long negotiations, to a happy end. (The
negotiations are described in detail in some of the biographies
of the founder.)

Adapting the building meant even more financial
problems, since it involved a substantial amount of

enlargement and reconstruction. The suppliers and the laborers had to be paid every Saturday. When necessary, Don Alvaro pounded the streets—even when it meant getting out of bed with a high fever—to solicit donations and loans from friends (such as an attorney named Merlini) and to get mortgages, commercial loans, and letters of credit. He won not only people's confidence, but, quite literally, the gratitude of those who did him favors. It was at this time that he made fast friends with Leonardo Castelli, the owner of the construction company which eventually took charge of this project.

Don Alvaro's only concern was to relieve the founder of as much work and worry as possible. He tried as hard as he could to take care of those pressing financial needs himself. To this end he even made a trip to Spain on a day (sometime in 1954) when his doctor had said he should stay in bed. But years later, when speaking of those difficult times, he forgot about his own efforts. "Our Lord made it possible," he would say, "for us to make it with loans and balancing acts. It was like robbing Peter to pay Paul. It was really crazy, and the cause of a lot of suffering. And how *did* we pay? It was a miracle. I don't know how we did it, but somehow or another we always did pay."

Andreu Barrera recalls an observation which the founder often made about Don Alvaro at that time. "At the side of this man," the founder used to say, "it is impossible not to have faith."

Francisco Monzó, the man who worked most closely with Don Alvaro in those days, remembers a conversation in which he exaggerated to Don Alvaro the possible legal consequences of those financial maneuvers. If they kept going this way, he told him, they might end up in jail. Don Alvaro answered in a slightly sly tone of voice, "Well, if that happens, I'll take a typewriter and lots of paper to my cell!" Monzó was impressed. "He didn't care in the least about what might happen to him," he said. "His only fear was of not being able to give our founder all the help he needed."

Don Alvaro lived in Christian austerity, but with great naturalness and common sense. Encarnación Ortega remembers that in the fifties, in Rome, when they had almost no money, he told them that they must not skimp on the food they needed to keep themselves strong. And he gave them a reason based on faith. If, he said, they kept making an effort to get money, and if they managed very well what money they did have, the Lord would make sure they did not go without.

Francisco Monzó also remembers that at this time, Don Alvaro "gave bonuses to workers who had done their jobs exceptionally well. In this matter he was especially generous." How well Don Alvaro understood the inseparable relationship between authentic Christian poverty and Christian solidarity. Monsignor Escrivá many times praised his sensitivity to social problems. He liked to tell, for example, the story of a property to the south of Rome, in Salto di Fondi, which in 1953 became a summer residence for students of the Roman College of the Holy Cross. "The Marquis of Bisletti," he said, "who liked Don Alvaro very much, mentioned to him a large property which might be of interest to us. Well, when he told me about it, I said, 'But, my son, we can't even eat!' But he insisted. He said, 'Father, we could at least try. The boys need a place to take it easy during the summer. Without one, they will get sick.'" And so Don Alvaro talked him into it. And the upshot was that, in those times of great scarcity, this property fed all those members of Opus Dei who were living in Rome and also gave Don Alvaro a chance to help out the local farmers. "He managed things," the founder said, "such that three hundred of the farmers in that area ended up owning the land they worked on. Parcels were made over to them through an arrangement with a bank whereby they could pay off the loan with a portion of the harvest, while still having enough to live with dignity."

Don Alvaro himself would tell the story—though only much later, and only to illustrate the modesty of the founder—of another initiative he undertook during those first years in Rome. In 1947, not long after Opus Dei received its first pontifical approval (the *Decretum laudis*), Don Alvaro, in his capacity as Procurator General of the Work, requested that the Holy See make Father Josemaría Escrivá a monsignor. "The then Monsignor Montini not only approved my initiative, but actually took it under his wing," said Don Alvaro. The document arrived soon afterwards, along with a letter from Monsignor Montini which praised Opus Dei and its founder. Don Alvaro had not informed the founder of any of this, because, knowing his humility, he feared that he would not have stood for it. And as a matter of fact, when the business had already been settled, Father Josemaría said he did not want to accept any such honor. But Don Alvaro, with the help of Salvador Canals, won him over with an unassailable argument: that this title would make even clearer the secular nature of Opus Dei.

Ten years later, in Rome, Don Alvaro took on a heavy burden in connection with the death of Carmen Escrivá. Early in 1957 she was diagnosed with some kind of cancer, and on April 20 the doctors gave her two months to live. Monsignor Escrivá asked Don Alvaro to be the one to break the news to her. It was, of course, a very hard thing to do, but he did it with total honesty and great charity. Later he would often comment that "she took the news with total tranquillity and serenity, without tears, like the holy person she was." She told her brother and other members of the Work, "Alvaro has given me the sentence."

It was Don Alvaro who asked Father Fernández, an Augustinian priest and a deeply spiritual man, to come over once a week to give her spiritual help. At the insistence of Opus Dei's Central Secretary, Don Alvaro also talked the founder into allowing some of his daughters to take turns caring for her.

In June, a few days before his sister's death, Monsignor Escrivá went to her home to give her the last sacraments. He was assisted by Don Alvaro—and, as it turned out, he really needed that assistance. When he started praying the prayers of the last rites, his voice broke, and when it came time for Carmen to answer, he broke down in tears, and asked Don Alvaro to take over. He took off his vestments, and Don Alvaro immediately put on the surplice and stole and continued with the ceremony. A few women of Opus Dei were present. Afterwards, Monsignor Escrivá took them aside, into a nearby room, and said to them, "My daughters, I want to apologize to you for the bad example I have given you—for having cried, when I've told you so many times that in the face of adversity you have to stay strong and not cry." And Don Alvaro said very gently, "But the Father has also often told us that we have to have a heart, and today he has shown us that he has one. In this, too, he has been an example for us."

Only a little while before the death of Carmen Escrivá, Don Alvaro had borne the death of his own mother, Doña Clementina, with that same supernatural outlook and big heart. Her death came suddenly, on March 10, 1955, in Madrid, near the close of a retreat she was making in the church of San Manuel y San Benito. On the last day of the retreat, she came home in the morning very happy; not only had she just been to Mass, but she had also made a general confession. During breakfast she suffered a cerebral hemorrhage from which she never recovered, though the doctors did everything possible. She died that night, in great peace.

A telegram was sent to Rome. Monsignor Escrivá suggested to Don Alvaro that he check out the possibility of leaving immediately for Madrid. This was over forty years ago, and it's not easy to imagine how difficult travel was at that time. But it is certain that Don Alvaro could not have made it to Madrid in less than three or four days. And so he wrote to his brothers and sisters, "I have to offer to God the sorrow of not being able to give our mother a last kiss and all of you a big hug." He was always sure, though, that his mother had benefited from this deeply personal sacrifice that he had offered to God.

On March 11, the day after her death, he celebrated Mass at a quarter past seven. "Never have I prayed with greater devotion, and never have those words of the liturgy, 'Life is changed, not taken away,' given me greater peace," he wrote in that same letter to his brothers and sisters. After recalling how holy his mother's life had been, he continued, "Therefore, we can be quite certain that she has already received her reward. Our Lord has given me a certainty which is almost physical, not just moral, that Mama is already in heaven. And this has given me a deep peace, in the midst of all this pain. If it wouldn't sound strange, I would say that it has given me a *joy* in the midst of this pain. But I am feeling a lot of pain. Not for Mama, but for myself—because of all the good that I did not do, and all the bad that I did. For all this—for all my failings in relation to Mama—I ask forgiveness from God, from Mama, and from you."

Those years in Rome were very hard for both the founder and Don Alvaro. In the midst of countless other difficulties, the two of them had to bear the brunt not only of the battle for juridical recognition, but also of the work of expansion. Don Alvaro never voluntarily excused himself from anything on account of illness, not even on days when he was scheduled to work on many fronts towards the canonical approval of Opus Dei and also had to take care of those constant and serious financial binds they were in. His spirit never flagged; but sometimes his body just could not hold up under the strain and he did come down sick. Several years later Monsignor Escrivá said that the medicine Don Alvaro had really needed was "two poultices of a million dollars, one on each side."

Even when a fever forced him to stay in bed, Don Alvaro never lost his smile, and he always showed great gratitude and affection towards those who kept him company. "One day," says Francisco Monzó, "he even sat up in bed to show me the tricks of using a slide rule—he saw one peeping out from my jacket pocket—so that it would be easier for me to do the building accounts. He did it with such good humor, with such affectionate playfulness and cheerfulness, that you would have thought he was in the best of health."

Don Alvaro did, however, occasionally suffer more serious illnesses, and these caused the founder great concern. In February 1950 the abdominal pains that he had suffered for years suddenly grew much worse and, as I mentioned before, he was told (by Dr. Faelli, who was treating the founder for his diabetes) that he urgently needed an appendectomy. Many years later Don Alvaro admitted that the pain had been quite severe—but he did so only to show the great affection and charity that Blessed Josemaría lavished on his children when they were sick. On this occasion, to distract Don Alvaro and make him laugh a bit, he had gotten up and done a funny little dance in front of him. (See Cavalleri 1996, 84–85.)

Juan Masía, among others, remembers that although the operation was successful, the effects of the anesthesia lingered on. A few days after the surgery, Juan accompanied Monsignor Escrivá to the hospital. Only the two of them were in the room with Don Alvaro, and, whether because of the anesthetic or because of the fever, he was delirious. He kept saying over and over, "I want to work with the Father, with all my strength, until the day I die." Blessed Josemaría and Juan, with tears in their eyes, stayed by his side for a long time and then returned home in silence.

In 1959 there was more surgery, followed by a complicated and slow recovery. On February 2, the day that

Don Alvaro was hospitalized, Monsignor Escrivá went to Villa Sacchetti (the part of Villa Tevere that was reserved for women of Opus Dei) and lit a candle in Madonna Hall. Then he talked to his daughters about how important Don Alvaro was to the Work, and said that when this candle burned out, he would like for them to replace it with another one and keep doing this until Don Alvaro returned to Villa Tevere.

In the summer of 1973 Don Alvaro came down with another serious illness. The founder was with him when this happened; they were in a little rented house in the town of Civenna, near the Italian city of Lecco, about two miles from Switzerland. After a bad night spent tossing and turning in bed, Don Alvaro would not think of excusing himself from going with Monsignor Escrivá on his morning walk, even though he went out there looking terribly pale and feeling feverish. Monsignor Escrivá, with his history of heart trouble, absolutely needed that exercise, and Don Alvaro was not about to take any chances on his not getting it. So out he went, but soon he came down with a very high fever which made him break into a heavy sweat. Years later I heard him say that not only the sheets, but even the mattress had gotten soaked. The doctor he usually went to in Rome came and took care of him there; he was spending a few days in Castel d'Urio, which was not far away. His diagnosis was a kidney infection, and his recommendation was that when the fever died down, Don Alvaro should see Dr. José María Gil Vernet in Barcelona to find out if more surgery was needed. And it was. Don Alvaro underwent another operation, this time at San José Clinic in Barcelona.

Alfonso Balcells, a professor of general pathology at the University of Barcelona, was with him in the operating room and during his convalescence. "I was impressed," he says, "by his tranquillity and peacefulness. He had not the slightest anxiety or nervousness at any time. He never complained about anything."

11

From Pius XII to John Paul I

Don Alvaro would always be visibly moved at the recollection of June 4, 1943, when he was received in audience by Pope Pius XII for three-quarters of an hour. The Holy Father would likewise remember the young Spanish engineer who spoke to him about new ways to achieve holiness in the midst of the world. Not at all had he forgotten him by the time of the second audience, on April 3, 1946, after Don Alvaro's ordination. Nor by 1950, when he received Don Alvaro's mother, who had traveled to Rome for the Holy Year. Her son Carlos recalls that Pope Pius greeted Don Alvaro with an affectionate "Hello, engineer!"

During this pontificate Don Alvaro was named to several posts in different offices of the Holy See. He was highly regarded in the Roman Curia for his personal qualities, his pastoral experience, his solid theological background, and his legal expertise.

I have heard Don Javier Echevarría tell stories of a trip he took with Don Alvaro in 1958 to Cantabria and Vasconia, to help him do research on his family tree. Don Alvaro had been asked to do this by Pope Pius XII—twice, as a matter of fact. On the advice of Monsignor Escrivá, he had not started doing it until the request was repeated. But he never found out the reason for the request, because Pope Pius died that same year.

The founder of Opus Dei followed very closely the official reports of the Pope's illness. He suffered greatly when he saw morbid pictures of the Pope in his deathbed agony being broadcast on Italian television. This was so unethical that the Italian medical association suspended the doctor who had authorized the filming in the Pope's bedroom. According to Don Javier (this is in the above-mentioned article in the 5/2/94 issue of *Epoca*), when Don Alvaro saw those scenes he remained silent for quite a while, and then he said, "The Father is right. This is outrageous. What kind of son would make a spectacle out of the deathbed agony of his own father or mother?"

Pope Pius XII died on October 9, and on October 28 Cardinal Angelo Roncalli was elected as his successor. From the very beginning of his pontificate, Pope John XXIII kept in close touch with both Monsignor Escrivá and Don Alvaro, especially through his personal secretary, Monsignor Loris Capovilla. The founder's filial talks with Pope John, starting with the very first audience, on March 5, 1960, opened up new horizons of apostolate for the Church. Don Alvaro admired the priestly virtues of the Holy Father. As he put it, "he was very friendly and simple, which made it easy for people to say things freely, without worrying about protocol."

Pope John had, as a matter of fact, already come to know Opus Dei quite well when he was a cardinal. I was at one time director of the Miraflores residence in Saragossa, and I have happy memories of the time that he spent there, and also at the La Estila residence in Santiago de Compostela, during his trip to Spain in July 1954. As pope, he continued to follow the apostolic work of Opus Dei very closely and with great affection. He was always wishing he had more time to spend with the founder. "We must get together more often," he used to say. And he gave Don Alvaro one job after another with the Roman Curia. In 1959 he named him a consultor for the Congregation for the Council, and in 1960, a qualificator for what was then called the Supreme Congregation of the Holy Office. In 1963 he was also named a consultor for the Pontifical Commission for the Revision of the Code of Canon Law.

With Blessed Josemaría, Don Alvaro was thrilled when Pope John convoked an ecumenical council. The founder immediately offered the Church authorities whatever help the Work and its members could give. Many of them did participate directly in the work of the council, but none more so than Don Alvaro. Pope John entrusted him with weighty responsibilities, both in the work of preparing for the council and in the work of the council proceedings.

But soon came those sorrowful days of Pope John's final illness. Those who were living in Rome at the time remember the pained look that came over Don Alvaro's face whenever he or the founder alluded to the suffering of the Holy Father. When Monsignor Angelo Dell'Acqua told them that Pope John was in great pain, they prayed all the harder for him. Don Alvaro, by the way, also showed a great affection for Monsignor Dell'Acqua, who, along with several workers within the pontifical household, took such great care of the Pope in his last days, right up to the very end.

Pope John died on June 3, 1963. On June 21 Cardinal Giovanni Battista Montini was elected as his successor, and three months later the council was reconvened. Pope Paul VI very much liked Don Alvaro. Ricardo Castelo recalls that on the twenty-fifth anniversary of their graduation from engineering school, the former classmates all went to Rome and he granted them an audience. He greeted each of them individually, and when he came to Don Alvaro, he said in an affectionate tone of voice, "What? You're here too?"

They first met in 1943, and had their first real

conversation on June 17 of that year. Monsignor Montini received Don Alvaro at 1:30 in the afternoon, which by Italian standards was late in the day, and yet they spoke for over forty minutes. Don Alvaro, who was still a layman at the time, explained to Monsignor Montini the main features of the spirit of Opus Dei, and he understood it right away. Don Alvaro also gave him a copy of *The Way*. Monsignor Montini, in turn, gave him medallions commemorating the jubilee proclaimed by Pope Pius XII, and promised to pray for the Work.

As pope, he too had great confidence in Don Alvaro. In 1964 he named him a judge in the Supreme Congregation of the Holy Office, and in 1966, a consultor for three organizations: the Postconciliar Commission for Bishops and the Government of Dioceses, the Congregation for the Doctrine of the Faith, and the Congregation for the Clergy.

At the memorial service given by the University of Navarre for Don Alvaro (its former Grand Chancellor), Father Pedro Rodríguez (head of the theology department) described a very telling scene. "A cardinal, a high-ranking member of the Curia," he said, "is discussing with Pope Paul VI a matter of great importance to the life of the Church. He outlines for the Pope the problem, the different opinions, and a possible solution. The Pope listens attentively and then asks, 'What does del Portillo think?' The cardinal says, 'Holy Father, he supports the proposal.' 'Well, then,' says the Pope, 'that settles it!'"

One indication of the closeness between Pope Paul and Don Alvaro is a little exchange that occurred just after one of the first audiences which Pope Paul gave the founder of Opus Dei. At the end of it, Don Alvaro approached and greeted him. Pope Paul welcomed him with obvious delight and reminded him that they had met each other years before. "But I have become old since then," he said. And Don Alvaro, quick-witted as ever, replied, "No, Your Holiness—you have become Peter!"

Years later, on March 5, 1976, Pope Paul received him once again. This was the first papal audience Don Alvaro was granted after becoming head of the Work. Pope Paul was kind enough to schedule the interview for just after an *udienze di tabelle* (a weekly meeting with those who work most directly with the pope in the governing of the Church). On the day of the week when this meeting was held, the Holy Father normally did not receive visitors—a fact which made a longer conversation possible. Theirs stretched out to more than an hour. At the end of it, Don Alvaro thanked Pope Paul for his words of congratulation, and then immediately asked him for his apostolic blessing and for many prayers, "because," he said, "I am the successor of a saint, and that sure isn't something that's easy to be." And Pope Paul immediately responded, "But that saint is now in heaven, and he's busy moving the Work ahead."

Just before saying good-bye, Pope Paul said to Don Alvaro, "Nowadays I can't get away from here except on very rare occasions. I would love to go to the crypt to pray, but that's impossible for me. So when you get home, please imagine that you are the Pope and, in my name, kneel before the tomb of the saint and pray for me and for the Church." "Your Holiness," answered Don Alvaro, "your wish is my command. As soon as I get home, I will go to the crypt right away." But Pope Paul, in a fatherly tone of voice, replied, "No, not right away. First you have to eat." (The audience had gone on for longer than expected.) "Do what I have said later on. But do it today!"

Pope Paul was quite familiar with the apostolic efforts of the members of Opus Dei, and he encouraged those efforts. During the years of the Second Vatican Council, some members took it upon themselves, with the help of friends and other interested individuals, to organize some family guidance programs. These programs soon spread all over the world, thanks in large part to the international gatherings initiated in 1976 for the sharing of experiences and the solving of common problems. The first Family Guidance Convention took place in Rome, and Don Alvaro had a lively get-together with the participants. On the following day they were received in a private audience by Pope Paul VI, and Don Alvaro was very moved by what he heard about it afterwards. "The warm and spontaneous affection of the Holy Father when he received us in Clementina Hall," wrote one of the participants, "gave us a new sense of the apostolic importance of those family guidance programs. Apart from what the Pope had to say (this was a discourse in French, interrupted several times by direct expressions of his affection for us), the looks of encouragement which the Holy Father gave us, and the constant feeling that he was really enjoying his time with us, as in a family, made very clear the appreciation that the Church had for this initiative." Furthermore, at the end he asked them to stay with him a little longer, because "he wanted to have a photo taken of himself with us, as a keepsake of such a warm, familial, 'precieux' meeting."

I myself witnessed Don Alvaro's reaction to the death of Pope Paul VI, which took place on August 6, 1978. Even though at the beginning of the month there had been news of an illness, no one foresaw that it would be fatal. We were at the Solavieya Conference Center at the time, and it came as a big surprise to us when we heard the terse announcement on television a little after ten o'clock that night. I turned on the radio in hopes of getting confirmation of the news and getting more details, but with no success. Don Alvaro phoned some of the Opus Dei members in Rome, but they were unable to give him any details. It appeared that the end had come with lightning speed.

After that initial commotion, we went to the chapel. Don Alvaro led a responsorial prayer for the soul of Pope

Paul VI, and then an Our Father for the next pope. In a few
words, he then added a special and constant intention for
this period. Besides offering suffrages for the deceased pope,
he said, we should also pray for the future pope, going to the
Blessed Virgin through the intercession of the founder. For
that intention we should offer everything, even our breathing.

The next day was the anniversary of the ordination of
three priests who were with us at Solavieya: Fathers Javier
Echevarría, Joaquín Alonso, and Juan Domingo Celaya. But,
naturally, all the Masses were requiem Masses for the soul of
Pope Paul.

After breakfast, we saw on television a documentary
about Pope Paul. It was badly done, highly critical,
disrespectful, and superficial. It made Don Alvaro so
unhappy that he started making acts of atonement then and
there, out loud. On August 8 he went to the Marian shrine
of Covadonga to confide to our Lady his concerns and hopes
for the future. We prayed with him a rosary, which was led
(as usual) by Don Javier. At the end, when it came time for
the Our Father which we always prayed for the Roman
pontiff and his intentions, he offered it for the next pope.

In those days, though he was now in Spain, Don Alvaro
expressed a sentiment that he had heard Monsignor Escrivá
express whenever the office of pope had been vacant in the
past: that even before the election, he already loved the new
pope, whoever he might be. "The pope," he said, "needs all
our loyalty, all our affection, all our piety and devotion, all
our longing to be saints, even if we are just poor sinners."

The death of Pope Paul caused Don Alvaro to change
his plans. He had just arrived at Solavieya on the fourth of
August. On the tenth—after delegating many jobs so that
others could chip away at the work he had planned for the
month—he went by car to Madrid and then, early in the
afternoon, took a plane for Rome.

All of this helped me to understand even better

something that I was already well aware of: namely, Don Alvaro's great love for that common father of all Christians, Pope Paul VI. I thought of how he was always wanting, like any good son, to make him happy. A good example of that had taken place earlier that same year, on Wednesday of Holy Week. Pope Paul usually held on that day a general audience for the participants of the UNIV Congress, an annual international conference for university students. But this time he was not feeling well enough to grant them an audience; the best he could do was to give them his blessing in St. Peter's Square. Don Alvaro encouraged all forty-five hundred of these students to go. He said to them, "The Holy Father will see all this youthfulness of yours, and it will make him very happy."

After Paul VI came John Paul I, whom Don Alvaro loved dearly, as did all other Catholics. He had often met Cardinal Albino Luciani in the Vatican or at synods of bishops, especially after Cardinal Luciani became the titular patriarch of Venice.

From time to time I heard Don Alvaro recall various aspects of the holiness of this pope. In 1990, for example, he told us that when Cardinal Luciani was elected in the conclave, he accepted the papacy knowing full well that he might die soon, because he was sick at the time. And he also told us about something that had happened just a few days before the election. Cardinal Luciani had come over for lunch at Villa Tevere. It was nearly *ferragosto,* that stiflingly hot time in August when Rome grinds to a halt. Cardinal Luciani was happily talking about the life of the Church, and the phone rang, and the call was for him. Afterwards he explained that he had a terrible toothache and had not been able to get hold of a dentist. Finally he had made contact with one—and he went straight to his office after our visit. Don Alvaro said that no one had had any idea he was in pain. "He was such a saint," he said, "that he hid his pain in a marvelous way."

Hardly a month had gone by when Pope John Paul I died, on September 28, and the See of Rome was vacant once again. Don Alvaro learned of his death early in the morning, in time to offer his Mass for the repose of his soul. He spoke words filled with serenity and consolation, and he asked, once again, for prayers for the soul of the deceased pope and for the pope to come.

Very soon there arrived at the centers of Opus Dei a short letter from Don Alvaro. He was writing it, he said, "heartbroken at the sudden death of our Holy Father John Paul I." The fiftieth anniversary of the foundation of Opus Dei was just a couple of days away; now it would have to be celebrated "during this time of *sede vacante,* which for all Catholics is a time of mourning." However, "it is our Lord who has decided that we are to feel the lovable weight of his holy cross at this time of the golden jubilee of the Work, and he wants us to bear it with a supernatural outlook. Let us not forget that the cross is a sign of divine favor." He gave the same kind of instructions he had given when Pope Paul VI died: he urged everyone to offer suffrages for Pope John Paul I and to seek blessings for the future pope and for the Church at the hand of the Blessed Virgin, Mother of the Church.

Don Alvaro's filial devotion to the pope was well integrated with his faithful love for the Spouse of Christ. I saw, year after year, the growing but always serene concern that he had for the Church; I saw it right up to the very last days I spent with him, in 1993. He lived through some really difficult times. I remember several occasions in the seventies when there were problems I had to discuss with him. Over his usually smiling and reassuring face there would pass a cloud of sorrow. He would then say just a few incisive words to the effect that we needed to pray more, to make atonement for all these failures, including our own, and to feel in all humility the pain of not having been more responsive and loyal. Many a time I heard him insist on the importance of being very faithful to Catholic doctrine. We must, he said, deepen and update our understanding of it, both by reading and studying good theology texts and by living a life of genuine piety.

Here is one instance, among many, in which I got a close-up view of Don Alvaro's passion for unity. One day in August 1976, the first person featured on the evening news was Archbishop Lefèbvre. Don Alvaro became quite upset and insisted that we pray hard for the Church. That night, everyone could see that he was worried. On the very next morning he sent a telegram to Pope Paul VI, reassuring him of Opus Dei's unity with him and letting him know that we would all be praying for him throughout this difficult time. And he stressed to us that although we should at all times be truly united with the pope and the bishops, this was more necessary than ever in these difficult times. He said this quite often over the next several days, since there was a lot of news about Archbishop Lefèbvre. And long after that, in November 1989, I again saw how it pained Don Alvaro to hear national news coverage that reflected and spread a certain hostility towards Rome. "We must pray more," he would always say.

In those turbulent times for the Church, just as in other times, he fulfilled his pastoral mission and led his flock to rich pastures. But he did it without complaint, and was always understanding and nonjudgmental of others. He highlighted the positive aspects of whatever happened. Always shining through was his love for the Roman pontiff and the Church—a deeply theological and affectionate love which was not at all naive or blind. "The Church is holy and immaculate," he used to say. "She is the Spouse of Christ, ever youthful, ever beautiful. Yes, from one perspective, she is made up of human beings, and we human beings are wretched sinners. But, from another perspective, it is not fair to focus on the flaws of the children and attribute them to their mother." And with another simple argument (which he learned from Blessed Josemaría), he fended off all the superficial criticism, rumor-mongering, and slander heaped upon the Church, the pope, and the bishops: "A good son always speaks about his mother with affection and understanding; he never goes around broadcasting anything negative."

Don Alvaro loved the Church deeply and wholeheartedly, and encouraged others to do the same. He rejoiced in her joys and suffered in her sufferings. Nothing in her earthly path was foreign to him. He used to tell the faithful of Opus Dei that the best way they could serve the Church was "to live a Christian life under all conditions, bringing it to the most disparate environments of society."

Even when he was questioned about the most sensitive issues, people were struck by his supernatural optimism and his charity towards others, as well as by his concern for the good of the Church and his insistence on fidelity to the pope. In the 3/31/94 issue of San Juan's *El Vocero,* Bishop Juan Fremiot Torres Oliver, president of the Episcopal Conference of Puerto Rico, summed it up very well. "In my long conversations with Bishop del Portillo," he said, "during those turbulent years in the life of the Church, I always heard words of understanding and excusing of others. I never heard a complaint or a word against anyone. It was edifying to see how intransigent he was with regard to error, but, at the same time, how understanding with regard to persons. He could see a positive side to everything."

12

The Second Vatican Council

Only on rare occasions did Don Alvaro speak about his participation in the Second Vatican Council. On one of them, he mentioned in passing—and only to illustrate the intense interior life of the founder of Opus Dei—a car accident that happened during that time. In February 1963 he had to travel to Venice to speak with Cardinal Urbani, who was on the council's coordinating commission. There was a problem under discussion in the Commission for the Clergy, and it was the responsibility of Don Alvaro, its secretary, to consult Cardinal Urbani. Monsignor Escrivá and Don Javier Echevarría accompanied him on the trip because they needed some rest. But on some of the roads there was a lot of ice, and a dangerous amount of traffic. Their driver, Javier Cotelo (an architect by profession), took every safety precaution he could, but somewhere between Rovigo and Padua, about two and a half miles from Monselice, the car skidded, spun around, kept skidding, and finally collided with a stone road-marker at the edge of a cliff. The car was hanging over the chasm, so it was not at all easy for them to get out of it safely. But for Don Alvaro the most memorable thing about this harrowing event was Monsignor Escrivá's amazingly calm and supernatural attitude through it all. From the very first moment of it, he simply kept invoking the protection of the Lord and of their guardian angels.

In his interview with Cesare Cavalleri, Don Alvaro said something more about his own involvement in the Second Vatican Council, though once again he put the spotlight on Monsignor Escrivá: "He encouraged me to accept appointments to various commissions of the council, and to dedicate myself to this work with all my energy." He also said quite a bit about the many conversations that the founder had with the council fathers: "Sometimes he would invite them to dine at our central residence. On other occasions, he would go to see them in the houses where they were lodging—nearly always to return visits they had made to him. There were days on which he would receive over half a dozen of these visits. And it was certainly not easy for him to take time away from his duties of governing Opus Dei in order to receive the various cardinals, archbishops, bishops, nuncios, theologians, and so on. . . ." But in testifying to Monsignor Escrivá's simplicity and affability, Don Alvaro had no choice but to make this admission: "I was present at many of these meetings." (See Cavalleri 1996, 11–12.)

However, he says nothing about what it cost him to be present at all those visits and meals, overburdened as he already was by his direct participation in the work of the council. Nor does he mention how often he was the one to arrange those meetings. When, for example, Bishop Onclin introduced to him some prelates from cities where the Work had not yet taken root, Don Alvaro spoke with those prelates and arranged meetings with the founder.

It is an undisputed fact that Don Alvaro played an important role in the Second Vatican Council, since he was named a *peritus* (expert observer) when the work of the council began. But even before that, Pope John XXIII had chosen him to be president of the preparatory commission on the laity, and he had served on other commissions as well. And during the council itself, he was secretary of the Commission for the Discipline of the Clergy and of the Christian People. He also served as a consultor for several commissions: the commissions for bishops, for religious, for the doctrine of the faith, and for associations of the faithful.

He never, of course, talked about what he did. But obviously the work of the secretary of a conciliar commission was an important responsibility, and the working sessions were exhausting. It strained both one's intellectual powers and one's social skills to give an accurate account of the many different opinions, to harmonize them, and to bring about some meeting of the minds so that things did not get bogged down. The esteem in which Don Alvaro was held in the Church at large, and in the Roman Curia in particular, grew by the day.

Not a week had gone by after the close of the council when Cardinal Ciriaci, president of the commission of which Don Alvaro had been secretary, sent him a note expressing heartfelt gratitude and congratulations for the happy conclusion of a great achievement. I translate from this note, dated December 14, 1965: "You steered to a safe harbor your decree, which is by no means the least important of the decrees and constitutions of the council." The decree he was referring to is *Presbyterorum ordinis*. The cardinal was congratulating Don Alvaro on its nearly unanimous approval by the council fathers; after a thorough debate, the vote on December 7, 1965, was 2390 to 4. History would regard this decree, said Cardinal Ciriaci, as "a fresh, and practically unanimous, confirmation by the Second Vatican Council of ecclesiastical celibacy and the exalted mission of the priesthood." Then he added a sentiment which he would later communicate also to Pope Paul VI: "I am well aware of the extent to which this is a result of your prudent, tenacious, and courteous efforts. Without failing to respect the freedom of others to have and to express their own opinions, you never swerved from the track of fidelity to the great principles of priestly spirituality."

In an article published in *Scripta Theologica* shortly after Don Alvaro's death, the theologian Lucas F. Mateo Seco summed up his contribution to the council in this way: "Those who worked with him recall his amiability and discretion, his orderly mind, his engineering efficiency, his legal precision, and his theological depth." He did not mention Don Alvaro's sense of history, but he did highlight one related virtue: humility. Don Alvaro, he said, wanted only to serve, and never to cut a grand figure. He cited this testimony from Pedro Lombardía, who worked with Don Alvaro in the Commission for the Reform of Canon Law: "In meetings he followed discussions attentively, always trying to get to the bottom of the problem, and spoke only to make specific and very concise contributions. He never made useless observations which would prolong meetings unnecessarily. These qualities of simplicity, depth, efficiency, cordiality, and respect account for the high esteem in which people held him and for the serious attention they paid to his opinions."

In 1995, in the memorial service at the University of Navarre, Professor Pedro Rodríguez talked about how loved and respected Don Alvaro was for the rectitude of his outlook on the Church and for his innate gentleness and goodness. In his own career as a theologian, Rodríguez said, he had taken part in many international conferences and congresses in which he met high-ranking ecclesiastics, "and when I introduced myself as a member of Opus Dei, their response was often something to this effect: 'The fellow in Opus Dei that I am great friends with is Alvaro del Portillo.' And often they would add, 'A great intellect, and a saint as well!' He had gained a certain authority through his depth and competence, his ability to solve problems, and his contagious certainty."

Don Alvaro, as I say, did not talk about the work he did for the council. However, his guiding principles can be gleaned from what he published afterwards. Many of his contributions have been collected in a commemorative volume published by the Pontifical Athenaeum of the Holy Cross as *Rendere amabile la verità* (Making the truth lovable). Here I shall refer only to two of his more important books.

His *Faithful and Laity in the Church* came out in 1969. This book originated in' his work with the Commission for the Revision of the Code of Canon Law. Don Alvaro was a consultor for this body (which changed names several times) until the promulgation of the new Code in 1983. He was a rapporteur for two study groups: one on the rights and duties of the faithful, and another on the rights and duties of priests.

Faithful and Laity in the Church is probably the first systematic exposition of the council's doctrine on the People of God. This exposition hinges on the distinction between "faithful" and "laity," which today is fairly familiar, but at that time was original and innovative. Don Alvaro's precise delineation of the two terms establishes a solid intellectual basis for the dignity of the person in the Church, for a firm defense of the rights of the laity, and also for the identity of the priest, as one who facilitates an active and responsible participatThe Second Vatican Councilion of all the faithful in the mission of the Church—a participation not tainted with either clericalism or worldliness.

Particularly original is the discussion of rights. This issue had hardly ever been addressed by canonists. In this book Don Alvaro discussed the right of association, the right of petition, the right to a public expression of opinion in the Church, the right to a spirituality of one's own, the right to a free choice of state of life. With respect to the juridical status of women, the thought of Alvaro del Portillo was basically this: women in the Church, since they are lay people, have no duties, rights, or juridical faculties which are different from those of the other faithful; nor do they lack any of those.

A year later Don Alvaro published *Consecration and Mission of the Priest*—a book with a different thematic context. Here he put together his theological thinking, his historical knowledge, and his pastoral experience and brought it all to bear on a key problem of the twentieth century: the identity of the priest in the Church. In his view, the solution to this problem depended (as the title of the book implies) on an integrated understanding of the consecration and mission of the priest.

In this book, constant reference is made to *Presbyterorum ordinis,* the great document which was the primary achievement of the commission presided over by Cardinal Ciriaci. As secretary of that commission, Don Alvaro had to chair many meetings attended by cardinals and archbishops, because Cardinal Ciriaci delegated much of his work and did not attend the meetings. To some extent, it was Don Alvaro's decision that a text be drafted. He argued persuasively that the priesthood was so important in the Church that it well deserved a decree of its own, rather than just a handful of propositions with a concluding message (a suggestion made at some point in the proceedings).

The drafting of the decree was very hard work, especially because of all the tension there was at that time over the issue of priestly celibacy. That conflict, in fact, got so bad that Pope Paul himself had to intervene. Also, the commission had to reach conclusions regarding the spirituality of priests. One of its decisions was to defend centuries-old traditions against those who regarded them as mere pietism. It discussed the presence of the priest in the world, and why he needed a good formation in the basic human virtues in order to serve the men and women of his time. But it also warned that priests should not adopt lay lifestyles, much less take on commitments of a partisan political nature. Finally, it asserted the freedom of priests to join associations which in one way or another could help them achieve personal sanctification in the carrying out of their priestly ministry.

As regards liturgy (another major concern of Vatican II), Don Alvaro's only writings were letters directed to centers of the Prelature. Because of his deep piety, it grieved him to hear news of liturgical abuses. He believed that they damaged souls because they weakened the devotion of the faithful. I heard him give some specific examples—in a way that was very delicate, but that made it very clear that the Church's instructions about the liturgy must be loved and followed.

He liked the variety provided in the liturgical books for ceremonies; he liked that flexibility introduced in the Church after the Second Vatican Council. At the same time, he advised priests to make their choices according to this great practical guideline: their call "to know and to live the sacred liturgy of the Church with an ever-growing love for God and concern for the good of souls." In this desire to be very devout and to heed the good of the faithful, he said, there ought to be a complete unanimity.

He followed to the letter the instructions given by the Church, because he was quite convinced that, to quote Monsignor Escrivá, "we are led to God, brought close to him, by the liturgy of the Catholic Church" (*The Way*, no. 543). He also reiterated the founder's directive that Opus Dei would never have a liturgy of its own, but only a finely tuned and loving obedience to the general norms of the Church. In all of this, Don Alvaro was simply perpetuating the spirit and example of Blessed Josemaría, who in 1969 had stated emphatically that "we will love this new liturgy just as we loved the old one."

Another great outcome of the Second Vatican Council was the ecumenical movement. Don Alvaro came to appreciate this not only directly, but also through the life and teaching of the founder of Opus Dei. And I'm sure this was not at all difficult for him, given his innate friendliness and capacity for understanding all kinds of people. It was his nature to think and act in an ecumenical spirit. Case in point: towards the end of the forties, an international committee went to Rome to thank Pope Pius XII for the help which the Jewish community had received from the Holy See during the occupation of Rome. Don Alvaro was one of those responsible for looking after these guests, and as they were leaving, they thanked him in particular. "In the Vatican," they said, "everyone has received us very kindly and treated us very well, but no one as well as you." "Oh, that was nothing," Don Alvaro replied. "Remember, the woman I've loved most in my whole life is Jewish." "Who is that?" they asked. "The Virgin Mary," he said, "the mother of Jesus Christ."

This kind of thing explains why Rabbi David Rosen, the director for interreligious dialogue for the Anti-Defamation League of B'nai B'rith, reacted as he did when he learned of the death of Don Alvaro. He sent a telegram, which also bore the signatures of Lisa Palmieri-Billig of Italy and Rabbi Leon Klenicki of New York, in which they expressed "our most heartfelt condolences for the great loss of Bishop Alvaro del Portillo" and said they were invoking "the help of God so that the good work that Opus Dei does throughout the world may continue to go forward."

If Don Alvaro treated with charity and understanding those who did not know Christ, he showed even greater affection for his separated brethren. As Monsignor Escrivá had always done, he lived very intensely—and wanted everyone else to live very intensely—the Octave for Christian Unity, which ends on January 25, the feast of the Conversion of Saint Paul.

He never let slip any opportunity to show his big heart. At the UNIV Congress of 1976, the first one after the death of the founder of Opus Dei, there were university students from many countries, and some of them were able to address Don Alvaro publicly. One of them, a fellow by the name of Said, asked him, "Father, I am a Muslim—how can I contribute to the Work with my poor help?" "Look," replied Don Alvaro, "your poor help is just as good as mine. In the eyes of almighty God we are all poor. . . . I respect your beliefs, your faith, and I tell you that your God and my God are one and the same: the one, all-powerful God who created heaven and earth. Pray to him that he will make you see things clearly, and that you will come to have, if it is his will, the fullness of the light of revelation which shines on Catholics. In any case, be consistent with your faith, and if God asks more from you, tell him 'yes.'"

In Nairobi, a Presbyterian fellow named Clark had recently started working at Strathmore, an interracial education center set up by members of Opus Dei. He asked Don Alvaro, "How can I find out the will of God for my life? How can I know what direction I should take?" "You have told me that you're a Presbyterian," Don Alvaro replied. "I respect you, and, with the grace of God, I would readily lay down my life to defend your freedom of conscience. Let's go from there, taking that as our starting point. But now I must add something. I am a man who is full of defects, but I am sincere, and I see myself as your friend. And as a friend, I have an obligation to be loyal to you. Loyalty is a virtue which we ought to have toward everyone in the world, but especially toward our friends, because where there is no loyalty, there is no friendship. I consider us friends, and you do too, right? Are you my friend?" "Yes, Father," Clark answered. Don Alvaro then spoke with him about things they had in common (such as their faith in the Triune God), and about their differences (such as their beliefs about the sacraments and the hierarchical structure of the Church), and finished by urging him to pray.

On another occasion, a German fellow named Mathias,

who belonged to some evangelical denomination, asked Don
Alvaro where he could get the strength to become a Catholic.
Don Alvaro spoke to him about the Gospel, about freedom
of conscience, and about the one Church founded by Jesus
Christ: the Catholic Church. "In the sixteenth century," he
said, "pieces were chipped off of that great Church of Christ,
but those pieces still have something of that divine richness.
Pope Pius XI used to say that it was like splinters from a
gold-bearing rock—even the tiniest piece has a few grains of
gold. You have a lot of gold in your faith. You believe in the
Father, in the Son, and in the Holy Spirit. You believe in so
many things... But I would be a hypocrite if I were not to tell
you that you're still missing something of the true faith, the
faith that your ancestors had before they separated themselves
from the one Church of Jesus Christ. The only thing I can
do is ask you for permission to pray for you, that the Holy
Spirit will give you the fullness of faith. . . . In return, I ask
of you one thing: that you pray for me. Let's make between
us a kind of pact—you pray that I be a worthy successor of a
saint, because I am a poor man, a poor priest of Jesus Christ."

Similar scenes were often enacted in Rome and during
Don Alvaro's trips all over the world. The few examples I
have given are representative of his approach to non-
Catholics. They show how he combined love for the truth
with love for freedom, and always with affection and respect
for the person.

When the council ended, Don Alvaro continued to
work in the Roman Curia. Implementing the teachings of
the council was certainly not easy. Along with very fruitful
innovations, there were nasty shocks and serious difficulties.
The founder of Opus Dei coined the expression "a time of
trial"; his heart was grieved by the profound crises taking
place in so many sectors of Church life. Don Alvaro always
gave a fitting echo to the anguish of Blessed Josemaría's
priestly heart. He reiterated the need to keep on praying

that this "time of trial" would soon come to an end. He agreed with the founder that the times, precisely inasmuch as they were bad, were also good because they called for more holiness, for a deeper spirit of prayer and penance. When insisting on love for the Church, he used strong and clear words, but in such a calm and pleasant way that they warded off any temptation to fall into pessimism, discouragement, or bitterness.

In October 1983 I traveled to Rome. A special assembly of the Synod of Bishops was taking place, and Pope John Paul II had made Don Alvaro a participant. This time I personally saw him do what I knew he had done throughout the Second Vatican Council. I saw him throw himself completely into this service to the Church and still take care of his pastoral responsibilities in the Work, seemingly multiplying his hours. And I wondered how in the world, despite all this work, he always managed to be in such a good mood during our brief get-togethers in the center for the General Council of Opus Dei.

In short, as Pedro Rodríguez said at the memorial service at the University of Navarre, "for Alvaro del Portillo, his service to the Roman Church and his service to Opus Dei were not just linked together, but perfectly united in the one *communio* which is the Church of Jesus Christ." In Don Alvaro's eyes, everything in the Church should facilitate progress in the spiritual life and in evangelization. That, after all, was precisely why Pope John XXIII had convoked the council. Don Alvaro often reminded people of this, and in a letter written on September 1, 1987, just before the Synod of Bishops was to meet to study the mission of the laity in the Church and in the world, he expressed it with succinct clarity. "Ask the Holy Spirit," he said, "for abundant light for the Pope and for the synodal fathers, so that the theological and spiritual study of the Church that is carried out in these days will bring with it a strong surge of sanctity and apostolate that will reach all corners of the world."

Considering the extent of Don Alvaro's participation in the Second Vatican Council, it is not surprising that Pope John Paul II appointed him a synodal father for the extraordinary synod convened in 1985, on the twentieth anniversary of the closing of the council. From the time the synod was announced, Don Alvaro asked the faithful of Opus Dei to offer up many prayers and sacrifices for this intention, that this meeting of the bishops would bear much fruit.

When it ended, on December 8, he could not hide his happiness. This synod had gone into the teachings of Vatican II in great depth. It had also spoken out against some customs which, though in fact contrary to the council's decisions, had been introduced as authorized by "the spirit of the council." Don Alvaro stressed these key points in the speech he gave, as Grand Chancellor of what was then called the Roman Academic Center of the Holy Cross, for the opening of the 1986–87 school year. (I had the privilege of being present at this event, which took place on October 16 in the main auditorium of the Palazzo di Sant'Apollinare.) He mentioned in particular the closing statement of the synod. "Not only," he said, "does it explicitly propose that certain topics of special contemporary interest be studied—and that ecclesiastical athenaeums should pay special attention to them—but it also describes the lights and the shadows which the People of God are going through at the present time. To deal with these responsibly, it says, we must with constancy and fidelity deepen our understanding of the doctrine of the council." That great inspiration, to the Grand Chancellor's way of thinking, should set the tone for all the teaching and research to be done at that pontifical athenaeum.

In the United States, at the beginning of 1988, Don Alvaro spoke—perhaps more than he ever did in any other nation—about doctrinal controversies which were troubling the Christian conscience and being much discussed by the media. At the end of his visit, he traveled from New York to New Jersey for a dinner with Archbishop McCarrick and seven other bishops. During their after-dinner chat, the archbishop wanted to know more about Don Alvaro's participation in the Second Vatican Council and in the 1987 synod. All the bishops listened to Don Alvaro with great interest, in tacit recognition of his moral authority—for, after all, only one man at that table had actually attended the council...

13

The Death of the Founder

Despite the outstanding serenity that he showed even then, one of the hardest moments in the life of Don Alvaro was the unexpected death of Monsignor Escrivá, on June 26, 1975. He would, indeed, always regard that day as a "new Pentecost" for Opus Dei—a day of mystical enrichment, since its head was now in heaven. Nevertheless, the human pain of that separation was a wound in his heart which would never in this lifetime be healed.

The final chapter of *Immersed in God,* the book recording Don Alvaro's interview with Cesare Cavalleri about the founder, is entitled "June 26, 1975." A single question evokes a response of over twenty pages, a response that is essential for understanding how deeply Don Alvaro loved Monsignor Escrivá. He tells what happened and what he did; he speaks much more in first person than in the previous chapters. Though his focus is, of course, still on the founder and not on himself, what he says here communicates very clearly who Don Alvaro was, how he felt, and how he acted.

First he gave Monsignor Escrivá all the supernatural help he could. He gave him sacramental absolution and attempted to cure both soul and body with the Anointing of the Sick. He called up Carmen Ramos, the Central Secretary, and asked her to have all the women drop whatever they were doing and pray "for a very urgent intention." At the same time, he did not overlook natural means. He enlisted the help of two doctors, José Luis Soria and Juan Manuel Verdaguer.

When the doctors confirmed that Monsignor Escrivá had died, Don Alvaro submitted to the will of God and embraced the cross—literally. He took the relic of the True Cross which Monsignor Escrivá was wearing around his neck and told those around him, "Until the successor of the Father is elected, I'll wear this True Cross."

Calmly he dealt with an unending stream of business: arranging the funeral chapel, informing the Pope and the members of Opus Dei, and especially having Masses *de corpore insepulto* (before the burial) said continually, one after the other, until the beginning of the funeral. He himself said the first of these Masses.

Don Alvaro spent many hours praying before the body of the founder. At midmorning on June 27, he knelt by the casket and rested his forehead on the head of the Father. It was a symbolic moment. Not only was it a striking portrait of Don Alvaro's whole life, but also it was a key to understanding what fidelity means to every member of Opus Dei: always working *ad mentem Patris,* in accord with the mind of the Father.

Nearly twenty years later, at the memorial service for Don Alvaro at the University of Navarre, Bishop Javier Echevarría (who succeeded him both as Prelate of Opus Dei and as Grand Chancellor of the university) stressed this quality very forcefully. This was, in fact, the first thing he said: "Fidelity—this is certainly the best summary of the life of Alvaro del Portillo, and the fullest explanation of his profound influence on the Church, on Opus Dei, and on the University of Navarre. He was always faithful, even heroically faithful—faithful to Christ, faithful to the Church, faithful to the inspiration of the Holy Spirit, faithful to the apostolic mission passed on to him by Blessed Josemaría."

A subtext of *Immersed in God* is the great solicitude that Don Alvaro had for Monsignor Escrivá. The book's intent is to reveal details of the latter's heroic virtue. But Don Alvaro's warmhearted concern for him shines through in all kinds of homey details: his purchase, for instance, of a woolen undershirt when the founder catches a bad cold in Turin; his insistence that the founder get new glasses; his installation of wall-to-wall carpet after the founder collapses and lies unconscious for a while on the cold tiles of his bedroom floor... (see Cavalleri 1996, 34–35).

Such was the loyalty of Don Alvaro that he never neglected his responsibility as *custos* (guardian, or advisor) of Blessed Josemaría for fear of upsetting him. With clarity and simplicity he made whatever observations he thought necessary. Sometimes it was hard for Monsignor Escrivá to accept these, and occasionally he would say in front of the Blessed Sacrament (I heard this from the present Prelate), "Alvaro doesn't let a single thing slip past. And this doesn't feel like affection, it feels like cruelty!" But then, right away, he would turn this around and say, "Thank you, Lord, for keeping by my side my son Alvaro, who loves me so much that he never lets a single thing slip past!"

The life of Don Alvaro was a continual assisting of the founder of Opus Dei. On May 1, 1962, from Rome, Blessed Josemaría wrote to Spain's regional vicar, "Alvaro is in the hospital, but we have good reason to hope that another operation will not be necessary. Pray for him, for if among you I have many children who are heroic and even saintly— and I am not misusing either term—Alvaro is a model, and the son of mine who has worked hardest and suffered most for the Work, and the one who has best captured my spirit. Pray for him." Blessed Josemaría had a talent for synthesis, and these few lines sum up very well the fidelity for which Don Alvaro was famous among all who knew him. The founder himself had these words from Proverbs 28:20 inscribed on the lintel of the room where he worked with Don Alvaro: "Vir fidelis multum laudabitur" (A faithful man will abound with blessings).

In 1973, on Don Alvaro's birthday, at Villa Tevere, Blessed Josemaría took advantage of his absence at one moment to praise his cheerful spirit of sacrifice, which, he said, had led Don Alvaro into "a heroism which appears very ordinary." He went on to say to the people there, "I would like for you to imitate him in many things, but above all in faithfulness. In these many years of his vocation, he has had plenty of opportunities, humanly speaking, to get annoyed and angry, and to be disloyal. But he has always kept an incomparable smile and an incomparable faithfulness. He has done this not out of natural virtue, but out of supernatural motivation. It would be very good for you to imitate him in this."

On the day that Don Alvaro died, Don Javier Echevarría was asked, "What did Bishop Alvaro del Portillo represent for the Work? What is his legacy?" This was his answer: "He has left a very deep imprint. One of its essential features is a strong sense of filiation, accompanied naturally by an effort to be faithful, first to our Lord God and then to the spirit of Opus Dei left to us by the founder. Don Alvaro incarnated to perfection all aspects of the spirituality of Opus Dei, making them flesh of his flesh, bone of his bone."

And he did all this with a graceful and good-humored humility. Among his papers there was later found an undated note with these words handwritten by the founder: "In a work of God, I am nothing but a hindrance. Mariano." ["Mariano" was one of the founder's baptismal names.] Right beside that message is written this one: "Me too. Alvaro."

Don Alvaro had the entire life of the founder etched

into his memory. But even so, he always showed the greatest interest and joy whenever he heard or related anything about him. No matter how many years went by, nothing became stale or tiresome to him; he always felt the wonder of newness and surprise. Throughout his life he kept intact the sensibilities of a young heart. He knew nothing of that cold indifference against which Blessed Josemaría had always warned people (see *Christ Is Passing By,* no. 26).

After 1975 he constantly called to mind events and aspects of the founder's life because, as he once wrote, "they exemplify the heroic struggle to achieve sanctity and serve the Church on the pathway of fidelity to the Work in service of all souls." They were not "history" in the sense of being over and done with and to be viewed only from outside. He had fully incorporated them into his own life, and he wanted them "activated" in that of each member of the Work. He wanted all of us to thus identify ourselves "with what God is asking of us, so that we can do Opus Dei."

To the responsibility that Don Alvaro had always felt, there was added the fatherly command given him by Pope Paul VI in one of the first audiences after his election as head of Opus Dei. As he expressed it on several occasions, "Pope Paul told me that he considered the founder to be one of the individuals in the history of the Church who had received the most charisms, and one who had always responded faithfully and generously to those divine gifts. And he repeated several times that he considered him a very great saint." And when Don Alvaro shared with him some other details about Monsignor Escrivá, Pope Paul asked him affectionately, "Have you written all this down?" Don Alvaro said yes. Pope Paul then said, "This is a treasure not just for Opus Dei, but for the whole Church." And then he stated emphatically, "Everything that has to do with the founder, with his doctrinal teachings, whether written or oral, or with the events of his life, does not now belong solely to

Opus Dei. It forms part of the history of the Church."

Don Alvaro worked hard on this task, which was also indispensable to the cause of beatification of Monsignor Escrivá. Father Flavio Capucci, Postulator of Opus Dei, remembers how happy Don Alvaro was towards the end of 1985. One day, while Father Capucci was finishing up the preparation of Monsignor Escrivá's unpublished writings for presentation in the examinational phase of the process, Don Alvaro came into his office and chatted with him for a while. Father Capucci does not remember what their conversation was about, but he does recall what Don Alvaro said at the end of it. "Suddenly he said to me—this is not verbatim, but in meaning it is exactly what he said—'Now, my son, I can intone my *Nunc dimittis.*' Like old Simeon in the second chapter of Saint Luke, he had lived only in the hope of seeing fulfilled the promise which he had received from the Holy Spirit. . . . He was telling me that his life's work was now done. 'But, Father,' I said, 'what are you thinking of? Why are you saying this? There are still so many things left for you to do.' He said, 'No, I had three things to do before I die, and I have already finished them.' And then he listed them. I have spun this out, but his words were terse and to the point. He said, 'I had to obtain the configuration of the Work as a prelature; I had to finish my testimony for our Father's beatification process; and, finally, I had to write the notes to his 'Personal Notes.' And now I'm done.' And that was all he said."

Father Capucci describes the "Personal Notes" as "eight handwritten notebooks in which Blessed Josemaría, at different stages of his life and without the continuity and detail of journal-keeping, jotted down certain insights he had received from our Lord during his prayer, some pastoral experiences connected with starting and developing the apostolate of Opus Dei, and some possible channels for future development." In 1968 Monsignor Escrivá reread those notebooks and indicated those points for which it seemed necessary to add explanatory footnotes so that they could be understood in the future.

The material was left in a package marked with instructions from the founder that if he died before being able to do this himself, his son Alvaro should write the explanations for the points indicated. These explanations should give the contextual background, the historical circumstances or possibly the deeper motivations behind these things (most of which were written on the spur of the moment), so that people who lived much later could really understand them.

When, late in the summer of 1985, Don Alvaro finally finished annotating those notebooks, he was openly elated. He still had to make some minor stylistic revisions in the text and write an introduction, but the main job, the one entrusted to him by the founder, was over. On September 15, in Rome, he very cheerily said to us, "That's a load off my mind! I had that command from the Father weighing on me, but in all these years I couldn't carry it out."

Don Alvaro never tired of bringing up ordinary events and other recollections of his life with Monsignor Escrivá. These had to do with everything from salient features of his sanctity and of his zeal for souls to details of his personality, sense of humor, and so forth, revealed in both unusual and everyday situations. Often he even related incidents from the founder's childhood, or about life in the Escrivá household, having heard these things from Monsignor Escrivá.

Most of these remembrances have been published. But one which may not have been was the great affection which Monsignor Escrivá's mother, Doña Dolores Albás, showed to a Gypsy woman from Barbastro, named Teresa, who had a very hard life. Not only did she give her money, but she even tried to console her and give her good advice in her own bedroom; she often invited her in for a chat. This was most exceptional, for Doña Dolores never brought even her closest friends into her room. She just really took to heart the intense suffering of that good gypsy woman.

I even heard from Don Alvaro, who had never met Don José Escrivá, that he had been a very good dancer. Doña Dolores, he said, used to apply to her husband the old saying, "He could dance on the tip of a sword." Don Alvaro also knew of a saying often repeated by Don José: "Las medias, para los pies" (Stockings are for the feet). This summed up for Don José his negative experience of having gone halves (*a medias*) in business.

Other true stories were told purely for the fun of it, such as the one about an inexperienced chauffeur in Spain. This happened sometime during the forties. The man, whose name was César, must not have been a very good driver. One day he was taking the founder, along with Fathers José López Ortiz and Casimir Morcillo, through Madrid, and when they got to Paseo de la Castellana, near Plaza de Colón, he swerved off the road, almost ran into a few pedestrians, and finally collided with a streetlight. Blessed Josemaría burst out, "Ave, Caesar, morituri te salutant!" (the gladiators' greeting to the Roman emperor: "Hail, Caesar, we who are about to die salute you!"). And César, who had no idea what this meant, could think of nothing else to say but "Thanks, Father!"

The filial affection of Don Alvaro for Monsignor Escrivá showed itself in some very simple, down-to-earth ways. On September 6, 1993, for instance, on his way from Torreciudad to Madrid, he stopped for lunch at the Opus Dei center in Saragossa, and along with some important events from the life of the founder that had taken place in that city, he mentioned to his companions some Aragonese expressions that the founder had occasionally used, such as "desgana" for "hambre" (hunger), "laminero" for "goloso" (having a sweet tooth), and "lagotero" for "cobista" (sycophant). Then he thought also of an adjective that the founder had once used to describe the bad-smelling, not well laundered bed linens in a house that he had had to stay in: "arguellada." And, finally, of what the Aragonese call someone who transports people from one town to another: "el tío traidor." This would literally mean a messenger—the equivalent of what in Castile is called an "ordinario" and in the southern regions is called a "cosario."

Because of his great affection for Monsignor Escrivá, Don Alvaro had a special place in his heart for the founder's hometown, Barbastro. This was quite noticeable whenever the conversation had to do with the people or the countryside of Aragon, and especially when Don Alvaro stayed at Torreciudad. Whenever possible, he did not limit himself to visiting places directly connected with the family of the founder, but also spent time with old friends of theirs, and even with the civil and Church authorities of Barbastro.

That sparkling flow of mutual affection was particularly visible on September 3, 1992, at the celebration held by the city of Barbastro in honor of its newly beatified native son, Josemaría Escrivá de Balaguer. In the middle of the afternoon Don Alvaro went up to the city hall, where he was received by the city council, and in the visitors' book he wrote these heartfelt words: "As a bishop and as a priest, I pray every day for Barbastro. This is a debt of gratitude which is a pleasure for me to discharge." You could feel his appreciation for those people—and for their dreams, their customs, and their landscapes as well. His affection for Barbastro was, indeed, perhaps stronger than it would have been if he had been born there himself. Even in this, he faithfully shared and communicated the sentiments of Josemaría Escrivá.

Especially after 1975, Don Alvaro felt a responsibility to start working on the founder's biography—to get underway the various tasks involved in reconstructing his life—in part because he did not want to risk losing any of the ideas or nuances contained in the founder's preaching.

He himself sent to the press previously unpublished manuscripts, quite sure of the great good that they would do for souls. The first of these posthumous books was *Friends of God,* which appeared in print (in Spanish) at the end of 1977. Don Alvaro was very much involved in the publication of this book of homilies about various virtues, and he wrote for it a long introduction. In 1981 there appeared the first Spanish edition of *The Way of the Cross,* which was set up according to the very detailed instructions of Don Alvaro. The section for each Station included a short but pithy commentary by the founder, and also some points for meditation drawn from his oral or written preaching.

A month after the release of *The Way of the Cross,* Don Alvaro spent a few days in Madrid. He mentioned then that he wanted to finish up some high-priority tasks so that he could get more of the founder's books published—another book of homilies and, especially, *Furrow* and *The Forge.* He told us that final checks would need to be done, with the help of Don Javier Echevarría, to make sure the texts were faithful to Monsignor Escrivá's originals. But all of this was, as he put it, "in a bottleneck phase," since at that time he had more urgent matters to attend to.

In the summer of 1985, as soon as he finished annotating the notebooks of the founder, he began editing *Furrow* and *The Forge,* with the help of Don Javier. This was a job which had been pending since at least 1950. In that year, in his foreword to the seventh Spanish edition of *The Way,* Monsignor Escrivá promised another book—*Furrow*— "which I intend to give you in a few months." But he actually never got the time to revise it. On September 8, 1960, in Aralar Hall in Pamplona, we asked the founder about this book, and he instantly responded with this Castilian saying: "You can't ring the bells and walk in the procession." As he told us on several occasions, he had more important things to do. He had more than enough work to do just in connection with the formation of the members of Opus Dei, who by then were already scattered across the globe.

Monsignor Escrivá did finish the first drafts of both *Furrow* and *The Forge,* including their beautiful prefaces. (He kept both manuscripts in ordinary envelopes, one for each chapter.) But to ensure that there were no repetitions, errors, or omissions, Don Alvaro needed a few consecutive days of peace and quiet, with no interruptions. By the end of the summer of 1985, he had finished these pending assignments also, and again was openly happy about it.

In January 1986, printed copies of *Furrow* and *The Forge* were given to the Congregation for the Causes of the Saints, along with other documents needed for the process of beatification of Monsignor Escrivá. Both of these books were quickly sent also to Opus Dei centers in regions outside Spain, for translation into other languages. Don Alvaro insisted that they be published just as the founder had written them, without any retouching. "This way," he said, "the language will be fresher and more spontaneous. The only kinds of things we will correct are the punctuation errors and the errors in transcription or printing which were found in the first copies sent to be translated." It seems that despite the overall unity of spirit and style, some sharp-eyed reader had noticed some verbal inconsistencies in points which were to be read one after the other, but which had been written years apart.

14

The Legacy of a Spirit

Early on, possibly even by the end of the thirties, the founder saw clearly that Don Alvaro would be the one to succeed him as head of the Work. This conviction, which was confirmed by several providential events, was certainly evident as early as 1948, when Monsignor Escrivá considered leaving Opus Dei to begin a new foundation for diocesan priests. At that time he commissioned a photograph of outstretched palms—the hands of Don Alvaro—receiving little wooden donkeys.

So no one was surprised when, on September 15, 1975, Don Alvaro was unanimously elected as the founder's successor. He himself later said to the electors, "You have chosen to place the burden of the Work upon the shoulders of this poor man, and I know why. I well know that I am worth nothing, that I can do nothing, that I am nothing. You did this because you knew that I spent more time than anyone else with our Father, and you wanted continuity. You have not voted for Alvaro del Portillo; you have elected our Father."

On August 21, 1981, some of us were having a nice relaxed chat with Don Alvaro a little before dinner. We were trying to remember a date that was not especially important, and someone said it must have been "in the times of our Father." Instantly Don Alvaro said with a smile, "In the Work we are always in the times of our Father." He encouraged us to use other phrases when referring to the past, such as "when our Father was on earth."

That instant reaction encapsulated what Don Alvaro had been saying insistently ever since 1975: that with the death of Blessed Josemaría, the foundational era of Opus Dei had drawn to a close and an era of continuity had begun. In September 1975 he wrote, "The founder's spirit is now unchangeable. That means no one can add to it or take anything away from it." He charged us with the tremendous responsibility of remaining loyal and faithful to the founder's spirit. We must, he said, "keep it pristine and spotless, and pass it on in all its fullness."

The electors would never forget the hard-hitting words that Don Alvaro spoke in his homily for the Mass of the Holy Spirit at the opening of the elective congress. These words confirmed the strength of the Paraclete in his gentle soul. "At this solemn and never-to-be-repeated moment," he said, "I ask God to have mercy on us should we ever not be faithful. However, since we all have the gift of freedom, someone could be obstinately unfaithful to the grace of God and to the spirit of our Father. If such a person is ever elected as his successor, may the bones of the Father, here below us, rise up to curse that man!"

A few hours later, after he had been elected, Don Alvaro explained during the family-style get-together what he had meant by that. "If a member of the Work," he said, "should ever have the misfortune to be unfaithful, the rest of us will all seek to understand him, to show him affection, and to be merciful to him, making every effort to help him get straightened out. But if we're talking about not just a member of the Work, but a successor of the Father, and if this successor ever decides to deviate from the Father's spirit, then let him be cursed. I fully realize that this is a strong word, and I ask you to forgive me for saying it so vehemently, but I do not take it back. And I'm sure you all agree with me."

That same day, a little before one o'clock in the afternoon, he went down to the crypt of Our Lady of Peace. It was the first visit he made to the tomb of the founder after being elected as his successor. When he entered, all those present stood up as a sign of respect. Don Alvaro gestured towards the tomb and said, "Where there is a skipper, a sailor doesn't give the orders. And the skipper is here." Then he knelt down, kissed the marble slab, and said, "Ask him to be the one to direct the Work, from heaven, and to have his successors be just his instruments and nothing more."

His wish to walk in the footsteps of the founder showed up even in little things of no real significance. When, for example, he started using contact lenses, he said that many years back, he had struggled against an annoying habit of wrinkling his nose to push his glasses up. Since he spent hours upon hours with Monsignor Escrivá, the founder called that habit to his attention and he eventually got out of it. But as time went by, the instinct began to reassert itself. So then he thought, "'Dead dogs don't have rabies.' If I get rid of the glasses, they won't slip anymore." In any case, he said, it had been a good excuse to get contact lenses, which the doctors had told him would probably help him see and read better. He then recalled something said in connection with Pope Pius XII, who had never chosen to wear the papal camauro—a kind of medieval headgear with white velvet across the forehead, and with side projections which covered the ears. When he died, it was put on him. Someone remarked that the Holy Father would not like that, and was answered, "The dead don't give orders." So now Don Alvaro added very emphatically, with reference to the founder and the Work, "Yes, the dead do give orders!"

Despite his already obvious identification with the

founder, Don Alvaro insisted that the members of Opus Dei pray that he become more and more like him. There was a Castilian saying he liked to use: "Quien a los suyos parece, honra merece" (A man like his kin has honor within). And after June 1975 he often said things similar to what he said in Rome at that time: "Ask God to make me think only as our Father thought, and to make me want only what our Father wanted. Then we will do well."

He used to drive home this point with an anecdote about some of his young daughters in Kenya. They had a hard time telling him and the founder apart, he said, since both wore glasses and had long noses. The only difference they could detect was the color of the hair. "Now, I know, my children," he would say to us, "that on the outside I am actually quite different from our founder. But the bad thing is that I'm this way on the inside too. Ask our Lord, because it will be good for the whole Work, to make me become on the inside more like our Father every day—so much so that someday it will be impossible to tell us apart."

He used to quote "with great delight," as he himself put it, the advice that Pope Paul VI had given him during his first audience after the death of Monsignor Escrivá. "He encouraged me," he would say, "to have always the most absolute fidelity to the founder's spirit. He said to me in a very assured and enthusiastic tone of voice, 'Always, whenever you have some matter to resolve, put yourself in the presence of God and ask yourself, What would the founder do? And then act accordingly.'"

His only desire was to be a visible manifestation of Blessed Josemaría. He expressed this in many different ways, some more direct than others. When, for example, he gave a blessing to faithful of the Prelature at the end of a get-together or when they were leaving on a trip, he would tell them, "In his last years, when giving a blessing, the Father often used to say, 'Alvaro, help me.' Well, now I'm asking him to give us all a blessing. I'm still here just to help him; I'm his visible manifestation. I'm the one that you see, but it's our Father who will bless all of us."

He wanted as much as ever to pass unnoticed. He brought souls to God, to the Church, to the founder, and to Opus Dei, but he himself disappeared. Some remarks made in June 1976, in Pamplona, showed in a very touching way his humility and his conviction that God was doing everything by means of the intercession of Monsignor Escrivá and his children's unity of spirit with him. With respect to the founder, he said, he felt like he was just his baton, or weather vane, or shadow. "But, my children," he said, "you need to pray hard for me, because whereas a baton is a lifeless stick, incapable of putting up any resistance to the conductor's hand, I, on the other hand, can say yes or no, like all other human beings." On June 13, in Madrid, he said, "I am like a weathercock—the *banderuola,* as the Italians say—not in the sense of being fickle, but in the sense that when the wind blows, the weathercock shows its direction. A well-oiled weathercock moves perfectly even when the breeze is ever so light. . . . But, now, if I were to rust up—if I were to get lukewarm or stop depending on God—I would not be able to point you in the right direction or set the pace for you, and you might go astray. So you see how important it is that you pray for me!"

Sometimes he confided to faithful of Opus Dei that he noticed he was always using Blessed Josemaría's ideas, expressions, and even gestures, and that this made him very happy. "I just hope I can learn also to imitate him in, and speak to you with, his deeds of love for God and of reparation. And I ask him for the same for you." Or again, "I should be telling you once more that I am offering you the sustenance that I received from his dedication. But if I don't do that, it's because you already know it, it's already clear to you. I've never tried to hide this: it is always my holy pride and joy simply to continue the preaching of our founder."

One day in July 1976, Don Alvaro happened to recall a few stories which reflected the founder's steadfast desire that he be elected his successor, and his conclusion was that the founder was on that account especially obliged to help him. These were, he said, what he considered his three greatest supports: (1) the duty of the founder towards him, (2) the prayers of the faithful of Opus Dei, and (3) his own defects, and ours as well, since these greatly pleased God if we struggled against them.

It was striking to see how, in all simplicity, he kept repeating his plea for prayers. He insisted that he was the one most in need of them, precisely because he was the head. He saw himself as a "bag of wretchedness" that needed much prayer and affection. He used to say that he was "the successor of a saint" while being "a poor sinner." And he would end his letters to the faithful of Opus Dei, as well as his get-togethers (big and small), with a priestly blessing and a heartfelt "And pray for me!"

He was very much aware that tens of thousands of people in a thousand places all over the planet were constantly keeping themselves united with his intentions in their work and their suffering, in the Mass and in their rosaries, in their dialogue with God. "When I think of this," he said, "I feel overwhelmed and, at the same time, immensely grateful to God and to our Father, to whose unceasing prayer this great miracle of the Work is due." Every day he used all that prayer as a letter of recommendation to the Lord, and on that basis called out to him, "Do not abandon me!"

Following the example of the founder, he asked with outstretched hands for "the alms of more intense prayer." He would harp on this and keep hammering it home—he himself used those expressions (*machaconería* and *martilleo*)—because he was convinced that "we can and must pray more!" In one of his letters to the centers of the Prelature, he wrote,

"Hold me up so that I can carry out what our Lord is asking of me. Don't slacken in supporting my intentions!" But while constantly making such requests, he was also constantly grateful, because day after day he felt—almost physically, I once heard him say—the ongoing help of the prayer of his children.

Don Alvaro never got used to having a multitude of souls look to him and give him so much affection. In November 1980, Juan Francisco Montuenga told him how grateful a friend of his had felt after meeting him in Rome, and Emilio Nadal told him of another person—someone with two children in Opus Dei—who had come closer to God after attending one of his get-togethers in Rome. Don Alvaro instantly responded with a quote from the Scholastic philosophers: "Quidquid recipitur, ad modum recipientis recipitur" (What is received is received according to the capacity of the one who receives). "These are good people," he said, "so of course they react well."

In his humility he regarded as unimportant anything that had to do with just himself. In the central headquarters of Opus Dei, he slept in the incredibly tiny corner room which Monsignor Escrivá had used for the same purpose. Shortly after the election he explained why. "It was very hard for me to obey him in this instance," he said, "but the Father said he did not want his bedroom turned into some kind of museum."

In October 1975 a small crosier, set on red velvet in a simple frame, was hung on the wall facing the head of the bed. Just above and below the crosier were two Latin inscriptions. Above it were these words from Saint Paul: "I have finished the race, I have kept the faith" (2 Tm 4:7). Don Alvaro's comment on this passage was, "It gives me an opportunity, as I go to sleep, to think about death. It is an invitation to clean my soul well and sweep away all the bad things so that someday I can say those words myself." The inscription below the crosier is an abbreviated version of something that Jesus said to Peter shortly before the Passion. About this inscription Don Alvaro would say, "It's as if the Father were saying this to me: 'As for you, . . . strengthen my children'" (see Lk 22:31–32). Later he came to understand these words in another sense as well. "Since you are now my children," he would say, "I also turn this around and ask the Father to strengthen you in your vocation."

His was not a gimcrack humility, as Blessed Josemaría used to put it. From the moment he became head of Opus Dei, Don Alvaro urged the members to "ask for whatever I am asking for." That, he said, was "the safe thing to do." Thus he brought up to date a motto he had coined years before, a motto which reflected how united he was to the founder's heart and mind: "Whatever the Father is asking for; whatever the Father wants; whatever the Father is praying for; whatever the Father does and thinks." And this is the way he explained it: "You can be sure, my children, that though I am just an ordinary man, you cannot go wrong by praying for what I am praying for."

He never thought of himself or of what he deserved. He did not allow himself to be served, nor exceptions to be made for him, even when such things would have been entirely justifiable. He was quite aware of being only a temporary instrument. I noticed this on innumerable occasions. For instance, at a family-style get-together in 1976, I don't remember what we were talking about, but he casually said that something or other would have to be done by "my successor." It was the first time I ever heard him use this expression, and it caught my attention because this was hardly a year after his election. Actually, he almost never referred to "my successor." He preferred to speak of "the successors of our Father," since in Opus Dei everyone is supposed to directly follow the founder and assimilate his spirit.

Precisely because of his humility, Don Alvaro also showed

great initiative—he never feared the opinions of others. Just by virtue of the faithful and active help which he had given Monsignor Escrivá until 1975, he would have had a prominent place in the history of Opus Dei. But his role unquestionably became even greater afterwards. His blend of creativity with loyalty stands out in all the important events of the history of Opus Dei between 1975 and 1994, that period which he defined from the very first day as "a time of continuity." He was quite sure that the initial spirit of Opus Dei would always be up-to-date and valid. Sometimes he spoke of this period as "a time of fidelity," to make it clear that the continuity he was promoting was not something mechanical, but was, rather, "a matter of giving a personal response with our lives, in all kinds of new circumstances, to the spiritual legacy which our founder left us."

True fidelity includes taking the initiative to meet, in each new situation, the demands of love and justice. It is a delicate, operative, and constant loyalty—the kind of loyalty, in other words, which ultimately constitutes what the founder called "the best defense against ageing of the spirit, hardening of the heart, and stiffening of the mind" (*Conversations with Monsignor Escrivá de Balaguer,* no. 1). As Don Alvaro explained to the editor of *Scripta Theologica* in 1981, on the subject of the mission to evangelize, "Fidelity is fruitfulness, and therefore it involves imagination, a capacity to invent new ways of doing things, that down-to-earth wisdom which allows us to speak always the same language of God, clothing it in different garments. This is what the saints always did. They did not invent a 'new Christ' or a 'new Church,' but they drew people in new ways to both Christ and the Church." He therefore never tired of reminding the faithful of the Prelature that "an attitude of spontaneity and personal initiative is indispensable if we are to assimilate and put into practice the spirit of Opus Dei in all its aspects."

This active receiving of a legacy—this receiving that did not admit of inertia or routine—proved very productive. Later I will show this in connection with the juridical path of Opus Dei and the beatification of the founder. But for now I would like to mention, among other things, a few details of Don Alvaro's work as head of Opus Dei which I remember with a special joy.

At the end of the seventies, Don Alvaro made possible the ordination of some of the first associates of Opus Dei. Long before, during the fifties, these men had started their studies in philosophy and theology. But their progress was slow, since they were at the same time working and often helping out their parents and siblings. Furthermore, the founder had said he did not want anyone to be ordained without having already obtained a doctorate in a Church-related field. So a program was set up, in conjunction with the departments of theology and canon law at the University of Navarre, which would give associates the help they needed (including plenty of time) to prepare themselves for ordination. (And it so happened that just when the first group was ready, the news came that Pope John Paul II would be making a pastoral trip to Spain. By a happy coincidence, those first associates of Opus Dei were ordained by the Holy Father himself, in Valencia.)

Don Alvaro's daring also showed itself in connection with the Basilica of Sant'Eugenio, which was so tied in with the history of Opus Dei: it was there that the founder's funeral had been held, in 1975. Monsignor Escrivá had always wanted to spend some time hearing confessions in a church in Rome. He had thought of the parish of San Giovanni Battista al Collatino, which had been entrusted to priests of Opus Dei. But this was not to be...

In May 1980, Don Alvaro told all this to His Eminence Ugo Poletti, the Cardinal Vicar of Rome, and just politely mentioned how nice the Basilica of Sant'Eugenio would be, since it was right there at Valle Giulia, so close to Villa Tevere. He did not make a formal request; he just confidently expressed this great dream of his. But Cardinal Poletti thought it was a wonderful idea. Hardly a month later, he told Don Alvaro that the Holy Father, at his request, had decided to entrust this church to Opus Dei. And this was the cardinal's explanation of how it all happened so fast: "You can see in this the intercession of Monsignor Escrivá. Without that, it's beyond comprehension." The new pastor, a priest of Opus Dei, began work on March 1, 1981.

I would like to mention briefly another of Don Alvaro's initiatives: the publishing of *Romana,* the bulletin of the Prelature of Opus Dei—something which the founder had wanted done when the time was right. This began in 1986. Contents include documents from the pope and from the Roman Curia, decrees and appointments and addresses and documents from the Prelate, information about the founder, Prelature news, and news about the apostolic activities of members of Opus Dei. Usually it concludes with an article on a theological subject or some point of canon law. Two issues are published each year—more than three hundred pages, all told—and mailed to subscribers all over the world.

Once the spirit of Opus Dei had been given an appropriate legal framework, it needed to be expressed theologically as well. Don Alvaro indicated as much at a seminar on Blessed Josemaría that was held in 1993 at the Pontifical Athenaeum of the Holy Cross. He already had had published many theological and canonical studies about the founder and his teachings, but a huge amount of work remained. "The central teachings of Monsignor Josemaría Escrivá," he said, "are universally known today. Some of them have even been incorporated into solemn declarations of the Magisterium of the Church. But most of them enter into areas which theology has hardly begun to explore. . . . The more deeply I study the teachings of Blessed Josemaría, and the more I meditate on them in my prayer, the more I feel that we have hardly begun to plumb the depths of their riches. They seem to beckon us on to ever new and more fascinating discoveries."

Don Alvaro presented a summary of the seminar to Pope John Paul II, at the beginning of an audience granted by the Holy Father to the participants. He was visibly moved by Pope John Paul's words about the founder—and especially by their theological depth. The Holy Father described Blessed Josemaría as one of those important figures "who light up the different eras of history with their life and message." And then he said this: "Theological research, which forges a much-needed bond between faith and culture, progresses and is enriched by a return to its Gospel sources which is prompted by the experiences of the great witnesses of Christianity. And Blessed Josemaría is certainly one of those witnesses."

On March 23, 1994, the day of Don Alvaro's death, Don Javier Echevarría summed up his work as head of Opus Dei in these words: "His period of governing Opus Dei has been a beautiful one. For many reasons, it has been a marvelous adventure. He had to preserve the witness of a saint, and he accepted the challenge (if I may put it this way) by moving ahead with the same gracefulness, rhythm, and energy that always characterized our founder."

15

Assuming the Mantle of Fatherhood

Not long after being elected to govern Opus Dei, Don Alvaro was asked what the founder had meant to his life. He answered by quoting words attributed to Alexander the Great, who, when accused of loving Aristotle more than his own father (King Philip of Macedonia), reportedly replied, "This is true. My parents have, indeed, brought me to earth, but Aristotle's teaching has brought me from earth to heaven."

In 1984, on Don Alvaro's name day (February 19), Father Flavio Capucci told him that he had looked up "Alvaro" in a well-known etymological dictionary of proper names, and found that it means "he who protects, watches over, and defends everyone." Don Alvaro replied that he himself was inclined to favor a derivation not from German but from Semitic roots, according to which it would mean "the son." "But this can be joined to the interpretation that you have suggested," he said. "Pray for this to be the truth: that I may be a good son and at the same time a good father who watches over the other sons."

Father Capucci probably had those words in mind when

he wrote in 1994, in an article in *Studi Cattolici,* that "the profound unity between the founder and his successor, this flowing of paternity from the one to the other (so different in temperament, but so identical in spirit), this continuity of filiation that we have in our spirit—these things bear witness to realities which have no natural explanation."

No doubt it is thanks to Don Alvaro that Opus Dei, with the grace of God, has kept in all its vigor the spirit of filiation and fraternity that is proper to the Christian family (see *The Way,* no. 955). Those bonds are anchored in the radically original charism of Opus Dei. They were brought into being by the founder, but they are not dependent on his natural personality, warm as it was.

On the first anniversary of his election, Don Alvaro explained this very concisely. Monsignor Escrivá, he said, had two kinds of fatherhood. One was foundational, and hence his alone, since he was the only founder of Opus Dei. But the other kind, the spiritual one, "will always exist in the Work, until the end of time, because we are a family with supernatural bonds."

Ten years after his election, Don Alvaro expressed his gratitude for the entry of God's grace in his life and in that of Opus Dei in these words: "The spiritual fatherhood which was incarnated in a unique way in our most beloved founder was passed to this poor man who is now your Father. Truly, *cor nostrum dilatatum est*—my heart has expanded to love you all, each and every one of you, with the love of a father and of a mother, as our Father asked that his successors would do" (see 2 Cor 6:11).

At the same time, the members of the Work had responded with obvious affection, which made him lift up his heart in thanksgiving also "because Opus Dei continues to be a *bella famigliola,* a beautiful family." Esther Toranzo tells a story about the visit that Don Alvaro made in 1989 to Kibondeni, a women's Opus Dei center in Nairobi. Don

Alvaro was welcomed with a Masai song—accompanied by sixteen drums!—one verse of which went like this: "I left the house to go see my father. When he began to speak, I asked him to be silent, because I wanted first to express my joy at seeing him."

There are countless anecdotes testifying to the paternal, yet never paternalistic, attitude of Don Alvaro. He loved all members of Opus Dei with the affection of any natural father or mother. And he still had that amazingly good memory. Great problems of the Church or of the Work notwithstanding, he could remember all kinds of details—big and small—of the lives of his children. Through the letters which so many of them wrote directly and spontaneously to him, he kept up with their worries, sorrows, and joys. I was astonished at his ability to retain so much information. Often he asked very specific questions which none of us could answer.

Many times I saw him react in ways typical of a father or mother, out of reasons of the heart which the head cannot explain. Usually this had to do with care or concern for sick people. But sometimes it had to do with situations which, objectively speaking, were of no significance. And sometimes he would get carried away with admiration of somebody's virtues or talents. This was never without basis, nor did it reflect negatively on anyone else, but it could at times come across to strangers as being somewhat exaggerated. For instance, a language teacher, Ana Echaide, a member of the Academy of the Basque Language, recalls that at a get-together at Torreciudad in 1980, Don Alvaro, thinking of the help she gave in translating the founder's writings into Basque, praised her as "the one who knows more Basque than anyone else in the world."

I myself will never forget how Don Alvaro took it when Jaume Tur, one of the regional directors of Opus Dei in Germany, came down with a life-threatening illness. One afternoon in August 1977, he told us that Jaume had been brought to Navarre and would probably have to have a very serious operation. He asked that we pray a lot for him. On the day of the operation (a Thursday), just before beginning the morning meditation in the chapel, Don Alvaro reminded us that the surgery was about to begin, so that we would keep this in our prayers. Later on, just after twelve, we heard that all had gone well.

On the next day, however, there were complications. From what I gathered, Jaume had to spend the next forty-eight hours under heavy sedation so that his heart would not have to work any harder than absolutely necessary. Only afterwards could his basic condition be known. Nonetheless, Father Juan Domingo Celaya spoke with the doctors on Saturday night. There was nothing new; Jaume's condition was stable, though serious. But I was struck by how grateful Don Alvaro was to Father Juan for just that bit of news. His head had accepted the doctors' reports, including the need for a forty-eight-hour waiting period, but his heart was eager to know at least if anything had changed. Any mother would have felt the same.

Little by little, Jaume improved, and on August 21, Diego Martínez Caro, Navarre's cardiologist, announced that he was ready to leave the intensive care unit. "I thank you all for having prayed for this son of mine," said Don Alvaro, "but please continue to do so, because his condition is still serious." Jaume did, as a matter of fact, keep having problems. For instance, he could hardly read. His condition steadily deteriorated, and although the doctors did everything they could, they could not pull him through. Don Alvaro, in Rome by now, followed his decline with a broken heart. On the day that Jaume died, October 2, Don Alvaro asked everyone at Villa Tevere to keep praying, since the doctors had said that "for him to recover would take a miracle, almost equivalent to reviving a dead person." He added that he had remembered Jaume in his Mass, both in the Memento of the living and in that of the dead. Jaume, he said, had worked and suffered a lot, and he was sure that God would take him straight to heaven, his soul all purified, if it was his will that he should die now.

Don Alvaro truly loved the sick. He always encouraged them not to neglect either the natural or the supernatural means that might help them recover their health. For me, another outstanding instance was the final illness of Seamus Timoney, one of the first members of Opus Dei in Ireland. On Palm Sunday in 1988, in Madrid, I took a call from Dublin, from someone asking if we could pick up Seamus at the Barajas airport and take him to Pamplona. I was told that he had some kind of leukemia and that the doctors had given up on him, but that when Don Alvaro found out about it, he had insisted that Seamus consult oncologists at the University of Navarre. Well, they confirmed the diagnosis, but they also said that there was a treatment which could give him at least a few more years of life. Seamus cheerfully submitted to this treatment, painful though it was, and he did go into remission. He was very grateful to the hospital personnel, to Monsignor Escrivá for his intercessory help, and to everyone for their affection, but most of all to Don Alvaro, for taking the initiative to get him there when no one else had given him any hope at all. He lived a normal life until the end of 1991, when he finally succumbed.

Another example: On April 19, 1990, at Aralar Hall in Pamplona, we were awaiting the arrival of Don Alvaro, who was coming by car from Barcelona. Judging from his time of departure, we estimated that he would arrive at about one in the afternoon. But at about that time, when we were ready to welcome him, there was a telephone call notifying us that there would be a long delay. We soon found out why. He had stopped in Saragossa to visit a daughter of his, Camino Sanciñena, in the burns unit of Miguel Servet Hospital. She had been in a terrible accident at the end of January and was still in very serious condition; practically her whole body was covered with burns. She was in an isolation ward—Don Alvaro had to talk to her on a telephone, and she could see him only through a window. But he told her that he had been praying for her ever since he heard, in Rome, about the accident, and that he was counting on her to advance the apostolic work going on all over the world by offering up her suffering. Four years later, when she was studying law at the University of Navarre, she wrote about this conversation in the school newsletter (*Diario de Navarra*, 4/5/94). "There are times," she said, "when it is very hard to keep a positive outlook on life, and one of those is when your whole life has changed because of an accident. . . . The Father told me that even though this is hard to understand, pain is actually a caress from God. He literally said that. And he said it with such conviction that it raised me to his level, the level of faith."

I myself, of course, was sometimes the direct recipient of his affection. Don Alvaro could show such great affection in the simplest ways. He noticed little things that no one else did. One day, for instance, at the beginning of August 1988, I told everybody at the breakfast table what I intended to be a joke on myself—a proof of how sleepy I had obviously been that morning. When I'd started shaving, the hot water had gotten cut off and I had to lather up with cold water. When I got finished, I turned on the hot water faucet to wash my face—I was on automatic pilot and expected the water to still be cold—and had to switch back to shaving again, because I almost got burned. I said all this thinking I had been confused and had made a mistake, and that's the way everyone took it. Everyone, that is, except Don Alvaro. Apparently not thinking this was one bit funny, he asked me what time it was that I had shaved. I guessed as best I could, and answered that it was at about ten after seven. "It must have been me," he said.

The next day, at breakfast, Don Alvaro wanted to know

how the water had been that morning. When he heard that everything was fine, he said, "Then it really was me." He had figured out that I was shaving at the very same time when, just one floor below me in this turn-of-the-century house, he was filling up his bathtub with hot water, as his doctors had recommended. It never ceased to amaze me that from that day forward, he took his morning bath earlier so as not to interfere with my shaving.

It was, of course, only natural that the first to feel the affection of Don Alvaro should be the faithful of the Prelature, and especially those who worked or lived with him. But to him this was not something to be just taken for granted; he showed it both by word and by deed. For example, he, like the founder of the Work, had a special place in his heart for the women whose professional work was domestic service in the centers of the Prelature. And one afternoon— this was in either 1987 or 1988, at the beginning of the summer—he heard on the radio that a heat wave was expected in the Lazio region [which includes Rome]. A few minutes later he called to ask if anything had been done to ensure that the heat would not affect a daughter of his who had suffered a heart attack some time before. Though she was by then completely recovered, Don Alvaro suggested that she leave Rome for a while and go to Casale d'Ocre, a cooler area in the mountainous region of Abruzzi.

In 1990 I saw up close the solicitude he had for Don Javier Echevarría and Don Francisco Vives, his vicars in the Prelature, both of whom underwent serious operations during the summer. It was quite an ordeal, but he took it with a supernatural outlook and even a sense of humor. On his way back to Rome, he encouraged us to pray for his two vicars whom he had left in Pamplona "descuajaringados"— fallen to pieces.

His admirable composure in such circumstances seemed to me to have three basic components: (1) leaving everything in the hands of God, without failing to make use of human means, (2) unflappable calm and good humor, and (3) continuous demonstrations of affection. At the same time, he was always pointing out what a tremendous treasure illness can be. Whenever a pope would speak of the "power" of Opus Dei, Don Alvaro would always think especially of the sick who were offering to God their pain, and even their loss of life, for his intentions. "This is," he would often say, "an enormous spiritual powerhouse which we'd have to be certifiable lunatics to overlook."

He was especially thankful to all those Opus Dei members in Pamplona who devoted a lot of time and energy to caring for the sick. For quite some time, many members with serious illnesses had been going to the hospital of the University of Navarre. Besides the doctors and nurses, many other individuals went out of their way to care for these patients and to share in their sorrows and joys. Don Alvaro, by one means or another, thanked them often. One of these was his letters to the Opus Dei vicar of Pamplona. In May 1988, for example, he included this message in a letter to Father Juan Domingo Celaya: "Keep up the good work, my daughters and sons; keep lavishing affection on the sick. This is a most important apostolate. It is very pleasing in the eyes of God, it is very necessary for maintaining a family spirit in Opus Dei, and it is a guarantee of supernatural effectiveness."

Whenever he himself went in for a checkup, he never failed to visit the Opus Dei members in the wards, to bring them consolation and hope. He would advise the terminally ill to pray for the miracle of a recovery, and would ask everyone else to pray for them that they not lose their awareness of the presence of God or their cheerfulness.

Like the founder, Don Alvaro insisted that the sick are the treasure of Opus Dei not only because sickness is good for a Christian, but also because of the spiritual energy that the sick can generate for others by becoming saints through their "professional work" of suffering. From this perspective, so full both of humanity and of theological meaning, one can certainly understand his great affection for the hospital at the University of Navarre. It contained so much suffering, prayer, charity, and joy that he regarded it as an "atomic bomb" of supernatural power. At the university's memorial service for him, Professor Natalia López Moratalla (its vice-rector) expressed it in this way: "In the hospital he had a holy envy of two things: the work done there by the hands of women, and the suffering of the sick—and most especially that of the children."

In Don Alvaro's affections, love for family also had a very high place. I got to know Tomás Niño and Pilar del Portillo in Segovia, during the summer months that I spent as a child with my grandmother Piedad in Plazuela de la Merced. (Their oldest son, José Ramón, was my age. They lived very close by, just down Daoíz Street, across from Alcázar Esplanade.) The example of her brother Alvaro, reinforced by some of her own children's vocations of dedication to the Lord, gave Pilar this strong conviction: "When people give themselves totally to God, this does not separate them from their parents or brothers and sisters. On the contrary, these are the children who stay closest to their parents. At least that is my experience." She has very happy memories of how Don Alvaro loved them all—with an affection that was deep and genuine, though not at all schmaltzy. "He never missed a name day, a birthday, a family event... And when he was with us, he certainly had a wonderful time, catching up on family news, chatting, joking..."

Naturally, he had a similar concern for the relatives of all other members of the Work. Sometimes it happens, especially in countries with very few Christians, that members of Opus Dei have non-Catholic parents. Don Alvaro advised these men and women to love their parents very much, to respect them, and to venerate them. In

February 1987, in Nagasaki, a woman asked him what she should do about her Buddhist parents. His answer was, "If you have received the gift of the Catholic faith, this has definitely come about by the will of God. But your parents have smoothed the way for you by living true to their own beliefs. Perhaps without realizing it, they made you a religious person—a person capable of receiving the seed of faith. You cannot give your parents lectures. You should love them and treat them with great respect. What you can and should do is pray for them." And then he added, also for the benefit of a medical student who had asked him about the true source of happiness, "Make sure they see how happy you are, how content. Then they will ask themselves, 'Why is our daughter so much happier than she used to be?' They may even ask you. I pray to God that they will. And then you can say, 'It's because I am a Christian.' And backing this up will be the example you give by how hard you work, how dedicated you are, how ready you always are to be at their service, how much you love them and help them."

At that same get-together was the sister of an Opus Dei member who was overseas at the time. Afterwards she wrote him a long letter in which she mentioned their parents' impressions of Don Alvaro. "They said he seemed very affectionate," she told him, "but at the same time very demanding, astute, and dignified. And they said he had a special light in his eyes." Then she said this: "As for me, although there were lots of people at that get-together, I felt like the Father was speaking to me alone, in private, looking straight into my heart and communicating to me all the depth and demandingness of his own life."

Precisely because Don Alvaro was so concerned about his children, and also about so many others who lived within the circle of his fatherly affection, he often received news of deaths. He would always pray the traditional responsorial prayer for the dead ("Eternal rest . . .") wherever he happened to be at that very moment. He did this immediately, before even asking about the cause of death or about other members of the family.

I noticed this for the first time in August 1976, when he was told of the death of a woman in Opus Dei, Sole Gracia, who had been a patient in the hospital at the University of Navarre. Just a few days before she died, he had sent her a long letter and she had managed to pen a reply, although writing had become difficult for her. It all happened very quickly. In the morning she received Holy Communion and managed to say the Angelus, and a little while later, after a very brief agony, she died. Don Alvaro, after praying the responsorial prayer, confided to us that he had prayed for her, by name, that very morning, using the Vatican-approved prayer to the founder of the Work.

On the morning of September 15, 1978, in Segovia, my own father unexpectedly died. It was the feast of Our Lady of Sorrows, but also the third anniversary of the election of Don Alvaro. Since I knew that Spain's regional vicar would be putting in a call to Rome that evening, I suggested that he say nothing to Don Alvaro about my father's death, so as not to inject a note of sorrow in what should be a day of rejoicing. Well, it was Don Javier Echevarría who took the call, and he listened to my suggestion, but he did not heed it. And a few days later, he told me this: "Don Alvaro very much appreciated your intention that he not be told that day, but he appreciated it even more that he was, because that allowed him to be with you right away, with the strength with which we all love each other in the Work and with the strength which his position as Father gives him."

I soon received a letter from Don Alvaro, dated September 16. It was a two-page letter in his unique expansive handwriting, with its long and elegant strokes. "Last night," he wrote, "Don Florencio gave me the sorrowful news of the sudden death of your good father. I immediately began to say prayers for the eternal rest of his soul, and I passed on to everyone on the council the sad news so that they would join their prayers to yours and mine. I will continue to pray for him—I offered my Mass today for him—even though I feel that God in his mercy has already rewarded the uprightness of your father and that he no longer has any need of our prayers. . . . Salva, stay serene. Help your loved ones to be at peace in the midst of this great sorrow, and don't fail to offer up the pain of it also for me. Stay very united with the intentions of my Mass. I, for my part, am always with you all—with you, your good mother, and everyone else in your family—with all my heart, and in a very special way at this time."

Early on the morning of June 9, 1991, when I was finishing up some work at Opus Dei's central headquarters, Don Alvaro called me from his office there to tell me of the unexpected death of Luis Jesús Soto, a member of the delegation of the Work in Seville. He told me that we now had one more intercessor in heaven, but that this was for him a very hard blow. He had heard, and he was very touched by this, that Luis Jesús had offered up everything in his last hours for the Father and the Work.

Barely two hours later, when I was in his office, he was handed a typed letter to Father Tomás Gutiérrez, Spain's regional vicar, about the death of Luis Jesús. And then, almost at the same time, he was told that Father Eduardo Labandeira, a professor of canon law, had died in Pamplona. So Don Alvaro added a postscript to this letter to the vicar. "I just got through writing these lines," he said, "in both pain and peace, when a fresh blow fell: the death of Don Eduardo. What can I say? Only that I resolutely abandon myself into the hands of the Blessed Trinity and humbly accept these crosses, convinced that this is the best thing for us to do. Also I ask our Lord that we may love the struggle to become holy, as did our Father and so many others—both men and women—who have gone before us." And so, once again, I witnessed the deep but amazingly peace-filled sorrow that Don Alvaro felt when he lost one of his children.

He never got used to hearing such news, even when it started coming so frequently because, as he himself put it, "there are so many of us now." Despite his complete abandonment into the hands of Divine Providence, his heart never grew numb. At the beginning of September 1991, just after the ordination of several new priests in Torreciudad, he spent a few days in Pamplona. On one of those days, upon returning (shortly before suppertime) from visiting some of the women patients, he heard that two Opus Dei women in the United States had died. After praying for them, he said, "After a great joy there always comes a great sorrow. What can we do? These are blows—or, rather, caresses—from God."

In all my years in Opus Dei, I have never ceased to be amazed by the critical attitude that some people have towards the obvious unity of members of Opus Dei in matters of faith, of spirit, and of apostolate, when there are such great differences in mentality, culture, and social standing. Certainly there is a strong common denominator, but outside of that, as the founder used to say, we only agree to disagree; long live freedom! Organizational matters relating to law or administration are handled in a very human, affectionate, free, really disorganized fashion. Demands are made with the force of law and with military urgency, but always within the context of the loving freedom of a family.

One cause of scandal has been how united everyone in Opus Dei is, both in mind and in heart, with the head of the Work. Some have even termed Opus Dei—perhaps not out of malice, but certainly unjustly—a personality cult. I, for my part, can testify that the mentality of Alvaro del Portillo was completely alien to any such thing.

In Don Alvaro, the members of Opus Dei saw a clear

reaffirmation of the reality that the Prelate—not just the founder—is and always will be primarily "the Father." That is the name by which he is normally addressed, even according to the Statutes of the Prelature (see no. 130.1). This inclusion in the Statutes amounts to an acknowledgment that there is no room in any family for a false opposition between person and institution, or between freedom and obedience. The person always comes first, even when the person is engrossed in exhausting work and feeling no enthusiasm for it. This primacy of the person is not rooted in sociological or intellectual principles. It is derived from a deep spiritual reality, and is best understood in terms of a mutual trust and a clear recognition of every person's dignity.

It was with this deep humanity that Don Alvaro fulfilled his canonical duties. Over and above his different legal and pastoral capacities, he was, as indicated in the Statutes of the Prelature, a teacher and father who truly loved everyone in the heart of Christ. He formed and enkindled them with a burning charity, gladly wearing himself out for them. This was the mainspring of his life, the focus of each and every one of his days, the kernel of his work and prayer. From 1975 on, his heart just kept expanding; day by day he felt his affection grow.

At the same time, he never ceased to insist on the importance of fostering a family atmosphere. This, of course, cannot be separated from the obvious, unarguable need for a development of each member's unique personality, and well he knew it. But he was very moved, nonetheless, to see Opus Dei become every day a more solidly united family. "The cement which binds us together ever more strongly," he wrote on November 7, 1976, to the Counselor of the Work in Brazil, "is the love of God. It is the spirit which our Father incarnated so perfectly and passed on with incomparable faithfulness. This cement will never crumble as long as we all keep struggling to be good children."

Covadonga O'Shea once asked Don Javier Echevarría (as reported in the 5/5/94 issue of the Madrid weekly *¡Hola!*) what had been the greatest lesson he ever learned from Don Alvaro. "Without a shadow of a doubt," he answered, "docility and simplicity. I have never seen a person more ready to serve others than Don Alvaro was. If there was ever a person who knew how to love, and who succeeded in loving, according to the teachings of our founder, it was Don Alvaro del Portillo."

He lived this way until the very end of his life here on earth. We have a short note from Don Alvaro, written in his own hand on March 7, 1994, with a few ideas he intended to develop in the letter he was going to write to the faithful of the Prelature on the occasion of his golden jubilee as a priest. After fidelity to the founder comes "horror at becoming bourgeois," and its remedy, "helping each other: fraternal correction." Then, "the more the Work spreads, the more unity." At the end, after an expression of gratitude for Opus Dei's spirit of filiation, there is just one word, underlined: "fraternity."

One did not need to be in the Work to be aware of all this. The writer Vittorio Messori, who had interviewed Don Alvaro just a few months before his death, wrote in the 3/23/94 issue of the Italian newspaper *Corriere della Sera,* "He really was a father, as they call him in Opus Dei. You felt like making your confession to him, instead of asking him questions."

16

Zeal for Souls

Don Alvaro's fatherliness was particularly evident when he spoke, as he so often did, about apostolate. "Souls, my children, souls! There are so many people living around us who still don't know Christ. They are waiting for you to care about them, to make sacrifices for them, to love them." These words from one of Don Alvaro's letters sum up one of the great passions of his life. Elsewhere, with reference to the visit of the Magi, he expressed it this way: "How cold the world is, my children! We must warm it up with the fire of our loving hearts!"

This sentiment went so deep in his heart that when someone asked him—in February 1988, when he had just barely arrived in Chicago—what his favorite aspiration was, he immediately gave this half-joking, half-serious reply: "I go to confession to Don Javier, and I don't have to make a public confession. But all right, I'll tell you what I think would be a good aspiration to use for this immense city and this immense nation. I think you should use this prayer that our Father wrote in *The Way* [no. 804]: 'Jesus, souls! Apostolic souls! They are for you, for your glory.'"

In his plans for the apostolate, he showed the strength and optimism of someone who is sure that it is God who gives the increase (see 1 Cor 3:6). He encouraged people to work realistically and with a positive outlook, without what he called sterile lamentations. He was a firm believer in the supernatural effectiveness of the apostolic methods which the founder, by divine providence, had prescribed. In September 1975 he wrote, "Zeal for souls which is not preceded, accompanied, and followed by prayer and penance will be nothing more than a human undertaking. We have not come to Opus Dei for merely human motives. We have come to accomplish a divine task: nothing more and nothing less than the Work of God."

I recall that during the summer, he would inquire—year after year and day after day, with ever renewed interest—about the apostolic work being done, in so many places, for and with young people on vacation. He was especially happy to hear about apostolic activities begun in the winter and continued on through the summer. There should not be, he said, any vacation from the task of forming and helping young people and their helpers.

At the beginning of August 1977, during lunch, the regional vicar of Spain told him about a few letters he had read that morning. In one of them it was mentioned that a large number of boys had taken part in the summer activities. Don Alvaro's comment was, "And that number will increase, if we are faithful."

He also encouraged initiatives with broader horizons. He was happy, for example, to see parents help out in the formational activities organized for their children, or to see the participants' families also being well looked after. He was very much convinced of the effectiveness of such interlinked apostolates. As did the Magisterium of the Church, he stressed the importance of the human and Christian development of the family.

In those days, nearly all the centers of the Work were setting up more social service programs, especially in rural areas. The volunteerism which is so much in vogue now, in the nineties, got hardly any press back then. But even in this, some people in Opus Dei took the lead. Out of a sober and generous sense of solidarity, they went to forgotten and isolated areas of the country to lend a helping hand. In the letters they sent back to Don Alvaro, they often related, with great delicacy, some hair-raising incidents. These stories really got to him; he felt what his children were feeling. But he gave thanks to God for the "hairy apostolate"—that's what he called it, the *apostolado capilar*—described in these letters.

He never stopped urging people to practice the works of mercy, as had always been encouraged and done in Opus Dei, from the very beginning. "As much as possible," he wrote in 1981, "all of us have to make contact with those who are suffering, who are sick, who are destitute, who are alone, who have been forsaken by all." We find in them, he said, "our richness, enabling us to work harder; our treasure, enabling us to fall more deeply in love with God and to grow stronger in our vocation; our strength, the strength of God, enabling us to conquer."

Don Alvaro richly bore out the great claim of the founder of Opus Dei that "out of one hundred souls, we are interested in one hundred." In February 1976, at the Roman College of the Holy Cross, an American student named Mike told him that an "indio rojo" (red Indian) had asked for admission to the Work. After gently letting him know that the proper Castilian term was "piel roja" (redskin), Don Alvaro, quoting the founder, said to him, "We understood you perfectly, but in any case it doesn't really matter. We are all of the same race: the race of the children of God. Whether we're white or red or copper-colored or olive-skinned, and regardless of our social status or level of education, we're all children of God!" (see *Christ Is Passing By*, no. 13).

Then he took advantage of the opportunity and told this story. "Yesterday," he said, "I received a letter from a shepherd girl who is not in the Work. She wrote very well, with good spelling and grammar. She told me that she is a student in an agricultural school and that she takes care of some cows—she is a cowhand, I guess I should say. What a lowly job that is! Well, but then she added a few considerations which I found astonishing. Surely the Holy Spirit is leading by the hand this daughter of God. She told me about the affection she has for our Father, and about the sacrifices she has to make to attend the monthly day of recollection—she is caring for her invalid mother and cannot be away for a long period of time. She told me that although she is not in the Work, she loves our founder like a father— so much so that when she does ask for admission to the Work, she will consider herself a posthumous daughter. She explained that she had never met the Father during his life on earth, but that she had learned to love him because of what her older sisters had told her about their life in Opus Dei. Isn't this beautiful? It was written by a little country girl—clear proof that the Holy Spirit blows where he wills, and quite a lesson to us, who put on such airs about knowing so much and being so educated."

The universal character of his apostolic zeal was very evident. From Monsignor Escrivá he had learned to focus on the souls of all the people he encountered, even if he could not speak with them. When he was in a car and caught sight of a pedestrian, for example, or when, just out of politeness, he waved to someone whose path he crossed on a walk through the countryside, he thought about the spiritual and material needs they might have, and he prayed for them. We caught on to that from some casual comments he made.

On several of the trips we made together, I could hear for myself the friendly words he spoke, on both mundane and spiritual topics, to the people he met. He connected with them very easily. Right away it was clear that he was interested in everything about them, and a relationship of mutual affection would spring up. I then understood why Monsignor Escrivá so often spoke of his "knack for engaging people." In a eulogy for Don Alvaro, printed in the 5/1/94 issue of Montreal's *L'Informateur,* Denis Saint-Maurice summarized it thus: "His identification with the message of the founder of Opus Dei, his humility, and his great charity won him countless friends. He had a real talent for being interested in each and every person that he spoke with, whoever they might be, and hearts opened up to him immediately."

Many persons who first met him in another country later saw and recognized him in Spain, and he would always take the time to speak attentively with each one. He was motivated, of course, by his natural openheartedness and by his pastoral and apostolic spirit, but also by gratitude to God, because he found out in these conversations how Opus Dei was growing in the most diverse settings.

On January 28, 1985, Don Alvaro phoned from Madrid the vicar of the delegation of the Prelature in Pamplona, Father Juan Domingo Celaya. He wanted to thank him for all he had done for him during his recent stay there, and also to ask him to look after a young patient in the hospital at the University of Navarre. This was a twelve-year-old boy, a diabetic, who had recently undergone surgery. One afternoon, in the corridor, this boy had told Don Alvaro that he was going to have an operation the next day, and Don Alvaro had said he would pay him a visit. At about 2:45 the next afternoon (on his way to the hospital chapel, to make a visit to the Blessed Sacrament), Don Alvaro stopped by his room and found him crying and fighting off sleep. The operation had left him drowsy, but he didn't want to fall asleep, since Don Alvaro was coming. As soon Don Alvaro came in and said a few words, the poor boy burst into tears again but then happily fell asleep.

When he came to see him the next morning, the boy

was already up. He said to Don Alvaro, "Look how well I'm doing. It's because of your prayers." Then he told Don Alvaro that he'd like to draw him something, because he was very good at drawing. (And he really was; he had even won a prize in a national contest.) After some deliberation, he decided to draw a picture of the Blessed Virgin and then send it to Don Alvaro by way of a nurse. When Don Alvaro told him that he might be leaving Pamplona the next day, the boy said, "Well, I'm still going to send it to you, one way or another."

Don Alvaro told us all this when he was already back in Madrid. At the end he said to us, "I felt so sorry for him. The poor kid must be so lonely." And that was why he asked Father Juan Domingo to keep looking after him.

At the end of a stay at Solavieya, Don Alvaro would always give a very affectionate, unhurried good-bye to Emilio de Francisco, the maintenance man, and Manolo Lougedo, the gardener. Many years later, Manolo recalled that he had very quickly begun to feel like part of Don Alvaro's family, for one thing because Don Alvaro had told him, on his very first day on the job, that he was. And as if that were not enough, Don Alvaro had given him a hug, notwithstanding Manolo's protest that he was too sweaty from his work. "It was a big hug," he said, "cheek to cheek. He wasn't in the least put off by the fact that I was covered with sweat. I tried not to hug him too hard, because of this. But he went all out, with great affection, even though he ended up soaked."

Manolo was also very touched by the interest Don Alvaro took in his family—his father, his wife, his children. He asked about his studies, and also about his football games. He told him that he hoped to go to one of them someday. "He talked with me," said Manolo, "as though I were someone he'd known all his life."

Not allowing himself to be served, Don Alvaro greatly influenced Manolo's life with just the example of his goodness. "When Don Alvaro talked with me," he said, "it always gave me a lot of joy and satisfaction. He said things that filled your spirit—things that went so deep inside you that you could never forget them. It made you want to pray. Many times he told me that I had God to thank for my family, my wife, my beautiful kids, that I should work hard to provide for them, and that I should offer up all this work to God."

In 1989 Don Alvaro heard that Manolo was seriously ill. He was so ill, in fact, that although he could still work, another gardener had started to work with him part-time. Don Alvaro let us know right away, so that we could start praying for him. He himself kept on praying for him, day after day, and asking him what the doctors were saying. Those short but very affectionate conversations took place at the end of the morning, when Don Alvaro, after four hours of work, went out to the garden to say a rosary. "I am sure," said Manolo in 1995, "that he prayed for me absolutely every day. The only reason I am standing here today is, I am sure, because he never stopped praying for whoever was in his family, and we were all in that family, as he had told me. And he prayed especially for whoever was sick. Now more than ever, I look upon him as a friend, and I ask him for many things."

I myself remember very clearly an incident which took place in El Grado, a town very close to Torreciudad, early on the morning of September 3, 1991. Don Alvaro was going by car to Pamplona, and I was behind him, in another car, with Father Joaquín Alonso. All kinds of people waved to him when he crossed the esplanade of the shrine at Torreciudad, when he approached the entrance to the shrine, and when he was out on the road that goes along the seashore. But he stopped at only one place—in the middle of El Grado, where a woman was signaling to him and holding out to him a bouquet of roses wrapped in silver paper. She was very neatly dressed, in a uniform; I later heard that she worked as a cook in this town. Don Alvaro rolled down the car window, and, after a short conversation, the woman knelt down on the road, kissed his hand, and waved him good-bye with one hand, while with the other hand she kept the roses in her lap.

When we got to Pamplona, I found out that she had wanted to give him the roses in gratitude for all the good that he had done, through Opus Dei, for her soul and for her family. But she had also asked him to pray for one of her sons. So he had gratefully accepted the roses, but then, insisting that they now already belonged to the Blessed Virgin, he had asked the woman to take them on his behalf to the shrine, and there to pray for her son with great faith, knowing that a mother's prayer is most powerful before God.

I've told these stories in detail because I was there when they happened, and because I was so struck by the affectionate connectedness that Don Alvaro had with all kinds of ordinary people. But he was also famous for the deep friendships he had with persons in very high positions, such as Pope Paul VI, Pope John Paul II, and Francesco Cossiga, who was president of the Republic of Italy from 1985 to 1992. Many bishops, archbishops, and cardinals happily opened their doors to him, or visited him where he was staying, when he went to such places as Cologne, Prague, Mexico City, New York, Manila, Singapore, Nagasaki, and Hong Kong. Cardinal Bernard Law, the archbishop of Boston, said in the memorial homily that he gave on March 25, 1994, "I often enjoyed his hospitality in Rome. He was extraordinarily affectionate; whenever I was with him, I always had the feeling that I was one of the family."

Actually, Don Alvaro was always giving himself to others, always bestowing affection on somebody. In May 1987, in Rome, he told us about something that had happened just a few days before, when he and another priest were in some country in Northern Europe. A drunk man approached them and said he was surprised to see Catholic

priests out on the street. To give him a quick explanation of
what had brought them there, Don Alvaro gave him a holy
card with a picture of Monsignor Escrivá on the front and a
concise introduction to Opus Dei on the back, and asked
him to pray for them. The fellow was lucid enough to be
able to respond that he never prayed. Don Alvaro then
explained that God is our Father, and that he eagerly awaits
the prayers, the petitions, of his children. The man grew
thoughtful (inasmuch as his condition would allow) and then
said, "Well, if I pray, I'll pray for you guys."

Don Alvaro's great capacity for making friends also had
to do with the sincerity and clarity with which he spoke. In
January 1987, for example, when he was at Warrane College
in Sydney, one of the boys told him that the college was
being criticized for not allowing girls to go up to the boys'
rooms. Don Alvaro explained the reasons for such a policy—
it made life easier for others in the residence; it facilitated
everyone's studying, it was just one of those conditions
necessary for a good coexistence. But he also pointed out,
with a certain sternness, the injustice of that criticism.
"Sydney is a big city," he said. "Everyone here is free to leave
the premises and go somewhere else. Are all the boys so shy
that if they can't have girls visit them in this building, then
they can't get together with them at all? Or are they little
animals that just have to have a female with them at all times
or else they can't live? The residents in this College are men,
and men let their heads rule their hearts!"

Don Alvaro had many good friends because he was a
good friend. He practiced what he preached, and what he
preached was this: "Friendship requires common interests
and a real affection for people—an affection which leads to
loving them as they are, spending time with them,
understanding them, and not abandoning them even when
they show little or no responsiveness."

He encouraged people to be generously affectionate, and

to cheerfully give way in matters of personal preference. "Welcome everyone with a smile," he would say. "Make sacrifices for everyone, and learn to overlook the little annoyances of daily life—don't give them any importance. Look for what unites, not for what divides. Be positive. And always, *always,* do this in a natural, tactful, unobtrusive way." He truly gave himself without holding back. He was always ready to understand other people, to excuse them, to lend them a hand. In January 1981, at the Torrescala Street residence in Milan, he defined friendship as "generosity, self-giving, sacrifice, and love." He lived to the hilt that kind of friendship. It was inseparable from his personal apostolate.

Friendship was something he cultivated right up to the very end of his life. When he died, there was on his nightstand the business card of one of the pilots who had flown him back to Rome from the Holy Land. They had chatted with each other during the wait at the Tel Aviv airport and also during the flight. Their friendship was short but deep; as soon as the pilot heard of his death, he came to pray before the body of Don Alvaro.

It was with the same human and supernatural sensitivity that Don Alvaro followed the progress of the corporate apostolates entrusted to Opus Dei. I saw this especially in connection with the University of Navarre, from the time he succeeded Monsignor Escrivá as its Grand Chancellor. His faithfulness to what the founder wanted was something very active and creative, even with regard to long-standing wishes or projects which had not been realized by 1975.

I'm thinking, for example, of the centers for ecclesiastical studies which were set up in Pamplona and Rome to serve ever more effectively the universal Church and local churches in many countries. Don Alvaro often reminded the professors of the radical Christian identity that they ought to have. They should all, he said, be believers who lived a consistent life and who wanted to help others share in the enriching lights which flow from Christian doctrine. He made them see that society needs their Christian witness—one that is resolute, appealing, respectful of freedom, and mindful of the most abandoned and weak—in all the different fields of knowledge and of human and social activity. Active Christians, he said, use their freedom to respond to the needs of those around them; they are nourished with a spirituality which cannot be separated from the building up of social life. And, he said, all of this must be achieved with great affability and cordiality. Don Alvaro was very serene and composed, but he was also very warm and human, and he expected others to be so as well.

He had in his heart a real passion for helping others. He did this with great courage and daring, without any concern for human respect. He was demanding on himself and understanding with others. How much he liked to serve! How often he used the word "service," even in the context of those collective apostolic works! He followed with great interest the progress of existing corporate enterprises and often thought about how to increase their apostolic fruitfulness. And he never forgot the necessity of maintaining their basically lay and professional character, in accord with another great foundational criterion from Monsignor Escrivá. Those educational and social-service undertakings arise and develop when ordinary people, including non-Christians in many cases, freely exercise their sense of responsibility. Therefore they are not and cannot be denominational, even though their directors entrust Opus Dei with the responsibility of giving the appropriate doctrinal instruction and spiritual help.

One major concern for Don Alvaro was the spiritual formation of business people, because of the important role that they play in society. He wanted them to learn how to do their jobs well and in a way that was consistent with their Christian faith. I myself, as far back as the seventies, heard him talk about his dream of setting up business schools which would have the professional competence and reputation to help forge sound solutions to the enormous social inequities in so many countries. He was thoroughly convinced that these terrible injustices, though they do not justify hatred or class warfare, do cry out to heaven and appeal to the Christian conscience for solutions.

The priestly heart of Don Alvaro—here, too, in full resonance with that of the founder of Opus Dei—was wrung by the terrible poverty of the Third World. Although he was, of course, very happy about the many projects begun and run by members of Opus Dei in those countries, he encouraged people to do much more to relieve at least the most serious needs. He was open to a wide range of solutions, from additional corporate works entrusted to Opus Dei to more individuals participating in nongovernmental organizations in the less developed countries.

I'll never forget how strongly he spoke of the demands of justice, as expressed in the social teachings of the Church. My impression is that, particularly after the collapse of Marxist regimes in Europe, he felt moved to encourage the practice of Christian virtues not just to help each man and woman to develop their personality on the basis of their own intrinsic personal dignity, but also to make the faithful aware of their responsibility to build up a just social order. It is important, he said, "to fully respect the freedom that everyone has in matters of opinion, but also to never use our freedom as 'a pretext for evil' by looking for excuses not to do what we can to help solve these many injustices" (see 1 Pt 2:16).

In a eulogy written for the Madrid newspaper *ABC* (the 3/24/94 edition), Don Javier Echevarría gave a quick overview of Don Alvaro's apostolic concerns. Don Alvaro, he said, had everywhere encouraged people to begin or develop "important social initiatives, always motivated by what constitutes the first and foremost responsibility of pastors: the spiritual goods of salvation." The present Prelate of Opus Dei pointed out that "some of these initiatives are outstandingly successful in helping to solve the social problems of the environments in which they operate. I am thinking, for example, of some new universities in countries which are struggling to form leaders capable of contributing to a homogeneous development that is respectful of human dignity. I am also thinking of educational and social-service institutions which operate in areas and among populations that are extremely deprived, particularly in Latin America and in Africa."

17

Apostolic Expansion

The day after Don Alvaro died, Ignacio Aréchaga had an article in the paper in which he mentioned the years just after the Spanish Civil War, when Spain was isolated and battered. "Nothing in that situation," he said, "encouraged even the thought of a worldwide undertaking. But it was in that setting that a young civil engineering student began to study Japanese." The reason for this, he explained, was that the founder of Opus Dei was already dreaming of spreading to all kinds of countries his message—a message without frontiers. "As it turned out," he said, "life took Don Alvaro in directions which did not allow him to master Japanese. But the mere fact that he made this effort gives a good picture of the man."

At the side of Don Alvaro, one could practically feel the beating of his big heart as it pumped the fresh blood of prayer and supernatural life, through the communion of saints, to every corner of the world. Just an article in the paper was enough to awaken in him a lively pastoral concern for some very remote place. In his company, one came to see—from the perspectives of the people living there—the circumstances, problems, and ups and downs of life in the most diverse lands.

By 1975, when Don Alvaro succeeded Monsignor Escrivá, Opus Dei had a presence on each of the continents. But much remained to be done. The founder had planned to initiate work in some new countries—for example, Bolivia. Under Don Alvaro, several trips were made from Argentina to La Paz, and in July 1978 the first Opus Dei center in Bolivia opened there, in the world's highest capital city.

The next Latin American country on the agenda was Honduras. Both the founder and Don Alvaro felt a special gratitude towards this country because its embassy in Madrid had given them shelter during the Spanish Civil War. Trips began in 1979, and at the end of 1980 a center of the Work opened in its capital, Tegucigalpa.

Don Alvaro also followed events in Africa very closely, with an eye to initiating apostolic work in some of the French-speaking countries. (Up to this time, the only Opus Dei centers in Africa were in Kenya and Nigeria.) Towards the end of 1979, at Don Alvaro's request, Juan Masiá and Benito Badrinas traveled to Zaire and to Côte d'Ivoire to do a study of what was needed to set up operation in those countries. Don Alvaro, meanwhile, in his Christmas letter to all the centers of Opus Dei, asked everyone to pray that stable apostolic efforts could begin in both of those places in 1980.

From then on, it became something of a tradition for Don Alvaro to use his Christmas letters to inform everyone of the immediate plans for apostolic expansion. In December 1980 he wrote, "This year I have the great joy of announcing that stable apostolic work will very soon begin in Hong Kong. Pray a lot about this new door which is opening in the Far East, and be filled with a holy and zealous desire that this seed from heaven may make its way, first by germinating and then by bearing abundant fruit, into all of humanity."

The following year, he spoke of "all those beloved countries in Asia." More specifically, he asked for prayers that a center might soon be set up in Kuala Lumpur, the capital of Malaysia. In some Far Eastern countries there were serious difficulties to overcome, such as that of obtaining residence permits for priests. This had to be taken care of before work could begin, since the apostolate of Opus Dei, as a Church structure, is an organically united effort of priests and lay people. Soon enough, however, regular trips to Kuala Lumpur began, and in October 1982 a center opened in Singapore.

By Christmas 1982, the apostolic panorama was expanding to "the chilly regions in Northern Europe: the Scandinavian countries." Don Alvaro finished the prehistory of Opus Dei in these countries with a weeklong trip begun on March 20, 1983. In that short time he traveled to Oslo, Helsinki, Stockholm, Uppsala, and Copenhagen. On March 25 the new cathedral of Stockholm was dedicated, and Don Alvaro, with the papal nuncio and fifteen other bishops from various countries, concelebrated the solemn Mass presided over by the papal legate, Cardinal Höffner. In December 1983, Don Alvaro wrote to the members of the Work, "Continue to keep in your prayers our work in the Scandinavian countries. Pray that we will soon be able to open a center in Stockholm."

A few months earlier, he had gone to Mexico to prostrate himself in thanksgiving before Our Lady of Guadalupe. I will have occasion later on to speak of this visit in some detail, so for now I will just say this: There he spoke very forcefully about the social obligations of Catholics. Although quite a few projects for human and cultural development were already in operation in Mexico, he encouraged the faithful of the Prelature to set up quite a few more, especially on the outskirts of big cities and in extremely impoverished areas, such as Valle de Chalco. Near the end of his stay he said, "My children, from what I have been able to observe in these travels around the country, I see a huge difference between the social classes. I say to you all, keeping in mind

the teaching of the apostle Saint John, that it is not true that
we love God if we do not love the neighbor whom we see,
whom we have right here next to us. Tell this to others, one
by one, each of you in your own way. Teach people to give
not just what they have left over, but even what they think
they need. Then they will know what it really means to
give." Soon afterwards there opened in Guadalajara the
Escuela Profesional Jarales, and to the north of Mexico City,
the Centro de Formación y Estudios Técnicos e Industriales
(CEFETI)—two social-service enterprises offering a Christian
education and a brighter economic future to people with
very limited resources.

A year later, when apostolic work had already begun
in Northern Europe, Don Alvaro set his sights once again
on the Far East. He wanted to set up operation as soon as
possible in some new countries. On July 7, 1985, the fiftieth
anniversary of his admission to Opus Dei, he received a great
gift: the news that on that very day, the Blessed Sacrament
had for the first time been reserved in a tabernacle of the
Work in Taiwan.

At the beginning of January 1986, Father Francisco
Vives arrived in Madrid, bringing with him a long letter
from Don Alvaro about a new evangelization of Europe. In
this letter—finished on Christmas Day—Don Alvaro noted
that Pope John Paul II had insistently and repeatedly
requested this new evangelization, and added that he felt he
was being faithful to the thinking of the Holy Father by
extending this apostolic outreach also to the United States
and Canada. In the pages of this letter he outlined an exciting
panorama of evangelization for the next few years. As means
for attaining these goals, he proposed a renewed effort in the
struggle for holiness and a continual recourse to the Blessed
Virgin, "refugium nostrum et virtus" (our refuge and our
strength), which would fill us all with the hope that
"Possumus!" (We can!).

This was the gist of many of his conversations and get-togethers in 1986, a year in which he traveled (especially during the summer) to Austria, Sweden, the Netherlands, Belgium, France, Germany, Switzerland, Italy, Spain, and Portugal. (He had been in the British Isles near the end of 1985.)

In November 1986 he simultaneously presided over two formation workshops for directors of the delegations of Opus Dei in Spain—one for the men's branch and one for the women's. Assisted by Don Javier Echevarría and Don Joaquín Alonso, he himself gave most of the meditations, classes, and talks. During those days, he gave the desires for sanctity and the apostolic ambitions of the members of Opus Dei in Spain a strong push forward by promoting this new evangelization of Europe.

The pastoral zeal of Don Alvaro was really most amazing. By now already over seventy, he was still actively concerned about the whole world. In his 1986 Christmas letter, he asked for prayers for the success of the preparatory work being done in South Korea and in the Dominican Republic. In the next few years, in these family letters, he encouraged the faithful of the Prelature to accompany him in spirit on the pastoral trips that he would be making first to Far Eastern lands, then to the countries of North America, and finally to the continent of Africa.

In January and February 1987 he visited Singapore, Australia, the Philippines, Hong Kong (with excursions to Macao and Canton), Taiwan, South Korea, and Japan. Ever eager to see the apostolate expand among the throngs of the Far East, he stressed different aspects of Catholic doctrine or of the spirit of Opus Dei in each country. In Australia, which, despite its geographical distance from the West, has a Western background and culture and mentality, he echoed the cry that Pope John Paul II had made during his visit there: "Come back!" For the Australian people, this was a call to return to their Christian roots, to a committed practice of the Faith. For the Prelature, it was a call to reach every area on that continent, as well as New Zealand and other nearby island nations.

In the Philippines, together with a reminder of its responsibility to be the vanguard of the Church in the Far East, Don Alvaro gave an incessant call for peace and concord. The country was going through a time of public disorder which could have resulted in a situation of virtually irreversible violence and hatred. At the same time, Don Alvaro was happy to see men and women from every stratum of society coming together at the gatherings that he held. Those who initiated the work of Opus Dei in that country had kept in their apostolic vision a vivid consciousness and concern regarding social differences, material poverty, and lack of education. These things constantly called out to their Christian conscience. Don Alvaro expressed great appreciation for the enterprises already under way, especially those directed to the material and spiritual advancement of people in rural areas. But he urged everyone to do still more with their love of God by enlisting the help of many others. Right up to his very last day in the Philippines, he kept insisting that "it is necessary for new social projects to begin as soon as possible." Soon afterward, another professional development center for young men of modest means opened in Cebu: the Center for Industrial Technology and Enterprise (CITE).

In Hong Kong, and in his brief excursions to Macao and Canton, Don Alvaro was well aware that he was standing at the threshold of China. He praised the industriousness and intelligence of the Chinese. But in his Masses, his private prayers, and his conversation, he also constantly mulled over the fact that "there are more than a billion people here, and very few of them know of the existence of Jesus Christ." In light of the fact that God wants the merits of the Redemption to be applied everywhere, his conclusion was that "China is a pressing concern for our Lord, and because of our love for him, the souls of China are a pressing concern for us as well."

In that context, his stay in Taiwan made very obvious the linguistic and cultural differences among the various parts of China. These differences posed difficulties that were serious but by no means insuperable, especially from the radical perspective of the universal message of salvation which Christ proclaimed from the cross. To my mind, the present which Don Alvaro gave to the faithful of the Prelature in Taipei was deeply significant: a reliquary with a fragment of the True Cross. In Taiwan he could see up close so many admirable human virtues, including industriousness and hospitality, and these only increased his eagerness for the doors of mainland China to be opened to religious freedom. The Gospel would illumine with a new light this splendid culture, he said, since the Christian faith does not destroy what is human, but, rather, advances and ennobles it.

The beginning of the history of Christianity in Korea— where the faith took root through the apostolic efforts of lay people, initially without the help of any priests—was to be repeated, in a way, in the case of Opus Dei. When Don Alvaro first traveled to this country, he found there a good number of cooperators. Having found out about Opus Dei through their work and professional contacts in other parts of the world, they were eagerly awaiting the establishment of the first Opus Dei center in their country. With the help of interpreters, Don Alvaro spoke personally with these Korean friends and even held a public meeting, which several hundred people attended. He spoke in Italian, and a language teacher translated for him. He left a solid foundation for the future development of apostolic work in Korea.

When he reached Osaka, he lamented that he had never made good on his early resolve to learn Japanese. "By now," he said, "I can remember very little—just a few verbs, how to count to ten, and a few other words. So much time has gone by. I studied it for one or two years, but since I didn't

practice it, I forgot it all." But what he could do during his
stay in Japan was to once again admire, and thank God for,
the richness of the spirit of Opus Dei, which was capable of
giving a Christian dimension to the noble human virtues so
typical of those lands—industriousness, refinement, loyalty,
love for the family, and so forth—and ward off the egotism
that so often follows upon ostensible material well-being.
He shared with the Japanese a great dream of his: that Japan
might be converted to Christ. "Oh, that it might become a
nation of fervent believers!" he exclaimed. "What a great good
for the whole world that would be!"

When he returned to Rome, he took up his pen to write
to the centers of Opus Dei. He began by expressing his
gratitude to the Blessed Trinity and to the Blessed Virgin for
the baptisms, conversions, and vocations in the Far East,
and for the unity of the faithful of the Prelature. "What a
joy it is," he said, "to see the spirit of the Work being
incarnated so perfectly in peoples of such diverse mentalities
and cultures, keeping intact the idiosyncrasies of each one
while uniting all in the same zeal for sanctity and the same
apostolic drive!"

Just eleven months later, in January 1988, he embarked
on a new apostolic adventure: a trip to Puerto Rico, the
United States, and Canada. (On the way, he made a short
visit to Mexico City to pray to Our Lady of Guadalupe.) He
went to the many cities which had Opus Dei centers, and in
each of them he basically repeated what he had said as soon
as he arrived in Miami: "The United States is a great country
with enormous human potential. The eyes of the world are
fixed upon you, for good or for ill. So you must be
distinguished by your sense of responsibility." During that
winter of 1988, he many times encouraged people to be "full-
time" Catholics, not "part-time" ones, and certainly not
"weekend" ones who do nothing more than go to Mass on
Saturday evening or Sunday.

When he returned from North America, he again visited nearly every country in Europe. As he expressed it in Brussels on August 31, "It is obvious that Europe needs a new evangelization. This continent from which the light of the Gospel has gone forth to illuminate so many countries is now in darkness." Now, he was thinking, of course, not only of the rest of Europe, but of Spain as well. In August 1989 he made a visit to the shrine of Covadonga. After quietly praying the rosary, he started praying out loud to the Blessed Virgin, placing in her hands the re-evangelization of all European nations, including our own, and asking her to rejuvenate their religious vitality. He also expressed his deep hope that many Spaniards would find in Opus Dei their vocations so that, together with people from other countries, they could work at evangelizing the whole world.

Meanwhile, he continued to look with special affection upon Africa. During the summer of 1988 he prayed hard that the imminent coming of the Work to Cameroon would be successful, and on August 18 he had the joy of passing on this fresh news from Rome: that on August 22, the feast of the Queenship of Mary, members of the Work would be arriving in Yaoundé. And in April 1989 another great dream of his came true: he was able to spend a few days in Africa, "the continent of the future" for the Church.

Upon his return from Kenya, he summed up his experience thus: "It gave me great joy to celebrate the Holy Mass there, and to be with so many good people who have so much human virtue, faith, and desire for God. I learned so much from them." He was very touched by the affection they had shown him, which went far beyond even the famous African hospitality. At the first public gathering, at Kenyatta Conference Center in Nairobi, in the presence of four or five thousand people, members of different tribes had come up and invested him as an "elder." Esther Toranzo, who spent twenty-five years in Kenya, says in her memoirs, "The designation of 'elder' or 'senator' is given to heads of families whose children are already grown and who have managed their homes with prudence. It is a basic feature in the governmental systems of all the tribes of Kenya, whether their origin is Bantu, Cushite, or Nilotic."

From there, Don Alvaro went to Cameroon and Zaire, and when he returned to Rome on September 15, he said this to the people at Cavabianca: "I was very edified to hear that in Africa, on the black continent, there are no atheists. Everyone there believes in God. Some have received the gift of faith in the true God; others are searching for it and are eager to know the Truth."

In October 1989 Don Alvaro visited Côte d'Ivoire, and a few days afterwards, Don Javier Echevarría came to Madrid and shared with us his impressions of the trips he had made with the Prelate to the different African countries. He was struck by how much affection and gratitude had been shown to Don Alvaro by people of such different cultures. They certainly reciprocated his obvious affection for them; they were deeply moved when they saw how he adapted himself to their ways, and how he adjusted his preaching to make it easier for them to grasp what he was saying. They were especially attracted by the way he kept trying to move into the background by pointing out that he was just continuing what had been so well begun by the founder of the Work. He had, of course, spoken out strongly against customs which were contrary or alien to the demands of Christian faith and morality, but he had done it from within that attitude of humility and affection.

Meanwhile, he continued to advance the Work into new regions. In October 1989 he announced the opening of the first center in Poland, and in his Christmas letter for that year he asked for prayers for "those new fields of apostolate which are opening up in some Eastern European countries." The Berlin Wall had just fallen, and shortly before that, the cathedral of Vilnius (the capital of Lithuania) had been ceremoniously restored to the Catholic Church, after years of being used by the Soviets as a museum.

In solidarity with the apostolic zeal of Pope John Paul II, Don Alvaro pondered in his heart the prospects for people on the other side of what used to be called the Iron Curtain. Soon he entrusted to Opus Dei's regional vicar in Austria the development of apostolic work in Czechoslovakia and Hungary. And on September 21, 1990, the eve of the reunification of the two Germanys, he wrote to Germany's regional vicar to highlight the importance of this event for "the many millions of souls whom, for so many years, they tried to keep from coming close to God."

In January 1989 the Work took root in New Zealand. In this connection I particularly remember the great affection that Don Alvaro had for a fellow named Mark. Relatively young for a man with eight children, Mark was for a while the only member of Opus Dei in that country. While on his way to do some business related to the setting up of the first center of the Work there, in the city of Hamilton, Mark was badly injured in a car accident. Thanks be to God, he survived, but he was in a coma for quite some time. Don Alvaro commented that our Lord had wanted to give the Work's beginning in New Zealand a special blessing with the cross.

In 1989 he also told us of the possibility that a house offered to us in Jerusalem would soon be ready to move into. It was a great dream of his to begin an apostolate near the holy places. In September, Father Alberto Steinworth moved there. Of German stock, but born in Costa Rica, Father Steinworth was a priest of the Prelature with a great gift for languages. Others soon joined him, and in 1993 two centers opened, one for men and another for women.

Back in 1935, when Don Alvaro asked to be admitted to Opus Dei, the Church celebrated on that day (July 7) the feast of Saints Cyril and Methodius, and he had a special devotion to those two saints. So he was very happy when, on December 31, 1980, Pope John Paul II named them, together with Saint Benedict, the patron saints of Europe. He prayed to them for the success of Opus Dei's apostolic efforts in Eastern Europe, including Russia and other countries behind the Iron Curtain. "I'd love to be able to go there," he said to us one day in 1983, during a short stay in Zurich.

In his get-togethers in 1991, he often spoke of the former Soviet Union and of his hope that it would open up to religious freedom after its painful breakup, full of uncertainties as it was. In July he told us about people from Russia, Belorussia, and other countries in the former Soviet bloc who were now studying theology at the University of Navarre or at the Pontifical Athenaeum of the Holy Cross. He was intensely interested in setting up operation as soon as possible in those countries, though he foresaw that it would take a lot of hard work after all those years of Communist rule.

On August 14, 1991, World Youth Day, Don Alvaro participated in the ceremonies held in Czestochowa, in Poland. He celebrated a Mass for the Spanish-speaking youth, and in his homily he said, "We are living in a time of tremendous importance. This is one of those moments in which is decided the fate of nations—the fate of millions and millions of souls. . . . God is the Lord of history, but he chooses to depend on our cooperation for the fulfilling of his salvific plans."

He had just returned to Rome when, on August 18, there came the alarming news of a coup by the Communists in Russia. It really hit him like a douse of ice water. In Poland he had dreamed about the apostolic horizons opening up all over Eastern Europe. He had even gone to a church in Warsaw to pray before Our Lady of Ostrabrama, an image venerated especially by Lithuanians.

Right away he encouraged us to unite ourselves with the intentions of the Holy Father, who was in Budapest that day. He said that we should pray for peace and for whatever would be best for the Church and for souls, ever sure that God knows best. He assured us that God would bring great good out of this apparent evil. He also advised us to pray to "Sancta Maria, Stella Orientis" (Holy Mary, Star of the East) about the international situation, and that the apostolic possibilities for the Church which had just barely opened up in Eastern Europe would not be crushed. He kept on giving us this kind of encouragement until late on August 21, when the news came that the coup had failed. Who would ever have imagined the scene that the whole world saw on television on December 25 of that year, when, in the Kremlin, the red flag with its hammer and sickle was pulled down and replaced by the old Russian standard?

Right at the start of 1992, Don Alvaro went to Prague and to Budapest to spend some time with the faithful of the Prelature who were working in those cities. On January 17 he celebrated Mass in the oratory of the Opus Dei center in Prague, and on January 19 he celebrated his first Mass on Hungarian soil. Soon the apostolic work of the Prelature began to take shape in both Czechoslovakia and Hungary— nations "which are so hungry for God after so many years of atheistic tyranny," wrote Don Alvaro on February 1. "This adventure of ours is absolutely marvelous," he continued. "We're contributing to the re-Christianizing of those places, and at the same time we're learning a lot from all these sons and daughters of the Church who have gone through decades of martyrdom."

From there he went to Vienna, where he spent some time with people from Croatia and Slovenia who still traveled to those countries from time to time. Along with encouragement of the apostolic work that was about to begin in cities like Zagreb and Split, he gave them reminders of the need for a spirit of magnanimity and concord.

In September 1992, in Rome, an ordinary General Congress of Opus Dei was held. Its resolutions included a consolidating of the work already begun in various countries in Central and Northern Europe and a starting of apostolic work in a good number of countries in Eastern Europe, Asia, and Africa. On New Year's Day 1993, Don Alvaro wrote, "In the physical sense, only a few people will move to those new countries to start the work of Opus Dei there, but the rest of us will be backing them up with all the strength of our prayer and sacrifice. That's what will make it possible for the Prelature to take root and be fruitful in those places."

In August 1993 I heard Don Alvaro outline plans for present and future work in Lithuania, Russia, and other countries in that general area. He talked about the trip he had made in April to Tallinn, the capital of Estonia, and about facts he had learned from letters received during the summer. About a year later, in September 1994, a center of Opus Dei opened in Vilnius.

And, finally, in India. Don Alvaro had been thinking about this subcontinent, with its hundreds of millions of people, for many years. I remember that in the summer of 1976 he was already talking to us about the possibility of working with Indian students at the University of Navarre to solve the problems standing in the way of setting up Opus Dei in India. The biggest one was the difficulty of obtaining residence permits for non-Indian priests. In late autumn of 1990 Roberto Dotta, a member of Opus Dei's General Council, went to India with some people who were from there. They explored old and new possible solutions and made some interesting contacts. During the summer of 1991 Don Alvaro alluded to that trip several times. He was, he said, dreaming of the day when the doors of that vast subcontinent would open for Opus Dei.

By 1993 he was already encouraging us to pray for the

beginning, now imminent, of direct apostolic work in India. He had decided to go ahead even though he knew—having been well advised of this—that there were still some unresolved difficulties. These would have to be worked out later, by those brave souls who first stepped foot on that great land. In the letters that he wrote to the centers in September and October, he asked everyone to pray for those first Opus Dei members setting out for that huge land, those members moving to New Delhi.

Whenever I think of the pace that Don Alvaro set for the expansion of Opus Dei throughout the world, there comes to my mind a get-together held one afternoon in March 1981. We were discussing a wide range of apostolic ventures in which the region of Spain would have to lend a hand. People were needed in some countries in North and South America to consolidate the work already being done. Then there was the possibility of entering China, with the opening of the first center in Hong Kong now imminent. And we had to reach all those other nations of the Far East, as well as begin work in Northern Europe...

In the face of all this, it was very clear that Don Alvaro was placing his hopes not in human means, but in the spiritual life of each person. "That is everything," he said. For him, success depended on an authentic fraternal charity and a spirit of sacrifice, especially in the work of formation, which was the responsibility not just of the directors but of every member of Opus Dei. That, he said, was almost the sole responsibility of the Work—to form people so that they would each work in an apostolic way, with freedom and a sense of responsibility, in their own place, whatever that might be.

18

Prelate of Opus Dei

In the fifties the heart of Opus Dei became localized, so to speak, in Pentecost Oratory, a chapel in the Villa Tevere complex. Dominating this oratory is a tabernacle bearing the inscription *Consummati in unum* (completely one) and standing before a broad stained-glass window which vividly depicts the coming of the Holy Spirit. On either side of the nave are traditional choir seats with the classic misericords (projections on the seats that give support when the choir members are standing), which in this instance are decorated with wood carvings of donkeys. In front of the tabernacle are seats for the Prelate and his two vicars.

Blessed Josemaría once showed Nisa González Guzmán this oratory, upon her return to Rome after a long stay in Canada. He paused for a moment before the seat reserved for Don Alvaro, who was Secretary General at the time. On the misericord of that seat was a donkey kicking a wolf. He explained, "This son of mine has, whenever necessary, defended the Work with tooth and nail!"

Opus Dei received its definitive approval from the Holy See in 1950. However, contrary to expectation, this did not put an end to problems from the outside. In fact, serious oppositions were launched right away, though they took a while to come to light. All through 1950 and 1951 Monsignor Escrivá felt, as Don Alvaro expressed it, "a great uneasiness, an interior disquiet, because our Lord let him sense that some terrible plot was being hatched against the Work." Though he had no idea what it was, he had a strong feeling that something really bad was happening. He said this to Don Alvaro time and time again, and he too suffered deeply.

It was in those circumstances that the founder decided to make a pilgrimage to the shrine of Loreto, in the hottest part of the summer, to consecrate the Work to the Most Sweet Heart of Mary on the feast of the Assumption. It was a difficult trip—a truly penitential one, as I so often heard it described by Don Alvaro, who went with him. A few months later they found out what was going on. Some people outside Opus Dei who had some influence with the Roman Curia were trying to divide the Work into two separate institutions, one for men and one for women—and both institutions would have been decapitated, for the founder was to have been expelled.

On another August 15, twenty-five years later, Don Alvaro invited us to give much thanks to God for (among other things) having inspired the founder to consecrate Opus Dei to the Most Sweet Heart of Mary in 1951, because this had instantly dissipated that menacing storm cloud hovering over Opus Dei. It had vanished, he said, like a "palla di sapone" (soap bubble). But, he added, the opposition had also been like a dagger thrust close to the heart—any added pressure would have been enough to kill. So in March 1952, Monsignor Escrivá decided to send a very forthright letter to Cardinal Tedeschini, the Work's Cardinal Protector (a position specified in the canon law of that time). With all due respect, he wrote in strong language that set out the problem quite bluntly. Don Alvaro considered it appropriate that he too, as Procurator General of Opus Dei, should sign the letter. Cardinal Tedeschini decided to read it to Pope

Pius XII—this was on the vigil of the feast of Saint Joseph—and afterwards Pope Pius exclaimed, "But whose idea is this, to do such things?"

As, of course, we all know now, that terrible attack came to nothing. But I would like to highlight one remark that Don Alvaro made whenever he mentioned the visit that Monsignor Escrivá made to Cardinal Tedeschini to speak with him about this horrible ordeal: "As always, I was with him."

The possibility of such problems arose from the fact that the canonical garb in which Opus Dei was clothed at the time was a bad fit for its foundational charism. Monsignor Escrivá was aware that this discrepancy put Opus Dei at risk, but, as he always used to say, in Rome he had learned how to wait. At the end of the fifties he once again pointed out the need for an adequate legal framework—this was, he said, the "special intention" for which he had prayed, and asked others to pray, from way back when he was young. As in the preceding stages, Don Alvaro helped him to formulate and dispatch these petitions. Again they were not granted, because of seemingly insuperable obstacles presented by the canon law of that time. But soon afterwards the Second Vatican Council began, and this opened up new avenues in Church law.

The prudence of Blessed Josemaría led him to do absolutely everything he needed to do, including convoking a special General Congress of Opus Dei in 1969, but without trying to bypass any step in the legal process. The goal was still unattained when God called him to himself in 1975.

Throughout this long journey, the fidelity of Don Alvaro was a bulwark—first for the fortitude and prudence of the founder, and then, after his death, for the task of completing the journey. When necessary, he could be quite assertive and forceful. But he also knew how to wait—in the clamorous silence of prayer and sacrifice—when waiting was the best thing for the Church and for the Work.

I remember that in August 1976 he mentioned in passing how important it was to pray for this intention. A few months before, on March 5, in his first audience with Pope Paul VI, the Holy Father had encouraged him to prepare the documents needed for working towards the new canonical configuration. But with the Holy Father's agreement, he said, he had decided to let some time go by before doing that, because the founder's death was still so recent.

In Don Alvaro's second audience with him, on June 19, 1978, Pope Paul suggested that he go ahead and complete the preparatory work and then submit to him the request. However, this turned out not to be possible, since the Holy Father died in August of that year.

Pope John Paul I, short as was his pontificate, was actually on the verge of giving Opus Dei a boost towards obtaining this "auspicata" (desirable) juridical framework. Just before his sudden death, he approved a letter which would have set in motion the necessary studies. But he never got to sign it. (Don Alvaro was told this by Cardinal Villot, the Vatican Secretary of State, when they met each other at the Holy Father's wake.)

A short time later, Pope John Paul II, through a letter written by Cardinal Villot, expressed his conviction that a resolution of this problem was an "unpostponable necessity." So Don Alvaro, at the end of 1978 or the beginning of 1979, started insistently repeating words to this effect: "Intensify your prayer for the special intention of our Father. Offer up your work and your sacrifices, your joys and your sorrows, and get others to do the same. A lot of good will come out of this for the Church and for souls. That's why our Lord makes us all pray so much before giving us what we want."

From then on, and precisely because he thought this would facilitate a better service of God and of souls, he told people to expect a lot of difficulties to arise. "The devil," he said, "will try to get in our way. But if we just do our duty of being faithful, then despite our personal wretchedness we will manage to move forward and to joyfully persist."

He worked very hard on this project, but always relying wholeheartedly on supernatural means. There was in the Work a crescendo of prayer and mortification which helped everyone to grow even more united with one another and with the Father himself. Only this can explain how, despite some rather hostile press reports which appeared in November 1979, the regional vicar of Spain could tell us after a trip to Rome that Don Alvaro was very happy with the progress being made. (The reports were based on distorted or very incomplete versions of documentation received by the Holy See and then published without its permission.)

However, that joy of his was a true *gaudium cum pace* (joy with peace), and thus not something intermittent. Throughout those years, I always saw him looking very content and kept hearing him say, to all sorts of people who came to Rome, that he was especially happy. Even in times of serious external oppositions, he radiated calm and lavished affection. When he was with one of his children, he never seemed to be in any hurry. I was also struck by the persistence and enthusiasm with which he encouraged people to offer much prayer and mortification for the Holy Father and for the special intention.

It was a long journey, but Don Alvaro completed it with an exquisite faithfulness to the founder of the Work. He combined a supernatural outlook and a right intention (better service of God and of humanity) with constant work and the use of all human means at his disposal. He did this with peace, with good humor, with total abandonment to the will of God, even when the attacks were at their worst. Through it all he kept praying, and kept getting others to pray. And so that the members of the Work would not get so used to this that it would become mechanical, he kept setting for them new goals. He said he was using the "hare trick" that middle-distance runners use when trying to break a record.

At other times the sports metaphor he used was the hundred-meter dash, and the tremendous concentration it takes, first of all, just to make the all-important good start. We must, he said, pray hard day after day, and month after month, "without losing one second." And sometimes he talked about the final sprint, about the approach to the finish line, when each of the athletes extends their chest so as to be the one to break the tape. "That's what I am now asking of you," he would say. "I want you to run with your body thrust forward, without wasting a hundredth of a second!"

It was impressive to see how peacefully he dealt with the most extreme hostility. Never for a moment did he doubt that God writes straight with crooked lines. As he explained one day in March 1981, the false accusations just meant that, thanks be to God, things were going well and the devil was infuriated by this. Also, they were a means by which God was testing the members of the Work. The important thing was to remain loyal, to endure the trial with great fidelity—and with a lot of apostolic activity.

On occasion he did point out, however, how paradoxical it was that the international media, who normally opposed the pope and the Catholic hierarchy, now gave the impression of wanting "to defend the bishops against us, when we exist to serve them."

Throughout the final lap of the race to its juridical solution, Opus Dei was led by the hand of the Blessed Virgin. There was, once again, a crescendo of supplication—prayers offered up every day, in work and in rest, in ordinary things and in visits to shrines and other holy places. More than once I've thought that this whole spirit was best summed up in something Don Alvaro spontaneously said in 1981, just after renewing the consecration of Opus Dei to the Most Sweet Heart of Mary—an act which had first been done by the founder in Loreto thirty years before. "From that moment

on," said Don Alvaro, "we have gone to the Blessed Virgin
in a very specific way, asking this Most Sweet Heart of our
Mother to prepare for us a safe path. We have asked her to
sweep off our path all the thistles and thorns and snares which
are always coming up on the road that we travel together
and also in the personal journey of each of us, in our interior
struggles. We have gone to her praying fervently, with faith,
perseveringly, "Iter para tutum!" (Prepare a safe way!). And
now we continue that prayer.

"O blessed Lady, you are our mother, because you are
the mother of God. Being the mother of God, you can do
anything; and you are our mother; and you are a good mother
who gives her children everything, as all good mothers do.
Actually, you do it even better, because you are uniquely
God's daughter. Greater than you, there is only God himself.
We live in the shelter of your heart. We want to live your
life, that life so full of the love of God—a clean life, a pure
life, a dedicated life, a life of love. And to do that—since we
know we cannot do it by ourselves, knowing as we do how
small we are—we come and beg you to help us more. By 'we'
I mean the whole Work. The whole Work is at your feet, O
blessed Lady! We are your sons and daughters. We fly to
your protection, we fly to your help, and we ask you to keep
on preparing the way for us.

"Specifically, we ask you for that juridical solution
which—I can't go around broadcasting this out there, but
I'll say it to you here, in front of these children of mine—
that we can almost touch with our hands. We ask you to
give it to us now. Now! Now! Please don't make us wait any
longer! Of course, if it is the will of your Son that we should
wait for years more—months, years, whatever amount of time
may be necessary—we love the will of your Son! However, if
it can be now, please let it be now! Please give it to us now! It
is all for your Son, and it is for you. You can do it—please
grant us this grace!"

As the years go by, one appreciates more and more the human and supernatural character of Don Alvaro. Pope John Paul II told him on November 7, 1981, that he had decided to establish Opus Dei as a personal prelature, but he asked him to keep this information strictly to himself, and Don Alvaro did so. He started giving thanks to God immediately, of course, but he went on praying and asking for prayers with redoubled tenacity.

In July 1982 he told us several times that we should be "impatient" in our praying and "patient" in our waiting. A new campaign had just been unleashed, based on the false notion that Pope John Paul wanted to change Opus Dei into a kind of universal diocese above other dioceses. I think that this tactic was intended to set the bishops against the soon-to-be prelature so that Pope John Paul would put the process into reverse gear. It was surely significant, for example, that this type of information reached the pages of Spanish newspapers in June 1982, when the plenary assembly of Spanish bishops was meeting.

The tranquillity of Don Alvaro was really most impressive. On August 15 the regional vicar of Spain made a phone call to Rome. It was a particularly crucial moment. But Don Alvaro did not forget to ask after Ramón Herrando's mother, who was quite ill at the time. (As a matter of fact, this lady, Monserrat Prat de la Riba—daughter of a former president of the Commonwealth of Catalonia—died on November 7, the very day that Pope John Paul went to visit her.)

Finally, on August 23, the Vatican Press Office made the official announcement that Pope John Paul had decided to establish Opus Dei as a personal prelature, although, for technical reasons, the publication of the documents would be taking place later. The time had come for us to increase our thanksgiving to God and to the Holy Father, but without slackening in our prayers of petition and in our mortification. That was the way Don Alvaro put it when, late that afternoon, he gave us the news in Our Lady of the Angels Oratory at Cavabianca. He also explained what Pope John Paul's decision meant, and spoke very movingly about the founder of Opus Dei.

And he continued to appeal to the Blessed Virgin. On September 8, the feast of the Birth of the Virgin Mary, I accompanied Don Alvaro to a shrine dedicated to her, for the first time since the news of August 23. When we finished the rosary, he went on praying for a long time about the special intention. He did this in silence, but after explicitly asking us to join him in this prayer. On November 18, in Rome, he began a novena of visits to shrines and churches dedicated to the Blessed Virgin, to ask the Mother of God to "put the last stone in place." This novena ended on Saturday, November 27, the day on which the pontifical documents pertaining to the establishment of the Prelature of Opus Dei became public.

Don Alvaro lived through this last phase, too, with an imperturbable peace. As usual, he spread serenity and affection to all those around him. Antonio Prieto personally experienced this during those November days. Upon his return to Madrid from a short trip to Rome, he told us how impressed he had been by Don Alvaro's great calm in the midst of the heavy workload of those days just prior to the event, and also by his deep humanity. Even under all that pressure, Don Alvaro had still asked for detailed news of Antonio's father, who was very ill at the time, and had also asked about his mother and sister.

In that historic moment for Opus Dei, Don Alvaro coined a new aspiration to our Lady which was inspired by the "Cor Mariae Dulcissimum, iter para tutum!" (Sweetest Heart of Mary, prepare a safe way!) which the founder used to say from as far back as the fifties, if not before. "Let us now," he told us, "also say, 'Cor Mariae Dulcissimum, iter serva tutum!' (Sweetest Heart of Mary, keep a safe way!)."

As the years went by, he said, this aspiration should become "a persistent cry which carries down through the centuries the prayer of our beloved Father."

At the express wish of Don Alvaro, a Marian year then began in Opus Dei. This was, he said, a time to give thanks to the Blessed Trinity through the Mother of God, "without noise or ostentation, just every one of us men and women, both individually and very much as a family, from the bottom of our hearts."

After giving thanks to the Trinity of heaven (the Father, the Son, and the Holy Spirit) and to the trinity of earth (Jesus, Mary, and Joseph), Don Alvaro gave thanks to the Holy Father. He would always be especially grateful to Pope John Paul II not only for having established Opus Dei as a personal prelature, but for having done it with strict adherence to the proper procedure, without skipping a single step.

After the Holy Father, thanks were due also to Cardinal Sebastiano Baggio, Cardinal Franz König, and the other Church authorities who had worked so hard on the lengthy and thoroughgoing studies preceding that juridical act. The news was published in the 11/27/82 edition of *L'Osservatore Romano,* and on December 5, Don Alvaro went to Vienna to thank Cardinal König in person. (He also prayed to the Blessed Virgin in Kahlenberg, which is near Vienna, and before the image of Maria Pötsch, in the cathedral of Vienna.) From there he went to Cologne to thank Cardinal Höffner, and then to Switzerland to thank Bishop Deskur. This journey of thanksgiving culminated in his visit to the shrine of Einsiedeln, which is so closely linked to the history of Opus Dei. But as soon as he could, he also went to Mexico to prostrate himself "at the feet of the Virgin of Guadalupe in gratitude for having heard the filial prayer of our founder on his pilgrim journey in May 1970."

In the end, the serious difficulties put forth by some people for such a long time served only to show and to increase Don Alvaro's humility. He vigorously dismissed any reference to himself. One person who noticed this was Father Rafael Pérez, O.S.A., who presided over the Madrid tribunal for the process of beatification of Monsignor Escrivá. In September 1983 he attended a large outdoors get-together at Retamar College in Madrid. It was the first get-together of this kind in Spain after the establishment of Opus Dei as a personal prelature, so naturally Don Alvaro described in detail the juridical journey. On that very day, Father Pérez made the comment that he was impressed by the Prelate's doctrinal soundness, but even more by the fact that "in almost an hour and a half, only once did he speak of himself—and then he begged our pardon for having done so."

Years later, a commemorative medallion was minted, as is the custom in Rome. "And they got their way," I heard Don Alvaro say in 1990. He was referring to what was on the obverse side of the medallion: profiles of both the founder and the Prelate, surrounded by the inscription "GRATIAS TIBI, DEUS, GRATIAS TIBI" (Thank you, God, thank you) and the date "XXVIII * NOV * MCMLXXXII." [November 28, 1982, is the publication date of *Ut sit,* the apostolic constitution establishing Opus Dei as a personal prelature.] Back when he had first been shown this design, Don Alvaro had not much liked it. "This is unnecessary," he had said. He thought it was not right that a profile of him should be with that of the founder. This was, in fact, the main reason for the delay in making the medallion. The designer, Jesús Gazapo, had to enlist the help of Don Javier Echevarría to talk him into it, just as he used to have to appeal to Don Alvaro when the founder was still alive. Finally Don Alvaro gave in, won over by the argument that this depiction was a way of showing continuity. "And so," he said, "although it makes me blush, I decided that since the less important figure is eclipsed by the more important one, it could stay."

From the very first moment after the establishment of

the prelature, Don Alvaro kept repeating this teaching that he had learned from Blessed Josemaría: to forgive and pray for those who had fought against this juridical solution for Opus Dei. In the Mass of thanksgiving which he celebrated on November 30, 1982, in the prelatic church of Our Lady of Peace, he included in the General Intercessions this intention: "For all our benefactors, and for all those who in one way or another have tried to impede or make difficult the journey of Opus Dei—for, in imitation of our Father, we not only forgive them with all our hearts, but we regard them, too, as benefactors." And the response was, "May the Lord, in the richness of his mercy, fill them with true goods in this life and grant them heavenly glory."

19

A Strong and Prudent Shepherd

When Pilar Urbano asked Don Javier Echevarría (in the previously mentioned interview) if Don Alvaro had been somewhat naive, his answer was an emphatic "Not in the least!" He then explained, "He was a very good and holy man who was always ready to serve other people. But he had a well-defined character with a lot of strength. In his work of governing Opus Dei, for example, I heard him give firm reprimands whenever there was any delay in the sending of paperwork requested from another country. He would say, 'You can't let yourself forget about the paperwork. There's nothing more disheartening than administrative silence.'"

He really was an outstanding administrator, very knowledgeable and prudent. As a good shepherd, he cultivated a unity based on a refined charity and a genuine affection. He practiced what he preached, and part of what he preached was that directors of Opus Dei must love people, make demands on them, push and pull them. They must, he insisted, pray and then pray some more, and guide people, direct them, give them suggestions. They must not make any allowance for the lovelessness of indifference, as though some fields of endeavor were alien to holiness and to apostolic activity. And in everything they must be one with the person and the mind of the founder; he was a pillar they must lean on.

Don Alvaro was very attentive to all that went on around him, thinking always of the good of souls. In August 1977, for example, he encouraged us directors to pray a lot and to keep up with current events. Only in this way, he said, could we be really on the alert, as good shepherds, to discover in every set of circumstances the best helps for the interior life and doctrinal formation of Opus Dei members and of the countless other individuals reached by the apostolates of Opus Dei. He wanted us to feel the weight of our responsibility and, in a sense, to have a thin skin, so that our hearts could beat in synch with the heart of Christ. He used to insist that alertness—not wariness, but the wakefulness that people in love have, as is so beautifully expressed in Song of Songs 5:2—that this kind of alertness is a serious obligation for directors, especially when social and cultural changes give rise to new doctrinal or moral problems for which people are unprepared.

Many times I myself observed how he studied such matters. He did it in great depth, after listening to all those who could and should express their views. He was so approachable that no one hid their opinions or failed to give voice to doubts or questions out of fear of looking bad or making a mistake.

He applied without any exception, but also without getting into a rut, the founder's guidelines regarding a supernatural outlook, collegiality in decision-making, and professionalism. He was not attached to his own ideas; he was ready to correct them whenever necessary. It was impressive to see how he grasped the whole picture, approached everything with a positive attitude, and inspired confidence and freedom in all those around him.

Above all, Don Alvaro governed Opus Dei through affection, with that closeness to each soul which is typical of a true shepherd of souls. One day in August 1988 he was praying out loud that the Lord would give him and the other directors of the Work such a great sense of responsibility that they would be truly concerned about each person, and he was giving examples of what he meant. He mentioned praying for everyone, getting to know people on a one-to-one basis, going ahead and giving special help to those who have serious problems or who need more attention, and being demanding with oneself while being both understanding and demanding with others. And here he interrupted himself to give an important clarification. "Thanks be to God," he said, "this is the way we have always lived in the Work. I talk a lot about being demanding. I want you to understand that I'm talking about a demandingness that is full of affection, full of the respect and gentleness that the Father asked of us in our treatment of others—but at the same time really demanding. We have to call a spade a spade. If we don't, we're not fulfilling our obligations as directors."

One morning in 1991 I spent some time in the office where Don Alvaro was working. We had a long conversation in which several different topics came up, and in his apostolic zeal he was setting ambitious goals both for himself and for me. Well-prepared persons were needed in so many places, he said, that one had to make a choice, and the choice would inevitably involve considerable sacrifice. I told him that at times "the Prefect of Studies has a divided heart." (Prefect of Studies was my job at the time in the regional commission of Opus Dei in Spain.) "Well, then," he immediately suggested, "ask our Father to give you a bigger heart."

Don Alvaro never confused pastoral prudence with the timidity, cowardice, or love of comfort which induces paralysis and which often hides behind a false "objectivity" that is incompatible with faith and hope. "I remember," he said in Paris in March 1982, "a friend who served with me in the Spanish Civil War. We were planning to escape together from the Communists. But nothing could be done with this fellow. He immediately found problems with everything. We didn't have the wherewithal; we would be caught right away... But so what? We were prisoners anyway, whether hidden in an embassy or locked up in a jail. He had that kind of 'objectivity' which arises from fear and self-centeredness and which sabotages all plans."

Don Alvaro's prudence had nothing to do with apprehension, nervousness, or confusion. His concern was calm, but at the same time vigorously active. Prudence is, after all, according to Saint Thomas Aquinas's classic definition, "the virtue which commands" (*Summa Theologica,* I-II.61.3). In January 1993, in response to an Italian university student who said that he sometimes felt confused because of a lack of preparation, Don Alvaro cited the Italian proverb "É che, camminando, si aggiusta la soma" (Only when the donkey starts walking does its pack settle comfortably into place). And he added, "We learn to walk by first putting one foot forward, and then the other, and so on. Sometimes we fall, but then we get up and start going forward again. That's how children learn to walk."

He was no less outspoken about the need to spend time studying matters in depth, or about the fact that the founder had stipulated that the governing of Opus Dei should be done mainly in writing, to facilitate a balanced point of view and to discourage partiality and arbitrariness. These things, he said, were essential to the apostolic effectiveness of the Work. It was necessary that we act with at least the effort, exactitude, and seriousness of any good professional.

Don Alvaro worked hard, and he worked well. I don't think it's necessary to describe his typical day or schedule of activities in Rome—one can get a good enough idea of all that by reading Cesare Cavalleri's extensive interview with him, *Immersed in God.* In chapter 3 of that book, Don Alvaro describes at length Monsignor Escrivá's typical day in Rome. Back then Don Alvaro spent most of his time at the founder's side, and after 1975 he kept to that same schedule, day after day and year after year. However, I would like to highlight the rectitude of intention with which he did his work.

To Don Alvaro, effort became worthwhile when one offered it to our Lord and sought in it the glory of God. In February 1990, at a workshop for the formation of directors, he encouraged the participants to do battle with two great enemies of the sanctification of ordinary work: laziness, and what he called "professionalitis." By this he meant the attitude of those who do a good job for merely self-seeking purposes—to win, to look good—forgetting that they should be struggling to raise that human activity to a supernatural level and turn it into prayer.

Actually, he said, the best spur for a thorough fulfillment of one's duty is precisely the desire to sanctify one's work. Here he cited the well-known words of Saint Paul, "The love of Christ controls us . . ." (2 Cor 5:14). The urgency, the intensity, of one's love for Christ should be, he said, all the motivation one needs to do every job well, to use one's time well, to accomplish everything out of a desire to serve, to transform every task into a means of apostolate, to keep alive one's professional aspirations, to stay up-to-date, to make the best use of one's natural talents and supernatural gifts, to imbue one's social relations with Christian morality and meaning, to carry out the social demands of the Faith in professional and civic life; in short, to give one such a unity of life that one's professional work will not become a pedestal for one's ego instead of a throne for Jesus.

In 1991 Don Alvaro wrote, "A job well done is not the same as a job that goes well. Bees build a perfect honeycomb and produce delicious honey, but they don't *work,* because they are not able to love. What matters is the interior attitude, not the results. 'The Lord looks on the heart' (1 Sm 16:7). That is where we find the key to telling whether a job has been done well or badly."

As for Don Alvaro, he spent himself in his pastoral work with real human and supernatural dedication even when his health was not good. The first time I ever saw him sick was at the beginning of August 1976, when he suffered a bad attack of lumbago. Despite the enormous inconvenience of it—the pain making it very difficult for him either to walk or to sit—he went on living his life as usual. He tried to stay warm, although in general he much preferred cold to heat. But he didn't let this illness keep him from his work. He even wrote by hand a long letter to the members of the Work who were going to be ordained a few days later in Madrid.

I was always amazed at how little importance he gave his aches and pains. He just did whatever the doctor told him to do, and that was that. He took the prescribed medication without giving it any thought—without so much as asking what it was, or what it was for—and went on working. I remember one time in 1977, this was around the feast of the Assumption, a new denture had caused some sores in his mouth, and he must have been feeling awfully bad. He went to see Dr. Guillermo Rehberger, in Oviedo, and when he got back he felt great—"as if I just got out of jail," he said. Then I realized that I had spent the whole day with him without having any idea how he was feeling. Nothing had shown on the outside. On the contrary, he had not only followed his regular routine but had been even more active than usual. He had talked about a lot of things in our get-togethers and had also given two meditations, on August 15 and 16.

I did notice, and I found puzzling, the fact that our Lord did not spare Don Alvaro even during those times when he needed to rest. For Don Alvaro certainly did not disdain that indispensable rest which forms part of the virtue of industriousness. He often used this expression which the founder of Opus Dei had used with reference to his own body: "taking care of the little donkey." And he was always teaching that we must not only work and struggle and fight, but also rest. In May 1983, just after his trip to Mexico, he said this in Bogotá: "In Mexico they have a wonderful expression: 'to rest by laying adobes.' An adobe is a very simple kind of brick—unbaked, or only sun-baked. Well, that's what I do to rest a bit from my usual work. For me, one day of working in Rome is much harder than a whole year of preaching in all these different places. It is such a joy to come into contact with so many souls and to see how God stirs them up and draws them to himself."

In July 1975 he started setting aside some quiet times when he could work without interruption on matters which required many hours of study and an especially clear view of the big picture. An example would be the work of getting together the documentation needed for Monsignor Escrivá's cause for beatification. This was the main reason he spent parts of several summers at the Solavieya Conference Center and at similar places in Spain, Germany, and England. But during those times he also got plenty of fresh air and all the physical exercise recommended by his doctors, which did him a lot of good. In fact, he even looked better. With a touch of the sun his skin immediately took on a tan. And despite his being out of condition, and therefore inevitably tired and sore for the first few days, he would nevertheless faithfully complete his scheduled amount of work.

As the years went by, Don Alvaro's health declined. For one thing, he suffered more from hypertension and resultant complications. Serious problems surfaced at the beginning of 1985. In January he went to the hospital at the University of Navarre for a thorough examination, and it was discovered that he had a blockage in his left renal artery. After an angioplasty he immediately resumed all his usual activities. When he came through Madrid he was much thinner and, of course, tired, but despite his fatigue he kept up his regular pace. It was, perhaps, in those situations where he was obviously exhausted that one most appreciated his habitual good humor, which showed itself in the simplest remarks.

I have already mentioned the two workshops he presided over in November 1986, at Molinoviejo. The participants remember the resonance of his words and the deep impact they made on them. No one had any idea that during those days his mouth was very sore. He was, in fact, in so much pain that he had to go to a dentist in Madrid (Dr. Miguel Lucas) and postpone a trip to Portugal.

Obviously he had a lot of ability to bear up under pain and illness. Only something very serious could keep him from fulfilling his duties, whatever they might be, including the daily physical exercise prescribed for him by his doctors. I saw this for myself during the summer of 1993, when he underwent a cataract operation. It was impressive to see how serene he remained through it all. Sometimes, too, we overheard things that showed how he dealt with this situation in his everyday conversation with God. He asked our Lord, for example, to make his eyesight keener so that he could fix his gaze upon him. And then he made that same request also for all his children and all souls, recalling words uttered long before by Blessed Josemaría: "May my children look to you." He even made a brief comment about this in his next letter to the centers of Opus Dei, dated August 1: "I applied those words to myself, and I turned to the Holy Trinity, begging of each one of the three divine Persons that in all circumstances we might look to God, talk to him, and love him."

He was then on the verge of turning eighty. Despite excellent medical care, he had suffered much illness in the course of a life of hard work. It was ever more difficult for him to walk or to climb stairs, and the strokes of his handwriting were getting weak. But such things were hardly noticed, except by those closest to him, because of his sense of humor, his cheerfulness, his good manners, and his constant concern for others.

During that summer of 1993, I saw him act with incredible mental and physical agility in any situation having to do with serving God and the Church. At such times, if you'll allow me the expression, he couldn't sit still; he had to be involved, one hundred percent. Though he quoted only rarely those famous words of Saint Martin of Tours, "Non recuso laborem" (I do not refuse to work), his immediate and total responsiveness to the requirements of love was truly resplendent.

He kept going with his pastoral work until the very end, taking apostolic trips to various European countries, such as Austria, Switzerland, Poland, Germany, and, of course, Spain. In each country he talked with many persons individually and tended to whole crowds of them at once at huge get-togethers. In 1994 he would return to Spain to preside at a ceremony at the University of Navarre, in his capacity as Grand Chancellor. And then there was the pilgrimage to the Holy Land, which was the culmination of his life on earth.

His soul—in other words, his love for God—pulled his body along. He bore fatigue and illness with remarkable grace, showing more concern for others than for himself. Don Javier Echevarría mentioned this in connection with the time they spent at Ben Gurion Airport in Tel Aviv on March 22, 1994, just hours before Don Alvaro's death. "He was very tired," he said. "We all thought that this tiredness was just due to those days spent in pilgrimage, which did involve a lot of physical exertion... Well, when you leave Israel, it's customary for them to put you through a very long security check—it takes at least twenty minutes and can take up to two hours. I was surprised by the patience and matter-of-factness with which the Father answered all the questions. You might think this was only to be expected. But the fact is that he was obviously worn out, and yet he answered every question with his usual kindliness, frankness, and simplicity so that everything would go smoothly for that security officer."

From 1976 on, I also noticed the extraordinary combination of strength and affection with which he spurred on his immediate coworkers. He worked hard, and he made everybody else work hard. He was a very good organizer and had a special gift for cultivating a team spirit. He himself worked with a patient urgency that created an atmosphere of quiet effort. At his side one made great progress with great tranquillity, not running out of breath from running helter-skelter, but doing one thing after the other in an orderly fashion—in a *very* orderly fashion—and with a right intention, with the strength that comes of working not for one's own interests but for the glory of God.

As Lucas F. Mateo Seco expressed it in *Scripta Theologica* shortly after Don Alvaro's death, his life was "like a wide, gently flowing river. Beneath the serene peace which he exuded, and which he transmitted to those who worked with him, there flowed a powerful energy and an enormous capacity for work which he placed always at the service of the Holy Church and of human values."

He never felt burdened by his huge workload, because he had well learned from the founder of Opus Dei that "having a lot of work means having a lot of material to sanctify." In January 1986, in Sweden, a priest (Father Hayward) asked him about the problem of lack of time, and Don Alvaro spontaneously gave him this advice, which he himself lived by: "To multiply our time, according to the practical counsel given by our Father, we have to live more consciously in the presence of God. Then we will work with more peace and greater intensity, with a greater desire to do things well. Our time multiplies as a result, because we do things better, with more enthusiasm, with more interest in succeeding. We get less distracted and waste less time."

Don Alvaro's orderliness attracted attention because it was so clearly based on charity. This showed up in all kinds of things, both mundane and spiritual. His was a sense of order that was not mean or petty, but, on the contrary, openly magnanimous. Without being rigid about it, he simply did one thing after another. He did not like makeshift solutions; he preferred to think things through and get every little detail just right. However, he would change his plans on the spur of the moment, with no reluctance whatsoever, when this was needed for the good of souls or of the Church. In making his decisions, he used all the human means at his disposal, but at the same time he totally abandoned himself to the will of God. If need be, he would move up or delay a trip, or return early to Rome. As he expressed it to students at the Montalbán student residence in Madrid in February 1992, "I'm sorry I haven't been able to see you more, but what can we do? We can't do what we want; we have to do what we should."

In his sense of order there was, however, no scrupulosity or perfectionism. At the beginning of 1992 I was given a rather complicated assignment, and soon I was spending practically all my time on it. When Don Alvaro saw me on March 29, he took an interest in what I was doing. He wanted to know, among other things, how much longer I expected it to take. I told him I had probably ten or twelve days of writing to go. He turned to the others and said, "Well, then, take it away from him ten days from now."

He concerned himself with the smallest details, but did not pester or straitjacket anyone. His concern came basically from a solicitude of the heart, a mental knack for concretizing, and a strict fidelity to a very characteristic feature of the spirit of Opus Dei. He was so meticulous and observant that he would often notice details that escaped the rest of us. He always, for example, read things very carefully. But when he caught and corrected errors, he did it with a good-natured sense of humor. Once I had to type the fair copy of a document from a draft which had been seen and approved by several people before reaching Don Alvaro's desk. It had been circulated with this as its title, in huge capital letters: "PROYACTO DE. . . ." Don Alvaro, with red ink, crossed out that "A," wrote in the margin "/E," and then added, "y olé!"

Above all, he concerned himself with apparently inconsequential details when it came to the liturgy or to places of worship. In 1978 he saw for the first time Molinoviejo's new oratory, which had been dedicated some time before. The tabernacle in the Blessed Sacrament chapel was framed by glazed tiles representing the Blessed Virgin and the apostle John at the feet of the crucified Christ. As soon as he entered the chapel, Don Alvaro noticed an error in the tiny Latin inscription on the cross: the "a" was left out of "Iudaeorum."

On April 20, 1990, he was going to be giving the closing address at an international symposium sponsored by the theology department of the University of Navarre. So on the evening before, he went to the auditorium to check the microphones and the speakers. He wanted to work on both the sound system and his own tone of voice ahead of time so that what he said could be heard clearly. In September 1991 he took similar precautions before celebrating a solemn Mass for the university community. He wanted to check out for himself the liturgical dignity lent to the place that had been chosen for welcoming everyone: the gymnasium.

All of this vigilance, as I say, came from a magnanimous spirit of service, so there was nothing stingy or mean-spirited about it. When, for example, Don Alvaro heard that the women at Villa Tevere whose ministry was household services were in need of more irons, he immediately advised them to check into the possibility of getting the kind of ironing machine he had recently seen in a hospital. This machine, he said, might serve their needs much better. And sure enough, a mangle was purchased soon after, and with very good results.

Don Alvaro, affectionate as he was, did correct mistakes and faults quite clearly. But he did this, too, with such affection that it was impossible not to thank him for it. He had, even from his youth, a wonderful way of doing this. Basically, it was a combination of Christian fortitude and charity with a respect for the other person's freedom. He did not let slide any mistake or fault, no matter how small or slight, and he had no use for euphemisms. But this was because he cared so much about every person in Opus Dei— about every little thing that happened to them, whether in soul or in body. He used to insist that a good shepherd, besides anticipating the needs of his flock, must refuse himself the convenience of letting things slide which needed to be corrected. He used very clear examples—such as the propensity of some people to put on too much weight. Those around them, he said, should realize that this is a problem and should help them to overcome it—if necessary, by taking them to a doctor. And then he would say with a smile, "The more one eats, the hungrier one gets, because the body is very treacherous. People with this problem need to know how to offer up to the Lord their hunger. There's a joke about a donkey that had just about gotten used to not eating when he died. Well, they need not worry; this won't happen to them."

Because of his temperament and his supernatural outlook, it must have been very easy for Don Alvaro to assimilate Monsignor Escrivá's teachings on how to speak clearly and sincerely and not beat around the bush. In 1986 a father asked him how he could combine strength with affection in raising his children, and this was his reply: "Just let them see a smile on your face, and they will be happy. When you have to correct them, don't put on a long face. Say with a smile whatever needs to be said, and don't worry. When people know that you really love them, you can tell them anything, no matter how painful." Then he thought about a correction he had had to give to a member of the Work back in the fifties. The fellow had taken it very well, without saying anything. But some time later he mentioned to Don Alvaro that it had hurt him deeply. And then he had the nerve to add that this never happened when Monsignor Escrivá corrected him. Yes, Monsignor Escrivá did it loudly, but in a way that was full of affection. "You, on the other hand," he said to Don Alvaro, "did not raise your voice, but you left me feeling crushed." Don Alvaro's conclusion to this story was, "It was a good lesson for me."

As for me, I don't know who was exaggerating more— that fellow in his self-confident impertinence, or Don Alvaro in his modesty. But in any case, this story backs up something that Don Javier Echevarría said about Don Alvaro in his interview with Pilar Urbano: "He was a person without any duplicity or cunning—someone utterly transparent."

20

The Beatification of Josemaría Escrivá

Some of Don Alvaro's virtues and gifts, such as perseverance, organizational ability, and team spirit, became especially obvious during the preparation of the documentation needed for Monsignor Escrivá's cause for beatification. I myself caught glimpses of how he did his planning in the various stages, how he selected individuals to work on so many things, and how he was always thinking—without being at all overbearing or controlling—how best to advance the cause. The truth is that the solemn ceremony of May 17, 1992, was preceded by thousands of hours of diligent work which produced many pages bound in dozens of volumes. (At this same ceremony, by the way, was also beatified a Conossian Sister from the Sudan, Giuseppina Bakhita: "a luminous testimony to evangelical reconciliation and forgiveness," in the words of Pope John Paul II.)

Popes Paul VI and John Paul II, implementing the directives of the Second Vatican Council, instituted canonical reforms which did simplify the process. But there still remained the enormous task of collecting and studying all the pertinent documents. As Don Alvaro himself said, this work could never have been completed so quickly without the help of modern technology. Computers made it possible to work so much faster and better.

In its 5/17/92 issue, the Madrid newspaper *ABC* carried an article by Don Alvaro. It ends with these words: "I know that my personal debt to Blessed Josemaría is something I can never repay. I was privileged to witness for forty years his pursuit of sanctity, and consequently I feel a great responsibility. Many a time I have asked our Lord to give me at least a little bit of the love that I saw in his heart. In this moment of joy, as an insolvent debtor, I appeal to the mercy of God, to the affectionate loyalty of the members of the Work, and to the prayer of all sons and daughters of the Church."

In a way, though, he did repay that debt, from 1975 on, by tirelessly spreading both the teachings of the founder and private devotion to the future beatus. He advised thousands of souls to have regular recourse to the intercession of Monsignor Escrivá. Again and again he preached that Monsignor Escrivá, from heaven, would give more and better help to those who invoked him in their prayer to God.

Year after year, one could almost literally see that conviction growing in him when the news poured in of all the conversions and increases of love for God that took place at or just after the Masses said for the soul of the founder around June 26 (the date of his death) in many very different cities, such as Rome, Madrid, Bogotá, Manila, and Sydney. Don Alvaro was so moved that tears sprang to his eyes.

It was also with a view to the canonical process that he was eager to hear that the founder's reputation for holiness was spreading. So when he heard reports of special divine favors granted through the founder's intercession, he emphasized the importance of writing them down. And when they had to do with cures of illnesses, he never failed to ask if the relevant medical documentation had been obtained.

What touched him most was the supernatural instinct of the thousands of persons who put their trust in prayer and who looked upon the founder of Opus Dei as a direct and easy way to come to God. Don Alvaro was convinced that Blessed Josemaría served as a loudspeaker for the Holy Spirit within souls and also as a loudspeaker for our requests to our Lord. Through devotion to Blessed Josemaría, and especially at his crypt in Villa Tevere, many souls did indeed make decisions to take their Christian life seriously or to be reconciled with God through confession—some of them for the first time in many years. "Those are the most important miracles," Don Alvaro said in 1983, "though for beatification purposes they don't count and can't be used as such."

Don Alvaro constantly encouraged people to "use" the founder's example and teaching as "instruments" of apostolate. "During his whole life," he pointed out in November 1979, "our Father was a most faithful instrument in the hands of God. Now that he's in heaven, that's what he still is and forever will be, only with greater effectiveness. And now, good father that he is, he is also delighted to be an instrument in our hands. Let us use the example of his life and the richness of his teaching to speak to souls about the marvels of their God."

Already in 1975 Don Alvaro began working on the preparation of the necessary documents. He gave very specific instructions about gathering the founder's writings, accounts of the significant events in his life, and anecdotes. Everything had to be made ready for the canonical process, which would begin later on; as specified by the Congregation for the Causes of Saints, it could not begin until at least five years after the death of the candidate. Meanwhile, Don Alvaro set forth some basic guidelines which would often recur, like a refrain, in the years to come.

The first was the importance of a right intention. Yes,

it was a legitimate and noble thing for us members of Opus Dei to dream of the beatification of our founder with a view to the good it would do for the Work. But we should have as our ultimate goal the glory of God and service to the Church. We should realize that if a person so lovable and so contemporary were set up as a model of sanctity, this would be of great benefit to souls.

Secondly, Don Alvaro insisted that each one of the steps be carried out as well as possible. Monsignor Escrivá had taught and urged people never to do anything slapdash. Therefore, said Don Alvaro, no job should be done just so-so, but especially not any job so directly tied in with the founder.

Finally, since the devil would be opposed to the beatification, we would need a lot of help from God and a lot of humility. On August 6, 1978, at almost the very moment when, some distance away, several members of the Work were being ordained to the diaconate, Don Alvaro said that we should do what they were doing in that ceremony: we should prostrate ourselves on the floor. And, he added, "we should turn our whole life into a constant litany, a litany of continuous requests for help."

The formal petition for initiation of the process was presented to the Congregation for the Causes of Saints in 1980. Don Alvaro had wanted to accompany the postulator, but could not do so because on that day he had the even greater joy of being received in audience by the Holy Father. He did, however, notice a delightful detail: the fact that the registry number for the paperwork was 1339. Monsignor Escrivá often used to play with the numbers 1, 3, and 9 as an expression of his love for the Blessed Trinity. But when Don Alvaro told the students at the Roman College of the Holy Cross about this, he insisted on humility, on not making a lot of noise about it. "We are supposed to pass unnoticed," he said. "We can be sure that our Father does not want us to give ourselves an air of importance over this." And yet something similar happened again a year later, in 1981, when Cardinal Ugo Poletti, the Vicar General of the diocese of Rome, signed the decree introducing the cause and set a date for the constituting of the tribunal.

Don Alvaro kept warning us about possible attacks. They seemed to him entirely to be expected. After all, if we weren't getting somewhere, the devil would not provoke them; difficulties, therefore, would be a sign that we were on the right path. They would be a good way of verifying our progress—"like casting out nines," he would jokingly say. One day he told us that right after some negative pamphlets had been circulated, a bishop had written him to offer his congratulations. "The same kind of thing happened to us Salesians when we started the process of beatification of Saint John Bosco," said this good bishop. "There were terrible slanders against the saint and against his sons. Now that the Holy See has begun the process of beatification of the founder of the Work, it's only natural that the devil should get upset and cause trouble. Congratulations!"

On May 12, 1981, the official opening of the first stage of the process took place in the Lateran Palace, with Cardinal Poletti presiding. A handful of persons attended—just the limited number that the room could hold. It was a solemn and simple ceremony filled with a sense of the supernatural and with a spirit of prayer, as Cardinal Poletti said in his address. Six days later, on May 18, the archbishop of Madrid, Cardinal Tarancón, set up the tribunal for the process of interviewing witnesses who spoke Spanish or who lived in Spain. He appointed as presider of the tribunal Father Rafael Pérez, a well-known Augustinian monk who for many years had served as the promoter of the faith (or devil's advocate) in the Holy See. Father Pérez had a well-deserved reputation for doing things very thoroughly and by the book. Day after day the work went on, in long evening sessions, until June 26,

1984. The solemn closing ceremony was presided over by the new archbishop of Madrid, the Most Reverend Angel Suquía.

I was lucky enough to be present also at the official closing of this first stage of the process, which took place in Rome on November 8, 1986. This ceremony, too, was presided over by Cardinal Poletti and held in the Lateran Palace, but this one took place in the Sala della Conciliazione (the room where the Lateran Treaty was signed in 1929) and was attended by several cardinals and bishops, some ambassadors to the Holy See, and about a thousand other people. In his address, Cardinal Poletti stressed an idea that obviously went very deep with him: that Monsignor Escrivá was "a great founder who has left an indelible mark on the Church and especially in the city of Rome." He finished by expressing this desire: "What we are all hoping is that we will soon see him receive the honor of being raised to the altars and proposed as a model of Christian life for the universal Church. Let us pray to the Lord that he will grant us this grace."

The process continued, and on April 9, 1990, Pope John Paul II promulgated the decree recognizing the heroicity of virtue of the Venerable Josemaría Escrivá de Balaguer. This decree confirmed both the holiness of his life and the orthodoxy of his teaching. When Don Alvaro told the people at Villa Tevere about it, he spoke straight from the heart. "I ask God," he said, "not to let us become vain over this. The declaration of our Father's heroicity of virtue should not serve as fuel for vanity. It should, rather, give us a greater sense of responsibility. It should be the cause of an explosion of desires for holiness all over the world, within the Work."

At the end of April, Don Alvaro celebrated Mass in the oratory of the center on Diego de León Street in Madrid. He began his homily by applying to the founder these words from the Gospel: "Whoever humbles himself will be exalted" (Mt 23:12). He said that at this time, at the beginning of the exaltation of this man who had tried to spend his life hidden, we had to give thanks to God without any boastfulness— that we should, on the contrary, be renewing our own personal surrender to the Lord. That was why he wanted this thanksgiving Mass to be in honor of the Blessed Trinity. In our joy—a just and legitimate joy, the joy of good sons— we should savor, as did Monsignor Escrivá, these words included in the liturgy: "What shall I render to the Lord for all his bounty to me? I will lift up the cup of salvation and call on the name of the Lord" (Ps 116:12–13). We too should embrace the cross and, with the grace of the Lord, do his will. We should reciprocate this great gift from God by trying to be better sons. We should live the spirit of Opus Dei as well as we could, with complete fidelity to the legacy of the founder and with initiative. And, he said, we would do well to imitate the founder by practicing the "Nunc coepi!" (I begin now!).

A little over a year later, on July 6, 1991, the Holy See made public the *super miro* decree on the Venerable Josemaría Escrivá—the official recognition, that is, of the miraculous nature of a physical cure attributed to his intercession. The reaching of this new milestone, of course, put the whole process on its homestretch. The only thing that remained to be done was to set the date for the beatification. To determine the best date, the Holy See would have to take into account not only Pope John Paul's schedule of trips and ceremonies, but also the inevitable organizational concerns, since a huge crowd was expected to attend. The date would be determined after the summer holidays—"post aquas," as Don Alvaro put it, using an expression often used in the Roman Curia. "Do not forget," he wrote in a letter to the centers of the Prelature on July 7, "that this step is a new ringing of a bell by our founder, calling us to decide to be saints and to struggle to belong entirely to God, without compromises or concessions."

Four days later, on July 11, we were awaiting Don Alvaro in Madrid, and on that same morning one of the daily newspapers had in it a highly inaccurate and offensive article about the founder of Opus Dei. It was a resurgence of that negative reaction that Don Alvaro had warned us about so many years before. At the end of the month another article appeared that was in the same vein. Don Alvaro felt sorry for the authors—"May God forgive them," he kept saying— and was pained at the thought of the damage they could do to the Church and to souls. At the same time, I noticed his filial delicacy towards the Holy See. I suggested the possibility of counteracting these negative articles by writing a positive one. But he preferred to wait, at least for a while, so as not to give anyone the impression that we were trying to pressure the Holy See into moving up the date of the beatification.

At the same time, during those days of July 1991, he also received some news which made him very happy, especially since he was from Madrid. Bishop Antonio Astillero, one of the episcopal vicars of Madrid, was in charge of finishing the construction of its cathedral, La Santísima Virgen de Almudena, and he had suggested that one of the side chapels could be dedicated to Monsignor Escrivá, after he was beatified by Pope John Paul. Don Alvaro was delighted. He encouraged us to start thinking of a good design that would commemorate the many times in the life of the founder when he prayed before the image of the Virgin of Almudena that was located outside the city, across from Cuesta de la Vega.

With each new step towards the beatification, gratitude swelled in the heart of Don Alvaro. After he heard that the Holy See had set the date, he confided to the centers of the Prelature what the first impulse of his heart had been. "'Thank you, Lord,' I kept repeating, 'for being so good, for raising up those who have wanted to humble themselves.' All his life our Father tried his best to hide and disappear so that God alone would shine forth, and now God wants to raise him to the altars in glory and set him up as a model of virtue and as an intercessor for everyone's every need."

From the moment that the date was announced, opposition to the papal decision surfaced—especially, by some strange paradox, among avowedly nonreligious media figures. Don Alvaro forgave them, made reparation for their offenses, and encouraged us to keep praying and working with full strength and peacefulness, without failing to state the truth with charity and clarity whenever necessary.

By way of example, in January 1992 an American magazine published some totally fabricated stories about Monsignor Escrivá. Two of the most bizarre were that he had considered leaving the Catholic Church to become an Orthodox and that he had exonerated Hitler with regard to the Holocaust. These pieces of disinformation reached and spread through Europe as well. Don Alvaro did not attach much importance to the first, but he issued a formal statement about the second. "It is absolutely contrary to reality," he said, "to affirm such a thing of a person who so deeply loved the Jewish people and who always so vigorously condemned any kind of tyranny. Today, as soon as I read this magazine article, I contacted the Israeli embassy and some representatives of the Israeli community and I expressed my solidarity with them and my indignation at such lies. I know that in so doing, I am doing nothing other than share in the pain felt by Monsignor Escrivá on account of the holocaust suffered by the Jewish people due to the criminal Nazi program."

On January 9, 1992, Monsignor Escrivá would have turned ninety. Cardinal Angel Suquía, the archbishop of Madrid, marked the occasion by publishing a long article in *ABC* in which he wrote of his joy that this Spanish priest had reached the altars. After all, he said, "it was here in the diocese of Madrid that he received the clear call from the

Lord to incarnate and spread a message of universal scope." On that same day, the *Heraldo de Aragón* carried an article by the Most Reverend Ambrosio Echebarría, the bishop of Barbastro. In 1976, the bishop said, he had heard Pope Paul VI refer to the founder of Opus Dei as "a dearly beloved son of the Church." The Seville edition of *ABC* ran an article written from a different perspective—that of Simón Hassán Benasayag, president of the Jewish community in that Andalusian city. "Apparently they ran out of new things to say about Opus Dei," he wrote. "The invention of a Nazism or an anti-Semitism on the part of the founder is fantasy at its most extreme."

Don Alvaro encouraged us to set the record straight about such preposterous slanders, and went right on finishing up the preparations for the beatification. In that same month of January he spent two or three days in Madrid on the way back from Valencia, where he had attended the funeral of the archbishop of that diocese, the Most Reverend Miguel Roca Cabanella. He took advantage of his stay in Madrid to go up one morning to the future cathedral of La Santísima Virgen de Almudena, which was still under construction, to see what progress had been made on that side chapel which might be dedicated to the soon-to-be beatus. But everything was so covered with dust, and the weather was so icy cold, that it was impossible to envision how it would turn out. On his way back, he joked that it reminded him of the old saying, "Don't show your mother-in-law, your sister-in-law, or your wife anything that's only half done."

At the beginning of April, in keeping with the liturgical season, Don Alvaro sent a letter to the centers of the Prelature about contemplating the cross and the resurrection of Christ. At the end he briefly mentioned "this campaign of calumnies and nonsense which a few people are promoting." He said, "Pray for them, and renew your acts of reparation to our Lord for the offenses they are committing, and let's not lose

a moment's peace over this. Let's conduct ourselves like this
every day, so as to drown evil in an abundance of goodness.
Let us in this way tirelessly spread the truth."

Antonio Prieto, who made a quick trip to Rome that
April, said he was amazed by the viciousness of the anti-
Opus Dei campaign. Don Alvaro said again that we had to
drown all that evil with lots of goodness, staying on guard
against omissions and not being at all sad or pessimistic. At
the beginning of Holy Week more slanders were published
in the biggest national daily newspaper. Those of us who
were directly involved in the matters in question naturally
felt hurt, but we did remain at peace. Don Alvaro's
combination of vigor with peace was a tonic for us. On Holy
Thursday, as a matter of fact, Father Tomás Gutiérrez, the
regional vicar of Spain, received two letters from Rome: one
from Don Javier Echevarría, and the other one from Don
Alvaro.

What Don Alvaro said basically boiled down to this:
what we were going through was a deepening of our identity
with Christ. Christ's followers were called "to endure, like
their Master, misunderstanding and suffering." This kind of
thing had happened throughout the history of the Church.
Actually, he said, these slanders and schemes just amounted
to one more proof of the holiness of the founder. The kernel
of this one-page, closely written letter was this: "Be cheerful,
serene, live *in laetitia,* in joy, with this little cross which is
now ours to carry. Remember what our Father said—that
when the Lord wanted to crown his Work, he placed on it
the seal of the holy cross. This is the divine coin which gives
proof, wherever needed, of its authenticity. And here is
something else I would like you to think about. Our founder
used to cheerfully remark that during and after the forties,
when the persecution got worse, 'in this Spain of mine I was
a spittoon which everyone thought they had a right to spit
into.' Because of his generosity in the face of opposition,

because of that cheerfulness which 'has its roots in the shape of a cross,' the Work grew. And now, in these times of trial for the Church, the Blessed Trinity allows a few people—really very few!—to go on treating the holy memory of our Father as a spittoon. Let us work serenely, because from this episode, too, there will come more glory for God." But just before his signature there is this terse statement: "As for all the nonsense about the process, don't worry at all—everything has been done entirely properly, strictly by the book."

The strength of Don Alvaro infused peace into all those around him. Jordi Miralbell came over from Barcelona to attend the twenty-fifth annual UNIV Congress, and on the last day of it he stopped by Villa Tevere. There he learned that Fernando Valenciano, who worked with Don Alvaro, was suffering from a bout of sciatica, so he decided to go see him. When he got to Fernando's room, he saw the Prelate, who was leaving after having kept Fernando company for a good amount of time. Don Alvaro greeted him very warmly, calling him by his first name and giving him a hug and a kiss, and astonished him with his strength of character. "In the midst of all those slanders," said Jordi, "Don Alvaro was totally calm, just thinking about his sick son. He had the peace of mind to be able to really give him this time, and he was so affectionate. I was very impressed."

A few days later, on April 27, Don Alvaro wrote a short letter to the centers of the Prelature. We were now, as he put it, on the final "sprint" of our preparations for the beatification ceremony, and he wanted to make a few suggestions for the now imminent pilgrimage. Above all, he said, everyone coming to Rome should do so with the spirit of the pilgrims of olden times—praying intensely, being very united with the Blessed Virgin, and generously offering up whatever tiredness or setbacks they might experience during their journeys.

On May 9, 10, and 11, interviews with Don Alvaro were published in several newspapers. At about the same time, a short biography of Blessed Josemaría was printed, along with leaflets for the beatification Mass and the Masses of thanksgiving, as well as practical guides for trips and various functions. Among the many reports and articles in the newspapers (not all of them favorable, of course), there stood out a short but substantial article by Don Alvaro and a long note from the Congregation for the Causes of Saints, both of which reiterated that the process had been carried out in rigorously regular fashion, with no shortcuts taken, notwithstanding defamatory reports to the contrary—which until the very last moment were still being circulated.

On May 17 I followed the ceremonies on television, from Madrid. Even though I was expecting this, I was astonished when I saw how full St. Peter's Square was. There was not the slightest gap anywhere, until fairly far along the Via della Conciliazione. It was harder to capture the atmosphere of fervent piety in that crowd from the microphones (which apparently were hidden), but it could be felt in the solemnity of the liturgy, especially at the end of the rite of beatification, when the images of the new blesseds were unveiled. One could not fail to be impressed by the recollectedness of that multitude; it clearly came from a deep inner joy. It was obvious that when the ceremony ended, the emotional silence would be transformed into a renewed strength for the life of the spirit.

The next morning, the Madrid press gave the beatification front-page coverage. All in all, given the parameters and basic points of view of the newspapers, the reports were very positive. My conclusion was that even those who went to Rome predisposed against it must have been caught by the wonderful atmosphere which they could see with their own eyes in St. Peter's Square. Shorter articles of much the same tenor appeared in the following days.

But Don Alvaro did not dwell on all that. For him the beatification was first and foremost "a powerful summons to all Christians to listen to their call from Jesus, 'who desires all men to be saved and to come to the knowledge of the truth' (1 Tm 2:4)." As for the faithful of the Prelature, he wrote, "every time is a good time for conversion, but especially right now our Lord is inviting us—every man and woman among us—to operate on the basis of a real 'Nunc coepi!'"

On June 3 he was received in audience by Pope John Paul, who told him expressly that he thanked God for the beatification of the founder and that he had been moved by the way everyone participated in the ceremonies celebrated at St. Peter's. That very day, Don Alvaro communicated this in a letter to the centers of the Prelature. "As many of us as there were," he said, "each and every one was a cause of joy to the Vicar of Christ, and was an instrument of apostolate. Let us faithfully respond to this ever new summons, for then the Lord will bless us.

"I feel a holy pride in being a son of our Father, and in being your Father. I see very well, in my own case, that *il sangue del soldato fa grande il capitano*—the soldier's blood puts medals on the captain's chest. I thank all of you, and I ask of you, echoing our Father, 'more, more, more!'

"Pray hard for the Pope and his intentions, and for those who work with him."

21

Culture and the Media

Don Alvaro was well aware of contemporary trends and cultural and social changes. In our get-togethers with him, we often discussed recent books and current issues. He paid attention to what was going on in the world. Because of his intellectual curiosity and his constant concern for the good of souls, nothing was a matter of indifference to him. But he was interested most of all in anything that might have an influence, either positive or negative, on the religious convictions or practices of believers. And he encouraged this kind of interest in the members of Opus Dei. He wanted them to get a good cultural and doctrinal formation, each of them within the context of their own personal and professional situations, so that they in turn could illuminate, with the insights of a well-considered faith, the many pathways of thought and art that our civilization has taken. A coherent Christian life, he said, requires study, time for reflection, intellectual effort—all those things that one needs in order to project the great Christian standards into the daily realities of professional work, cultural activities, and politics.

"It will always be necessary to give doctrine," Don Alvaro wrote at the beginning of 1985, "but there's no question that there are times, such as ours, when this duty takes on a particular urgency." He continually encouraged the one-on-one apostolate, but he also held all Christians responsible for the shaping of public opinion, each according to his or her own possibilities. These would be quite varied—ranging, for instance, from writing letters to the editor to publishing articles and books.

He felt and he preached "the urgency of *doing more*—of constantly carrying out a Christianization of society, and especially of those environments and occupations that are farthest removed from God." And, like Blessed Josemaría, he constantly held up the example of "those Christians of the first centuries—men and women who were quite ordinary, but filled with the Holy Spirit—who with the help of God were able to transform that whole pagan society, making it Christian and therefore also more human."

He expected the faithful of the Prelature to act with spiritual courage and understanding, and not to have complexes, or do anything underhanded, or indulge in sterile lamentation. He also expected them to have a lay mentality, with no hint of clericalism. "In a united effort with other good Christians," he said, "we must try to make sure there is no sphere of secular society in which the light of Christ does not shine. This would include professional associations, labor unions, political parties, city and state governments... This world is fleeing from God. Turning it around and giving it over to him is an important part of the mission we have received. You will accomplish this, my daughters and sons, with the grace of the Lord and with your self-denying efforts, always with personal liberty and responsibility, making use of your rights and duties as citizens."

Ever a lover of culture and knowledge, Don Alvaro wanted the members of the Work to follow faithfully the study plans set up by the founder, so that they would become men and women with an intelligent, informed faith. He did not want them to have a more or less fideistic mentality and either reject or undervalue reason and philosophy. To help them deepen their understanding of the unfathomable riches of the mystery of Christ, Don Alvaro, in his capacity as Grand Chancellor of the University of Navarre, made the publication of good philosophy and theology textbooks a priority. He wanted these books to integrate perennial Catholic teaching with a study of the new problems of the present time. He also wanted them to present the original contributions of the Second Vatican Council and to explain the novelty of the spirit of Opus Dei—a spirit "as old and as new as the Gospel," as Monsignor Escrivá used to say. I remember how happy Don Alvaro was when he held in his hands the first volume of a series published by the University of Navarre.

He also took a great interest in another project undertaken by the University of Navarre's theology faculty: a new, annotated, easy-to-read translation of the Bible. The idea had originally been suggested by Monsignor Escrivá, when he was the Grand Chancellor. Don Alvaro was always happy to hear how the work was coming along—both the work of translating and the writing of the commentaries. He just wished it could all be done even faster.

More than once I told him apostolate-related anecdotes about members of the Work who were teaching in Spain's public universities. On such occasions he would comment on how good it was for young people to choose this kind of career, because of its importance for souls. He completely respected everyone's freedom, but he also wanted everyone to realize that it is very worthwhile to forgo the possibility of a more glamorous or lucrative position for a chance to bring the light of Christ to so many persons by teaching in a university, by putting one's scientific or academic prestige to work in this way. By the same token, he was pained by what was going on in some countries on account of large-scale apathy: university professorships, departmental positions, and administrative posts were being avoided by believers. It grieved him that good people were steering clear of such things because they did not want to complicate their lives.

I sometimes watched with Don Alvaro some videos of a documentary or catechetical nature. He appreciated the value of film; he considered it an excellent means of transmission. And he thought it very important that more persons with good judgment, with the qualities needed to combine technical expertise with a sterling code of ethics, enter this field—if, that is, they freely wanted to. Just by being good at their jobs, they would be called upon to take part in all kinds of different activities... Sometimes, however, our discussions on the audiovisual media had to do with reports or programs which had a negative influence. At those times he would suggest, with a troubled look on his face, that we pray a lot more and get people to actively oppose such things, or at least not to let themselves get used to a kind of irresponsible and indecent coarseness.

One day, in that context, he quoted what Saint Paul said about "making the most of the time, because the days are evil" (Eph 5:16), and he reminded us that these difficulties for the Church, including heresies and persecutions, went all the way back to the first century. But, he added, quoting Blessed Josemaría, when the times are bad, they are for that reason also good. And he reminded us of something else said long ago by the founder of Opus Dei: that Christians should not grasp at planks as if they were seeking their own salvation alone; that they should, on the contrary, resolutely exert themselves to help everyone.

At the end of the 1992 Summer Olympics, which were held in Barcelona, Don Alvaro and those of us then with him naturally thought about the influence of the audiovisual media. Millions and millions of people all over the world had watched on television the opening ceremonies, and now millions were watching the closing ceremonies as well. Don Alvaro dreamed of the apostolic potential of that pivotal sector—a field in which practically nothing had yet been done from the point of view of Catholic faith and doctrine.

But these ambitious apostolic aspirations by no means called for a "corporatizing" of individual initiatives in the arena of public opinion. Members of Opus Dei must each act and make decisions on their own, as the founder had taught and as had been the practice from the very beginning. The formation given to the faithful of the Prelature is meant simply to fortify their own good Christian judgment, through a reviewing and bringing up to date of the doctrine common to all Catholics. It is supposed to develop their own personal ability to analyze events and ideas, so that in every moment and circumstance they can with the greatest liberty and prudence form their own assessment and act on it.

Don Alvaro also reminded us that the Prelature, as Blessed Josemaría had directed, never did or would invest one cent in a media-related activity, since the media necessarily take sides in matters of opinion. It was clear, in other words, that this was an area calling for free personal initiative—of the noblest kind—but never for a concerted apostolic effort on the part of Opus Dei as such. That is why, for example, the Statutes of the Prelature expressly forbid the publishing of newspapers, or of any kind of writing, in the name of the Work.

But freedom should not be confused with indifference. Don Alvaro was delighted with the spontaneous and active interests of members of the Work. Early in July 1993, for instance, the Spanish press gave a lot of coverage to the celebration of the fiftieth anniversary of the Adonais Prize for poetry. Don Alvaro immediately recalled the hopes that Florentino Pérez Embid, a member of Opus Dei who had died in 1974, had put into that contest, which had such a great and well-deserved prestige in Spanish literary circles. And then he mentioned other things, mostly connected with research and with university life, which make it possible to bring a Christian influence to bear in all kinds of areas when one has a high level of professional competence.

His intellectual bent also showed itself in his love for books. From 1976 on, whenever I spent some time with him, sooner or later he would ask me what the young people were reading. Like many other intellectual and cultured people, he worried that the growing influence of the media would have a bad effect on the human and cultural formation of the new generations. He expressed for that reason some well-founded reservations about the predominance of the audiovisual. He saw it as necessary to overcome that kind of "almost pathological dependence on the small screen" which afflicts so many people in every part of the world. Reading, he insisted, develops one's capacity for analysis, enriches one's personality, and allows one to use television in an appropriate and positive way—not passively, but with a sensible critical approach. Also, he said, reading is an essential means for acquiring good self-expression—for learning to articulate one's ideas with precision, clarity, and good style, both in speech and in writing.

In August 1990 he had to point this out to some university students who were taking a summer course in Los Robles (in Asturias). One of them asked a rather starry-eyed question, and he gave the feet-on-the-ground reply that everything nowadays is dreamed for us on television. He talked about the risk of getting attached to things by getting used to not thinking, and he said in conclusion, "Human beings are supposed to reason. Some people don't want us to think; they want us to be puppets that they can easily manipulate. But you must use your intelligence."

He worried about television addiction because of its bad effects not only on culture, but also on family life. It hurt him to see so many TV programs taking the place of dinner talk and other family conversations, and to see families so often splitting up to watch programs on different television sets. He compared the tremendous power of television to that of nuclear energy, which can be used to cure the sick, but can also be used to destroy entire nations and could even put an end to humanity. The solution, he said, was to know how to use television in the home in such a way that it would not pollute or snuff out the atmosphere of a Christian family.

At the same time, he expected parents to exercise their rights and take up arms in the great battle of promoting and carrying out the education of their children—a battle to be waged in love and in peace. He offered them a broad range of suggestions, centering on prayer, friendship, and patience. But he was realistic. "You must bear in mind," he said in Mexico in May 1983, "that children are, indeed, children of their parents, but simultaneously they are children of the times—and the times are very confused."

Not surprisingly, Don Alvaro himself took full advantage of all his contacts with the media, but always in a totally natural way. When the spotlight was on his own life, he never tried to project any kind of image. He just went on fulfilling his duties as Prelate of Opus Dei, without any personal agenda. As Bishop Ambrosio Echebarría summed it up on March 24, 1994, "he was not given to grandstanding."

I myself observed this on several occasions. For example, on his birthday in 1986, when he was in Rome, he took a call from Manuel Antonio Rico, a news reporter for the Madrid radio station COPE. His first remarks were so spontaneous and so unusual that the reporter asked him to repeat them.

"Seventy-two years," said Don Alvaro. "By now it's not just some days, but quite a lot of years, thanks be to God. Help me give thanks to God for all these years of life that he has given me, and to ask pardon for all the offenses I have committed against him. And ask our Lord to give me more help to be good and faithful in the time that I have left."

"It seems to me," said the reporter, "that you should be the one to pray for us, since I would imagine that the president of Opus Dei is closer to God than we are."

"Many people do pray for me. I have a great responsibility before God. So it is I who hold out my hand like a beggar to ask for the alms of your prayer and your affection."

"What you are saying, Monsignor del Portillo, is really beautiful."

"The important thing is not to say it with words that are more or less beautiful, but to actually be faithful to our Lord—that is the important thing. I wish you and all your listeners happiness, peace, and grace from God. And joy, because we Christians should always be joyful, no matter what happens."

That conversation, which lasted for about ten minutes, got across very well the naturalness and simplicity of Don Alvaro, as well as the warmth of his thoroughly priestly heart.

A few years later, during his stay in Asturias in August 1990, he went to visit the archbishop of Oviedo, the Most Reverend Gabino Díaz Merchán, who was celebrating the twenty-fifth anniversary of his ordination as a bishop. They were such good friends that they called each other by their first names, and since their patron saints had the same feast day (February 19), they sent each other greeting cards. Well, when Don Alvaro arrived, a television crew was already there, getting ready to film an interview with the archbishop, and they decided to film Don Alvaro as well and ask him a few questions. On that same day they broadcast some of his answers on the local news, and then, that night, on the national news. But the context was not mentioned, and as a result the remarks sounded rather odd. Don Alvaro was not at all concerned, though he did comment that the report was rather confused and that no one would know why he had said those things.

His natural openness was accompanied, of course, by the necessary reticence. He did point out that the demands of the law and the right to information are compatible with a respect for privacy. "Private things should be kept private," he said. "You don't need to go around talking about them. You don't need to flaunt them, like banners in the wind." But this he also said: "To do apostolate, you must say, 'I am in Opus Dei, and this is what Opus Dei is all about...' so that there is no possibility of secrecy."

He certainly did not shrink from difficulties. This has already been shown in connection with the juridical journey of Opus Dei and the beatification of the founder. To the bottom of his heart, Don Alvaro was utterly detached from human judgments. With Saint Paul he knew that "it is the Lord who judges me" (1 Cor 4:4). No matter what might happen, he strode forward without slackening his apostolic pace. Never was he deterred by arguments based on "what people are going to say." In November 1986 he wrote, "Are people criticizing us? Slandering us? Interpreting our activity in a twisted way? Lying about us? Conducting smear campaigns against us? We, with the help of God, must keep in mind that he is the one to judge us, and must keep moving forward without deviating one bit from the way that God has marked out for us. We must also sincerely love all those who are starting or spreading those vicious rumors."

On July 12, 1980, terrorists bombed the main building of the University of Navarre. Don Alvaro was in England at the time. When he heard the news, he insisted that everyone stay very calm and serene and make acts of atonement, and said he would send a letter. The letter was brought over by the rector of the university, Alfonso Nieto, who had also been spending a few days in England. When Nieto arrived, he talked about how moved he was by the words of affection that Don Alvaro had lavished on him and the university on the day after the bombing. But he was even more struck, he said, by Don Alvaro's insistence that they should with all their hearts forgive the culprits, pray for them, and carry on with a greater determination their work at the university, as well as appeal to many individuals and institutions that could help with repairing the damage.

The Spanish press highlighted the event, and several newspapers ran editorials condemning the bombing and expressing support for the university. Don Alvaro was very happy to hear of the spontaneous gestures of support coming from so many people in Pamplona—including the less educated. One laborer came and donated his July bonus. Others were not able to give money, but they offered free of charge their services as carpenters or electricians. Many letters arrived with checks, or with a promise to send a check as soon as possible. A good part of this support, of course, came from students, from parents of students, and from alumni.

Don Alvaro was not concerned about any obstacles in the area of public opinion. All he cared about was service to the Church. He accepted all obstacles in advance, with a supernatural outlook. "It is very good for us to suffer difficulties and misunderstandings," he said, "because this makes it clear that we are working not for applause, but for God. Many people, of course, love the Work and think that what we do is very good. But when we see someone giving a twisted interpretation to the good things we are doing, it makes it easier for us to look to God and not to human approval. It makes us keep rectifying our intentions."

He just kept working away with joy, with optimism, without any worrying. This became especially obvious in November 1985, in an answer he gave a reporter in the Netherhall House auditorium in London. Religious ignorance, he said, imposes on believers the clearest duty to work in the apostolate of communicating doctrine, so as to "bring light to minds that are in darkness." Of course, he added, we should do this "without trying to give lectures" and "with great affection, with charity, without offending or humiliating anyone."

Throughout all these difficulties, he also kept his sense of humor. During his visit to Australia in January 1987, he had a get-together with over a thousand people in Clancy Auditorium, at the University of New South Wales. An Opus Dei cooperator named Paul, who was living in Tasmania, said to him, "From what I have observed, and from seeing all these people here today, I can't help but be puzzled by the comments that some people make about Opus Dei. In my contact with the Work, I've never seen any indication that there was some kind of secret. Father, is there some secret?" Don Alvaro smiled and gave the answer that the founder sometimes used to give: "Whenever you hear someone talk about a secret, ask that person to tell me about it, because it isn't fair for me to be the Prelate of Opus Dei and not be in on its secrets!"

22

Ordination as a Bishop

On January 6, 1991, almost nine years after Opus Dei was established as a personal prelature, Pope John Paul II ordained Don Alvaro a bishop. This was very much in keeping with the jurisdictional and hierarchical nature of the Prelature. So, with that in mind, Don Alvaro showed in a particularly resplendent way his prudence and humility. When Pope John Paul decided to make him a bishop, Don Alvaro made it clear that he was happy about this because— and only because—it would be good for the Work. When, for example, he gave the news at Villa Tevere on December 7, 1990, he referred to himself mostly in third person. "I wanted to tell you," he said, "that the Holy Father has decided to make the Prelate of Opus Dei a bishop. The news was made public today, at noon. The Prelate will receive the sacrament of Holy Orders in its fullness. There will be a fresh outpouring of the Holy Spirit upon the head of the Work and, through the communion of saints, in some way, on all of Opus Dei."

He chose as the motto for his episcopal shield one that was often used by Blessed Josemaría to sum up the apostolic purpose of Opus Dei: "Regnare Christum volumus!" (We want Christ to reign!). As usual, he was thinking not about himself, but about service to the Church. That, he kept saying, "is the sole reason for our existence and for the existence of the Prelature." His thoughts also kept going back to the fidelity of the founder of the Work. On the day after his episcopal ordination, in the pontifical Mass which he celebrated in the Basilica of Sant'Eugenio, a good part of his homily consisted of a fervent act of thanksgiving to God and also to Monsignor Escrivá. He was convinced that this event was a fulfillment of the words of Scripture, "A father's blessing strengthens the houses of the children" (Sir 3:9).

That Don Alvaro did not think of himself became especially obvious in connection with these events in his life and in the history of Opus Dei. I saw this most clearly during the days just before the priestly ordination of members of the Prelature on September 1, 1991. It was his first time to ordain priests since his episcopal consecration. Shortly before doing so, he asked everyone present to pray hard to the Holy Spirit that in his laying on of hands, he would touch not only the souls of the new priests but his own soul as well, since it was going to be a channel for the outpouring of the Holy Spirit.

That basic idea of being an instrument must have gone very deep in his heart, because in those days, in one way or another, he mentioned it often. He asked everyone to pray for those about to be ordained, that they would receive the sacrament with a very deep faith. But he also asked everyone to pray for him, that he would confer the sacrament with great piety. When he got to Torreciudad, his gratitude to God for so many good things was quite obvious—he expressed it constantly, out loud. Also obvious was his continual sense of the presence of Blessed Josemaría. He never ceased to insist that all of this had been made possible by the founder's heroic fidelity to the spirit he had received from God. "Even more than usual," he said at the beginning of his homily, "my thoughts necessarily turn to our most

With Rev. Javier Echevarría and Rev. Joaquín Alonso in the summer of 1980.

With a young patient in 1985 in the hospital of the University of Navarre, of which he was the Chancellor.

With members of Opus Dei from India in 1993.

Being ordained a bishop by Pope John Paul II in 1991.

beloved and holy founder. By his exemplary dedication to God, he made possible what we are now beholding." On such occasions, when it would have been most understandable if he claimed for himself some human glory, he all the more considered himself just a shadow of the founder—a shadow inseparable from the being, the person, of the founder.

On September 7, just a few days after the ordination in Torreciudad, Don Alvaro celebrated a pontifical Mass at the University of Navarre, at the request of the board of directors. When he got to the homily, which he had put entirely in writing, he prefaced it with a few spontaneous words. "Before I start talking," he said, "allow me for a moment to raise my heart to God to thank him for the sight of this vast assembly of people, both men and women, who love God and who for that reason wanted to come to a Mass that has no purpose other than to praise God, to bless God, and to ask God for the graces we so much need."

Don Alvaro tried to make use of whatever he did, and of whatever things he was using at the time, to deepen his friendship with the Lord. For instance, one could easily see that he was using his episcopal ring and cross as reminders for his contemplative dialogue throughout the day.

One day, at the end of an audience with Pope John Paul, Don Alvaro asked him to do him the favor of trying on for a moment his pastoral ring. After Pope John Paul did so, Don Alvaro explained, "This ring gives me a great sense of the presence of God, because it is the symbol of my union with Opus Dei. It signifies that I am a slave, a servant of the Work, for love of the Church and of the Pope. But now that Your Holiness has worn this ring, it will also give me a great sense of the presence of the Pope." On many occasions I saw him discreetly lift the ring to his lips, evidently using it as a human device for renewing his love and rejuvenating his dedication.

By virtue of his ordination as a bishop, Don Alvaro became, of course, a member of the episcopal college. From that point on, he would live also sacramentally in the close union with the bishops which he had learned to value during his many years at the side of the founder of Opus Dei, and which he had cultivated with ever increasing generosity throughout his life.

I spent several summers with Don Alvaro, and people often would ask me afterwards to tell them my impressions and to relate anecdotes. One year I summed it all up with this expression from Saint Paul: "anxiety for all the churches" (2 Cor 11:28). To spend a few weeks with Don Alvaro basically meant getting a more universal outlook. One constantly heard a lot of news, both joyful and worrisome news, about what was going on in the Church in so many places all over the world. One example: in the middle of August 1992, Don Alvaro was delighted to hear that Pope John Paul was recovering very well from the operation he had just undergone. But he took that occasion to mention another great suffering that the Pope had undergone a few days before the operation: anxiety about the situation of the Church in a certain country. And, with great delicacy and prudence, he pointed out in general terms some serious problems in the life of the Church in countries on different continents. His observations and commentaries, all of which were preceded and accompanied by requests for much more prayer, clearly reflected his unity with and affection for all the bishops of the world.

A year later, when his health was in a bad state (following a cataract operation), I wrote in my diary, "He looks very tired, but in spite of everything, his 'anxiety for all the churches' is still very much in evidence. He constantly shows concern for his children and for the Work, always with a great naturalness, in the simple and ordinary things of family life." Actually, on that very day (this was in July), he had invited us to pray for a priest of the Prelature who was experiencing some alarming symptoms and was going in for a checkup; he had praised some work done long before by another priest of the Prelature, Father Victorio Lorente, editor of some widely disseminated prayer books; he had discussed some activities related to spiritual and apostolic formation; and, more to the point, he had commented on several matters relating to the Church in Latin America— this was right after the assassinations of a Mexican cardinal and of the military ordinary of El Salvador—and in Spain, which Pope John Paul had recently visited. Such topics came up in his conversation quite spontaneously, at any time of day, because they were so much on the mind and in the heart of this son of the Church.

Ever since I started working closer to him physically, I could observe and appreciate the cordiality with which he referred to bishops. I could also see his deep joy when members of the Work—especially the directors—showed them veneration and affection, following the example of Monsignor Escrivá. In a letter he wrote on August 7, 1976, to members of the Work who were going to be ordained in Madrid, there is a paragraph which summarizes very well this important aspect of the life of Don Alvaro.

"Always stay very united," he said, "to the Roman pontiff, the common father of the faithful, the Vicar of Christ on earth—the 'Vice-Christ,' as our Father so lovingly used to call him—and, in each diocese, to the bishop, showing him deep affection and great respect. Remember the immense love, both theological and human, which our beloved founder had for the diocesan ordinaries. He taught us, with his own holy example, to love them and to obey them in everything that falls within the scope of their holy, magisterial authority, as the legitimate pastors that they are. He reminded us a thousand times, using this very vivid image, that we must 'pull the cart' in the same direction in which they are pulling it; that the results of our apostolate remain in their dioceses, which we love; that we feel like and we are (as he so often liked to say) diocesan priests in all the dioceses in which we work; and that the bishops already have a heavy cross to carry, their pectoral cross, and we have no right to place new ones on their shoulders."

One of the reasons he worked so hard for Opus Dei's establishment as a prelature was to make it possible for the Work to serve the local churches by giving spiritual assistance to diocesan priests. This canonical structure would make crystal-clear, once and for all, that it was impossible for the associate and supernumerary members of the Priestly Society of the Holy Cross to be bound to what might be called a "double obedience." Since the Priestly Society is "inseparably united to" the Prelature, but not a part of it, its members have no superior other than their own diocesan bishop.

Don Alvaro was, as I have mentioned before, good friends with many bishops and other Church dignitaries. Some had been theology professors of his. One of these was Cardinal Bueno Monreal, the archbishop of Seville. In August 1987 Don Alvaro read in the paper that this archbishop had entered the hospital at the University of Navarre, and that his prospects were not good. In the next family get-together, he mentioned him with great affection, and from there his thoughts went on to the other Spanish bishops. One could tell that he really loved them, that he prayed for each and every one of them, and that he truly did want to "pull the cart" in the directions determined by those prelates in their respective dioceses. Not long afterwards, he was told that Cardinal Bueno had died. Immediately he prayed the "Eternal rest" prayer for the repose of his soul, and then called to mind events from his life of service to the Church. He thought, too, of the affection that this man had had for Monsignor Escrivá—an affection now matched by Don Alvaro's affection for him.

Another case in point was Archbishop Miguel Roca, of Valencia, who on January 8, 1992, was killed in a car accident. I myself was very saddened by the news, because Archbishop Roca had been very close to Monsignor Escrivá and because he had relatives in Opus Dei. But I hardly imagined that Don Alvaro would be showing up in Madrid on January 10, on his way to Valencia to attend the funeral. He had at that time an enormous workload. I had not realized the depth of his sense of friendship and gratitude, although he had already shown it some years before, when he went to Cologne to attend the funeral of Cardinal Josef Höffner.

From Don Alvaro I learned how to love the bishops even more. No detail, no matter how small, was unimportant to him. He immediately made his own every problem affecting the local churches. In August 1988 I read in the paper a news item about the percentage of Spanish citizens who had declared on their tax forms that they wanted part of their tax money to go to the Catholic Church. The total amount thus designated was less than expected and needed. Don Alvaro was pained by this. He encouraged us directors to help the members of Opus Dei become more apostolic so that they, in their own respective ways, could help remedy this situation, since it was so closely tied in with the formation of the faithful and with actual religious practice.

Naturally, the bishops were thankful for the apostolic work done by the Opus Dei members in their dioceses. More than once I heard bishops thank Don Alvaro in front of Bishop Juan Fremiot Torres Oliver, the bishop of Ponce (in Puerto Rico) and the president of the Puerto Rican Episcopal Conference, when Don Alvaro made his pastoral visit to that Caribbean island in 1988. He himself was so hospitable that he even gave Don Alvaro his first pectoral cross. And when he learned that there would be in San Juan a get-together for priests, he wrote a note to the rector of the diocesan seminary which read, "I declare tomorrow, February 22, to be a day of no classes so that all the seminarians who so desire may attend the meeting which the Prelate of Opus Dei is having in San Juan with the priests of Puerto Rico. The visit of Monsignor del Portillo is a source of spiritual graces for the whole island."

Many bishops spoke publicly of their friendship with Don Alvaro when they heard the news of his death. It then became quite obvious that his sincere affection had been reciprocated with deep gratitude by prelates on every continent. Cardinal Joseph Bernardin, the archbishop of Chicago, expressed his gratitude for the spiritual and moral support that Don Alvaro had given him during those months when he had been the object of those terribly false, slanderous accusations. Cardinal Jaime Sin, the archbishop of Manila, emphasized his good humor. During trips to Rome, he said, they had often dined together, and they had had such a good time, they had laughed so much, that people who didn't know them might have thought they were crazy.

To get a good idea of all this, it's enough just to glance at the closely printed pages of *Romana,* the Prelature newsletter, on which are listed the Masses offered for the repose of the soul of Don Alvaro by bishops all over the world. In their homilies nearly all of these bishops recalled times that they had spent with him, under all kinds of different circumstances. "For me," said Cardinal James Hickey, the archbishop of the District of Columbia, "these encounters were an inspiration." Cardinal Ernesto Corripio Ahumada, the primate of Mexico, gave during a Mass at the Basilica of Our Lady of Guadalupe a brief biographical profile of Don Alvaro, which ended as follows: "The result of all this was a fruitful service to the universal Church and to its visible head, the Roman pontiff, carried out in cordial cooperation with the local churches and their respective ordinaries, whom he loved as brothers and always helped with great generosity."

Don Alvaro really meant every word of what he had

written to the centers of Opus Dei five days before his ordination as a bishop: "The entire Prelature—I will never get tired of repeating this—exists to serve the universal Church and each of the local churches. This includes not just all the ones where we are now working, but also all those to which our apostolic efforts will eventually extend. For this reason, there weighs and always will weigh upon the Prelate a real 'anxiety for all the churches'—a loving solicitude for the Mystical Body of Christ, a solicitude founded on the virtue of charity. His episcopal ordination will confer on that solicitude a new sacramental strength, since on every bishop—as a member of the College of Bishops, which succeeds the College of Apostles—falls in a particular way, 'with Peter and under Peter,' a responsibility for the whole Church."

23

The Affection of
Pope John Paul II

On October 16, 1978, the archbishop of Kraków, Cardinal Karol Wojtyla, was elected pope. Don Alvaro had gotten to know him during the years of the Second Vatican Council. He had, in fact, been introduced to him by another Polish bishop, the Most Reverend Andrzej Deskur.

As Don Alvaro told it in 1983, "Between our working sessions in St. Peter's Basilica, we would walk up and down the lateral naves for a little while to refresh ourselves. And it was at one of those times that Bishop Deskur—he was the secretary of one of the council commissions, and I was the secretary of another—said to me, 'Would you like for me to introduce you to the auxiliary bishop of Kraków? He's a very good friend of mine.' He was walking toward us, with someone else. I told Bishop Deskur that I would be most delighted to meet him, so he asked Bishop Wojtyla to join us. I even remember the exact place we met. It was in the lateral nave that is on your right if you're coming in by the main door, and it was near the relics of an Eastern saint, Saint Josaphat. That is where I met the future pope, who was then a young, tall, strong bishop."

After the election by the conclave, Don Alvaro issued a press release saying that he was very happy "because we—all human beings—have received from God a great gift." He also mentioned that he had been quite touched "to see His Holiness John Paul II, in the balcony of St. Peter's, with the weight of Peter upon his shoulders, invoking the Lord and twice appealing to the Blessed Virgin for help."

On the first day of Pope John Paul's pontificate, Don Alvaro went to visit Bishop Deskur, who had recently suffered a stroke and was still in critical condition. No one could possibly have imagined that on his very first day as pope, Pope John Paul would leave the Vatican to go see his great friend Andrzej Maria Deskur. This happy coincidence allowed Don Alvaro to spend a few moments with the Holy Father. Pope John Paul gave him a big hug and a couple of kisses, in accord with both Polish and Italian custom, and a few affectionate words.

Over the years, there were all kinds of little things that showed the great affection that Pope John Paul had for Don Alvaro. As Don Javier Echevarría described it in his interview with Pilar Urbano, their friendship was very "natural, confident, and spontaneous." Pope John Paul, he said, "saw in Don Alvaro a loyal and sincere son who would tell him things just as they were."

The Holy Father also knew that the only power, the only strength, that Opus Dei has is the power of prayer. As Don Javier also mentioned in that interview, Pope John Paul was very impressed by "a letter which the then-Monsignor del Portillo wrote him in 1978, at the beginning of his pontificate, from the shrine of Mentorella. In this letter, he offered him the only treasure of the Work: the prayers and daily Masses offered by its members, who then numbered about sixty thousand."

In 1979 the annual UNIV Congress took place, as usual, during Holy Week. As Pope Paul VI had done, Pope John

Paul II granted an audience to all these students. Well, during this audience he received several rounds of applause, to which he responded with some off-the-cuff remarks. At first he was surprised by the applause—especially since the first round of it came when he mentioned the sacrament of Reconciliation. But from then on, he took the time to comment on and to recapitulate whatever topics elicited applause. So, towards the end of his talk, after mentioning an article by Cardinal Luciani (Pope John Paul I) about sanctifying ordinary work and turning it into a "daily smile," he said, "Now let's count again: The first round of applause was for confession; the second, for service; the third, for cheerfulness; the fourth, for Papa Luciani; the fifth, for smiles." Then he proceeded with his speech. "Finally," he said, "I ask the Blessed Virgin, *Sedes Sapientiae* [Seat of Wisdom]..." At that, all those present leapt to their feet and gave him a resounding ovation. Only after several attempts was the Pope able to go on and finish his talk. At the end, with a happy expression on his face, he once again did his summing up: "The sixth round of applause, louder than all the rest, *Sedes Sapientiae*..."

A Spanish newspaper headlined its report of the audience as "Almost a Party." The headline was prophetic, for one year later, on Easter Sunday, the Pope started a tradition of receiving the UNIV participants in the courtyard of Saint Damasus, in an informal gathering filled with questions and answers, news from the students and comments by the Holy Father, songs and applause, spontaneity and deeply felt emotion. Pope John Paul looked very happy, as if this was his way of recovering from an exhausting Holy Week. It also showed the affection he had for Opus Dei and for the one who would soon be its Prelate.

On February 7, 1980, Pope John Paul sent a letter with an apostolic blessing for Don Alvaro, for Opus Dei, and particularly for the women of the Work, on the occasion of the fiftieth anniversary of the founding of the women's branch. In his letter he evoked "the unforgettable figure of the founder, Monsignor Josemaría Escrivá de Balaguer, whose priestly heart pulsated with great zeal for the Church and, at the same time, for contemporary humanity." Then he spoke of the spiritual and apostolic fruitfulness of the work of the women of Opus Dei and urged that they, "in full fidelity to Christ and to the Church, in the spirit of the norms and guidelines given by the venerable founder, in loyal and sincere cooperation with the hierarchy, continue to offer a constant and growing testimony of Christian faith—a strong and crystal-clear testimony—in today's society."

In light of his filial affection for Pope John Paul, it is easy to understand how Don Alvaro felt after the attempt on the Pope's life which took place in St. Peter's Square in 1981, on May 13, the feast of Our Lady of Fatima. Immediately he went to Gemelli Hospital, where the Pope had been taken. From the very first moment he kept strongly insisting, in a voice full of emotion, on the need for prayer and reparation. Throughout that time, he tried to make a visit to St. Peter's every day. He would say the joyful mysteries of the rosary on his way there, a Creed in St. Peter's Square (often without getting out of the car, but nevertheless fixing his gaze in the direction of the Holy Father's room), the sorrowful mysteries on his way back, and the glorious mysteries when he got home. He kept praying and getting others to pray for the Pope's recovery.

After an initial period of recovery, Pope John Paul began to suffer some complications and had to be hospitalized again; this happened around June 20. Don Alvaro expressly asked the members of Opus Dei to intensify their prayer for the Pope. It was, as I learned at the end of July 1981, his primary concern. He was always talking about the Pope. And he prayed even harder on August 5, when he heard that the Holy Father would be undergoing another operation.

Incessantly he asked us to "pray for the Pope, that there will be no complications." We all listened attentively to the radio and television news, and he never let up on his prayer campaign until the news started to get better. I'll never forget how moved he was on August 15, when he heard the Holy Father on the radio. With great piety he fell to his knees to receive his apostolic blessing. I also remember his joy when he saw on television how much better the Pope looked during his Angelus address in Castel Gandolfo on August 23.

A year later, upon arriving in Madrid from Rome, Don Alvaro showed us some photos from the audience which the Pope had just given him. While he was showing them to us, he took plenty of time just looking at them himself, and we were struck by the affectionate, grateful, son-like expression on his face.

On January 15, 1984, as part of his regular Sunday schedule of making pastoral visits to the churches of the Rome diocese, Pope John Paul visited San Giovanni Battista al Collatino, a parish in the suburb of Tiburtino which had been entrusted to priests of the Prelature. Not even twenty years had gone by since Pope Paul VI, on November 21, 1965, had dedicated this parish. That had been an especially emotional day for Monsignor Escrivá. Upon leaving, Pope Paul had given him a big, long, very affectionate hug—right next to the papal car—and had said to him, "Tutto, tutto qui è Opus Dei!" (Everything, everything here is Opus Dei!). And now, in 1984, when Pope John Paul was finishing his visit to the parish, to Safi School, and to Centro ELIS, he took some time to speak with regional vicars of Opus Dei who had come from all over the world to spend a few days working in Rome. He greeted them one by one and then, at the end, made a few extemporaneous remarks. He encouraged the faithful of the Prelature (since they were represented by the Prelate and his vicars) "to be ever more Opus Dei and to do Opus Dei in every dimension of the world." Don Alvaro

was especially touched by this because, as he explained in
the letter he sent to the Pope to thank him for his visit to
Tiburtino, "Your Holiness said the very same thing that our
founder used to say to us."

In 1985, when requesting prayers for the success of one
of the Holy Father's pastoral visits, Don Alvaro said, "We're
always going to be very united to the pope, whoever he may
be. It makes no difference if he's Polish or Vietnamese, tall
or short, young or old; he is the common father of all
Christians. I am older than Pope John Paul, but in spite of
that, from the very day he was elected, I have felt that I am
his son. Thanks to the faith that God has given us, we all
feel the same."

He said something similar also at the end of that year,
when the international press made sharp attacks on Pope
John Paul in connection with the extraordinary synod he
convoked on the twentieth anniversary of the Second Vatican
Council. "We will continue to be," he said, "just as we have
been up to this point, very united to the pope—to John Paul
II, just as we were to his predecessors and as we will be to his
successors—because the pope is Christ on earth. Maybe
people will say that this is worshipping the pope... We don't
care what they say. We have the pride of knowing that we
are children of God and children of the pope as well, since
he is the common father of all Christians."

The occasion on which I saw most clearly and vividly
the depth of Don Alvaro's devotion towards Pope John Paul
was on Sunday, July 12, 1992. Late in the afternoon of that
day, Don Alvaro arrived in the town of Zubiarte (in Navarre),
having left Switzerland that morning. There he had visited
and looked after some of his sons, especially Father Augusto
Costa, who was seriously ill. (He would die a few months
later, on February 13, 1993.) He had traveled by car from
the Barcelona airport and was totally exhausted. When he
greeted me, I was surprised that he said nothing about Pope

John Paul's health, since that morning, during his Angelus address, the Holy Father had publicly asked for prayers—he had told everyone that he was going to the hospital for exploratory tests.

As I soon ascertained, Don Alvaro had in fact not heard about this, because he had not turned on the car radio. So I prepared myself to give him the news, even though this was very hard for me, since I had never seen him so exhausted. On his way to the chapel for his afternoon prayer, he saw in the living room a brand-new book about the beatification of the founder of Opus Dei, a book with some wonderful photos. As he turned the pages, he seemed to recover almost completely. He made comments about both Pope John Paul and Blessed Josemaría that were full of admiration and affection.

I finally gave him the painful news at about eight o'clock that night. He reacted with serene concern and a desire for more information. So we attentively listened to the nine o'clock news, but we heard little more than we already knew. A bit later, however, Francisco Vives called us from Rome and filled us in on more of the details.

Scarcely two hours had passed since I had broken the news to Don Alvaro, but those two hours were lived with a tremendous human and spiritual intensity. I remember that Don Alvaro was extremely tired, worn out, but also wonderfully calm and connected with God. He was truly worried about the Pope's health, but at the same time he abandoned himself confidently to the will of God. His anxiety about the situation in the Church coexisted with a quite evident supernatural peace. One could feel that he had begun to pray about this problem from the very moment he first heard about it. We sat in the garden for a while. A doctor, Alejandro Cantero, suggested some explanations and possibilities based on the few facts we knew. The conversation was broken from time to time with long periods of silence.

That very night, Don Alvaro decided to return to Rome immediately. A son, he told us, ought to stay close to his sick father, even if his father is in the hands of good doctors. By eleven o'clock we had made, by phone, the reservations for the different flights, and the next morning Don Alvaro flew from Pamplona to Barcelona and from Barcelona to Rome. He had forgotten all about his fatigue, though it was still quite obvious. Ignacio Font, a fellow who spoke with him during the layover in Barcelona, recalls that when it came time to say good-bye, he felt obliged to suggest to Don Alvaro that he take care of himself. Don Alvaro, he says, looked at him affectionately and answered, "The truth is, my son, that I am indeed very tired—but we have done our duty."

When he arrived in Rome, he went straight to the hospital to ask about the Pope's condition, although, of course, he did not get to see him.

Nine days later he returned to Zubiarte—an unmistakable sign that the Pope was enjoying an excellent postoperative recovery. Don Alvaro very attentively kept up with the news from Rome, hoping that Pope John Paul would soon be able to resume his regular activities, and he energetically encouraged us to pray for a complete recovery. And soon we did see, on the national nightly news, footage of the Pope leaving the hospital on his own two feet. He was thin, but he looked well. How happy Don Alvaro was! Several times he said in a loud voice, "Thanks be to God!"

In his governing of Opus Dei, as one would expect, Don Alvaro loyally supported the Magisterium and went along with all rulings made by the Roman pontiffs—both doctrinal and pastoral rulings. He zealously transmitted to the faithful of the Prelature every word that the Holy Father directed to all Christians. But this is surely so obvious that there is no need to expand on it. I shall therefore limit myself to pointing out how wholeheartedly he seconded Pope John

Paul in his fights for world peace.

Don Alvaro had had in his soul a passion for world peace from the days of his youth—even before suffering all those hardships of the Spanish Civil War. Ordained a priest in 1944, he celebrated his first solemn Mass on the feast of Saint Irenaeus. He had a special devotion to this saint, partly because the liturgy for his feast included a prayer for peace which he knew by heart: "Da nobis illam quam mundus dare non potest pacem." He said, "Let us indeed ask the Lord to 'give us that peace which the world cannot give.' Why? Because the peace that God gives is tranquillity in the order of subordination, of filiation, of love for our Lord."

In 1986 Pope John Paul issued urgent pleas to those responsible for the many conflicts then raging. Specifically, in an address given in Lyons on October 4, he asked them to observe "a complete truce for at least the whole day of October 27." On October 27 he was going to be holding, in Assisi, an ecumenical and interreligious day of prayer for peace. So on October 11 Don Alvaro wrote a letter to the centers of the Prelature. Its purpose was very clear. "We must exert ourselves," he said, "so that to heaven will rise a great clamor of prayer, together with a fast, for peace in the world."

As for me, it was quite an emotional experience to be on that day in the central headquarters of Opus Dei and to attend there a Mass "for peace and justice," as Don Alvaro had asked us all to do. In such times as these, he said, we should in a special way have recourse to the maternal intercession of the Blessed Virgin Mary, the Queen of Peace. He asked us also to reflect deeply on the realities involved. "Peace," he said, "is a good of incalculable value. For individuals and nations to be able to live and to progress with human dignity, with the dignity proper to the 'image and likeness of God,' peace is necessary. But there is so little peace in the world! There is, instead, so much injustice, hatred, and division!"

At the beginning of the Pope's address in St Peter's Square on the day after the beatification of Opus Dei's founder in 1992.

With Rev. Javier Echevarría, the present Bishop Prelate of Opus Dei.

Celebrating his last Mass in Jerusalem in the Church of the Cenacle, on 22 March 1994.

Pope John Paul II praying before the body of Don Alvaro on the day of his death.

In 1989 Pope John Paul asked all the bishops to proclaim a day of prayer for peace in Lebanon. As the ordinary of Opus Dei, Don Alvaro asked the faithful of the Prelature to dedicate October 7, the feast of Our Lady of the Rosary, to prayer for this intention, in addition to whatever day was decided upon by the bishops of their own dioceses.

A few months later, he insisted that we pray that war would not break out in the Persian Gulf. When, in spite of everything, hostilities did commence, he communicated to the faithful of the Prelature his desire that we keep praying for peace, staying very united to the intentions of the Holy Father. He did the same at the beginning of 1993, and again in January of 1994, on behalf of peace in the Balkans.

Here is a little something that he also did, right up to the end of his days on earth. He used to keep for a while the holy cards of our Lady—under her various titles—which he had been given on his trips or had received in the mail. He would keep a few of them on his desk as a reminder of the reality of the Queen of Peace and as a help towards keeping up a personal relationship with her. From time to time he would set those aside and replace them with others. The last holy cards he had on this big desk of his were these two: an image of Our Lady of Bonaigua (near Barcelona) and one issued by the Holy See for the day of prayer for peace in Bosnia.

Death took him by surprise in March 1994, just after his return from the Holy Land. During his last days, Don Javier Echevarría later wrote, "he held, with many of the faithful, pastoral meetings in which he encouraged them to work for peace. Social peace is a consequence of interior peace, which comes from a personal correspondence to divine grace—from, in other words, the struggle that each of us wages against the stains of sin that we carry within our soul."

On March 19 Don Alvaro held a get-together in Bethlehem. All kinds of people came to it: Christians of various denominations, Palestinians and Israelis, diplomats from various countries, and even a group of German seminarians that Don Alvaro had just met on this trip to the Holy Land. Someone asked him in Arabic what Christians could do to promote peace, and how they could open wide to others their arms and their hearts. "We have to love everyone," he replied. "Think of yourself as having no enemies, even if some people seem to you to be treating you badly. Think of Jesus Christ. He died on the cross to save everyone—every person, without exception. Jesus Christ did not see anyone as an enemy; he loved everyone in the whole world."

At 6:30 on the morning of March 23, Don Javier Echevarría telephoned Monsignor Stanislaw Dziwisz, Pope John Paul's personal secretary, to tell him of Don Alvaro's death. He was calling at this early hour, he said, in hopes that the Pope could be informed in time to remember Don Alvaro in his Mass. Monsignor Dziwisz assured him that he would tell the Pope immediately, and that he would indeed remember Don Alvaro in his Mass. Don Javier soon learned that not only had the Holy Father offered his Mass for Don Alvaro, but he had even invited all those concelebrating this Mass to join him in this intention. Soon a very expressive, tenderly worded telegram arrived at the Opus Dei headquarters, with condolences and a blessing from the Holy Father.

Late that same morning, the prefect of the pontifical household, Monsignor Dino Monduzzi, told Don Javier that the Pope would leave the Vatican at about six o'clock that evening to pray before the mortal remains of the bishop-prelate of Opus Dei. Pope John Paul arrived on schedule, accompanied by Cardinal Angelo Sodano (the Vatican Secretary of State), Monsignor Monduzzi, and Monsignor Dziwisz. In the central nave of the prelatic church they all prayed on their knees for about ten minutes, in an impressive silence. When they rose, it was suggested that the Holy Father might like to pray the responsorial prayer for the dead, but instead he said the Salve Regina and three Glory Be's. Then he said the prayers "Requiem aeternam dona ei, Domine" (Eternal rest grant unto him, O Lord) and "Requiescat in pace" (May he rest in peace) three times and sprinkled the body of Don Alvaro with holy water. Afterwards he knelt again on the prie-dieu for a moment, and then, just before leaving, he gave his blessing to all those present.

When Don Javier, in the name of the Prelature, thanked him for coming, Pope John Paul answered, "Si doveva, si doveva" (I had to; I had to). And he wanted to know the exact time of the last Mass that Don Alvaro had celebrated in the Holy Land.

The Vicar General of Opus Dei expressed it very well on the next day, during the pre-funeral Mass that he said in the church of Our Lady of Peace. "I can assure you," he said in his homily, "that Don Alvaro constantly offered his life to God for the Pope and for the holy Church. I told the Holy Father this yesterday, when he came to pray before the mortal remains of the Father. I told him, because it is the plain truth, that the very last Mass of his life—the one he celebrated in the Church of the Cenacle in Jerusalem—was offered, as always, for the Roman pontiff and his intentions."

24

A Marian Time

Throughout his life, Don Alvaro was touched by the words and gestures of the popes whom he came to know. But he particularly admired the devotion to the Blessed Virgin, and the spirit of prayer, of Pope John Paul II. And he felt particularly united with him in September 1979, when he made a penitential pilgrimage to the shrine of Our Lady of Czestochowa. He went there to pray for the Church and for the Holy Father, and, as he had done in so many other holy places all over the world, to renew the consecration of Opus Dei to the Most Sweet Heart of Mary. He wanted to place it at the feet of Our Lady of Czestochowa. When he went to Warsaw to visit the primate of Poland, Cardinal Wyszynski, he summarized in this way—in Italian—the purpose of his pilgrimage: "Siamo venuti per pregare, pregare, e poi pregare" (We have come to pray, and to pray, and then to pray some more).

When he returned to Rome, he told us that he and his companions had planned to do this by going from Warsaw to the Düsseldorf airport, with a stopover in Frankfurt. But when they arrived in Frankfurt, they found waiting for them the regional vicar of the Work in Germany. So from there they went by car. On the next day, Hans Thomas went to the airline company to get a refund for the flight that they had not taken, and while he was at it, he asked the favor of being allowed to keep the tickets as a memento, for their historical value. The lady at the counter thought that some important business contract must have been made. Well, when Don Alvaro heard about this, his response was, "It's true—we have made a contract with the Blessed Virgin. We have gone to her and said to her, 'All of Opus Dei is for you, and so is each and every one of us. Our prayers, our mortifications, our work—it's all for you, so that you can present it to God.' She, in return, puts us under her mantle, protects us, enlightens us, and carries us forward."

At that time Opus Dei was quietly observing a Marian Year of its own. October 2, 1978, was the fiftieth anniversary of its founding, and Don Alvaro had decided that the Work should spend this jubilee year in a special closeness to the Blessed Virgin. This idea arose in his soul during the afternoon of December 31, 1977, while he was meditating in the crypt where the founder was buried—though there was, as he himself made clear when he communicated this at Villa Tevere, nothing miraculous about it. A little while later he sent to the centers a long letter. He expected this Marian Year to be, he said, a time of thanksgiving and of many benefits for the faithful of Opus Dei, since they would be living—each in his or her own way—much more united to the one who is both the Mother of God and our Mother. "Go more to our Lady in everything and for everything," he said. His hope was that the members of Opus Dei would thus make a "qualitative leap forward" in their lives. He wanted them to make this a year of gratitude, but also a year of renewed compunction, spiritual struggle, and apostolic endeavor.

The faithful of the Prelature certainly did intensify their devotion to the Mother of God under the guidance of Don Alvaro. This Marian Year, in fact, was extended from 1978 into 1979, and then into 1980, since 1980 was another jubilee year for Opus Dei. [It was the fiftieth anniversary of the founding of the women's branch.] Throughout those three years, Don Alvaro made many visits to shrines dedicated to the Blessed Virgin. With the single exception of his trip to Fatima, those pilgrimages were not public events, but private times of silence, prayer, and penance.

Don Alvaro finished 1981 with a visit to a Marian shrine, and he started 1982 with another. He kept leaving in the hands of the Blessed Virgin the solving of the juridical problems of the Work, but he also kept thanking her in advance, because everything was going well. He prayed for the Church, for the pope and for the bishops, for Opus Dei as a whole and for each and every one of its members, for the spiritual effectiveness of all the different apostolic efforts. Especially he asked the Blessed Virgin to help the members of the Work become more holy and more faithful to their Christian vocations.

I was able to witness in person that Marian spirit when I first accompanied Don Alvaro to the shrine of Covadonga, in Asturias, on August 2, 1976. As soon as we glimpsed in the distance the towers of the shrine, he intoned a Salve Regina. We left the car in the esplanade, almost right next to the entrance to the gallery which leads to the holy cave. Don Alvaro went down to the chapel and, near the door to the sacristy, knelt down on a kneeler and began to pray. It was not easy to concentrate because the little chapel was full of people and more kept arriving. And then a priest came in and started celebrating Mass. Almost immediately Don Alvaro got up and went outside. He suggested that we go up to the collegiate church and say a rosary there. So we went there, to the side chapel where the Blessed Sacrament was kept, but a Mass was being celebrated there as well. Don Alvaro greeted our Lord for a moment but decided not to enter the chapel, so as not to distract the priest. We said the rosary in the central nave of the church. When we finished, we returned to the side chapel to make a visit to the Blessed Sacrament. Then Don Alvaro went back to the nave and greeted the Blessed Virgin again with a Salve Regina. He wanted to unite himself to the prayer of the faithful of the Prelature who at about this time would be singing this Marian hymn in the church of Our Lady of the Angels at Cavabianca. (Some decorative work was being done there.)

In the many Marian pilgrimages which Don Alvaro made in his lifetime, he always abandoned into the strong and tender arms of his Mother all worries and anxieties. All of his more or less pressing concerns, whether they had to do with the Church in general or with Opus Dei in particular, had that as a common denominator. He would speak with the Blessed Virgin—the "All-powerful Suppliant"—about the Church, about its pastors, about the People of God, about the world. He would consult with her about how to live in a deep piety, how to distinguish error from truth and good from evil, how to increase peace and faithfulness in people's hearts, and how to turn his own life into prayer, holocaust, and total dedication so that he could find in the Most Sweet Heart of Mary the Sacred Heart of her Son.

I was amazed at Don Alvaro's ability to stay recollected even at the most crowded shrines. I especially noticed this at Lourdes. In July 1978 he went there by car from Torreciudad—a trip that took three and a half hours. Upon arrival he went immediately to the grotto where the apparitions had taken place, he got down on his knees, and he prayed the rosary. He stayed very focused despite the hubbub of so many people coming and going and moving around. At the end of August 1984 he went again to Lourdes. It was about 5:30 in the afternoon, it was raining hard, and the place was packed. It took us a while to reach the grotto. Standing under umbrellas which gave us hardly any protection from the rain, we prayed together the rosary, a Salve Regina, and the prayer approved by the Vatican for private devotion to Monsignor Escrivá. The heavy rainfall did not let up, but Don Alvaro was very recollected and in no kind of hurry. At the end he said a short prayer in a louder voice. We were not saying farewell, he told the Blessed Virgin, because we would all be staying right there in her heart, *consummati in unum* (completely one). In her heart the Work would stay well united, would pray effectively for the intentions of the Prelate, and would multiply its apostolic efforts in service of the Church.

Actually, all the rest of his days became a true "Marian time." He used this expression himself, in a letter written on December 8, 1980, at the close of the Marian Years with which Opus Dei had quietly celebrated the jubilees of the 1928 and 1930 foundations. "These Marian Years have left in our souls," he wrote, "the profound conviction that all of our time on earth—and afterwards, with the grace of God, in the marvelous eternity of heaven—has become a Marian time."

Don Alvaro entrusted all his actions to the Blessed Virgin so that, "perfumed by her loving maternal hands" (a phrase I often heard him use), they would be pleasing to the Blessed Trinity. And he always recommended the time-honored devotion of the rosary. Like Blessed Josemaría, he would often give rosaries to the people who visited him. As he handed them over, he would say very insistently, "I want you to really wear these out. I want you to have to take them in for repair because you've used them so much."

In 1983, to thank the Blessed Virgin for the establishment of Opus Dei as a personal prelature, Don Alvaro again traveled to shrines and chapels all over the world. But this time he showed the depth of his gratitude with a particular intensity at the Basilica of Our Lady of Guadalupe. He went to our Lady's villa in Mexico City as soon as he possibly could. He had not been there in thirteen years—not since May 1970, when he had gone there with

Monsignor Escrivá.

He arrived in Mexico City on April 27, 1983, after spending two days in Canada. On that same evening, he made this comment: "Our founder said that when he returned to Mexico, he would start at Monterrey. The reason I'm not doing this is that I have come not to see Mexico, but to give thanks to Our Lady of Guadalupe."

He showed up at the villa on the very next morning. He explained, however, that he would not be starting his novena of thanksgiving and petition—a novena in which he would be accompanied by the faithful of the Prelature all over the world—until the following day, Friday. This visit to the Blessed Virgin was, he said, just "a preamble."

In the novena he retraced the steps taken by the founder in 1970. With him were Monsignor Javier Echevarría, Monsignor Joaquín Alonso, and four Mexicans. He recited the three parts of the rosary, interspersing them with times of personal prayer in which he spoke out loud to our Lady. On one of the first days, he said that he wanted to reciprocate this gift from the Mother of God with one from him: the faithful struggle of his children.

On May 1, after the basilica's closing time, Don Alvaro was allowed to pray for quite a while in the place where the image was kept. Special lighting enabled him to see clearly the delicate, unique expression on the face of our Lady. When he finished the rosary, he kissed the hands and feet of the image—or, rather, the protective glass covering them. At first he thought himself unworthy to give her a kiss on the cheek. "How could I kiss the face of the Virgin, when I am a sinner?" But then Don Javier gently reminded him that she is our Mother...

Later he remarked that no painting or photograph of Our Lady of Guadalupe that he had ever seen really captured the motherly look on her face. "On this part of the image," he said, "there is very little paint. Her face shows an utter simplicity. Her expression is one of sweetness, of humility, of purity, of honesty. It's a look of compassion, of love, and, at the same time, of suffering. I think that she suffered when she saw that no one was taking any account of poor Juan Diego, and that she is looking at him with compassion and affection. I thought of your sins and mine, and I realized that she is looking at us, too, with that great affection—because she is our Mother—but also, at times, with sorrow... Let us not give our Mother in heaven any sorrow!" Then, to sum it all up, he said, "How lucky we have been!" And for "lucky" he used a Mexican word—"suertasa"—which he had learned as a child from the lips of his mother.

On the last day of the novena—May 22, the feast of Pentecost—at nine o'clock at night, Don Alvaro went to the villa to say good-bye to Our Lady of Guadalupe. The basilica was packed with people who wanted to pray there with him. He went to the sanctuary, knelt before the image, and prayed in silence for about ten minutes. Then he stood up, and Don Javier intoned the Salve Regina. After the final prayer, Don Alvaro knelt down again and, with the microphone on, addressed to the "Madrecita de Guadalupe" (Little Mother of Guadalupe), in the name of Opus Dei, words full of love, gratitude, and hope. He said, "Our Mother, look upon us with those eyes of yours that are so full of mercy. You are now looking at us. We know it. We feel it in the depths of our hearts. And we love you so much. . . . We are children of God, and we are your children, and you are our Mother. Look upon us with compassion and never leave us! If you were ever to leave us, every one of us would go astray. We want to be very faithful."

Then came a filial and trustful request for the Church and the Holy Father: "O Mother of ours, make sure we never let the pope down—not Pope John Paul II, nor any successor of his, until the end of time." He then proceeded to pray for bishops, priests, and religious, for the nation, for families—for the fidelity of them all. And then, close to the end of his prayer, he exclaimed, "And now, our Mother, I tell you that all of us who have come here from Rome to pray before your image, and all those who have joined us here, will never leave you! We're not really saying good-bye or farewell. We will always be with you, because we keep you in our hearts and souls. You look at us with those eyes that are so full of sweetness, and your look fills us with strength. Make your divine Spouse, whose feast we celebrate today, grant us his gifts and fruits. Make us always be good children, completely abandoned into the hands of God. . . . We ought to be saints, and we are sinners. Oh, sweet Mother of ours, look upon us with compassion! Help us! Make us be faithful! Give us this kind of pampering. We beg you to give such a caress to your children who need it most—us!"

He followed those words with these few more: "And now we are going to sing you some popular love songs. We'll be able to sing them perfectly since we'll be thinking of you. Listen to us, Mother!" Then began the strumming of the guitars, with the first bars of the songs which in that very place, thirteen years before, had been sung when the founder of Opus Dei was taking his leave: "Gracias por haberte conocido," "La Morenita," and "María Elena."

When the last song was over, Don Alvaro knelt down again and continued to pour out to the Mother of God his gratitude and petitions. It was obvious that he was so deeply moved that it was hard for him to leave. He said, "I'm leaving my heart here, and no one will ever take it from here. I'm leaving it at your feet. I have dared to kiss your feet, your hands, and even your face. Think of it as the daring of a son who loves you very much. But you, O Mother of ours, you love us much more. You are the cause of our joy. You are the reason for our hope. You are the handmaid of the Lord. You are... our Mother! We are staying with you, our Mother, although we have to go. Give us your blessing!"

During that Marian Year of thanksgiving, he could not

fail to make a visit to the cathedral and shrine of Our Lady of the Pillar, in Saragossa. There his love for our Lady under this manifestation, which he had learned to appreciate during his school days in Madrid, seemed to blend almost physically with fond memories of the founder of Opus Dei. In September 1983 he stopped off at Our Lady of the Pillar on his way from Torreciudad to Madrid. The usual entranceway was closed for repairs, so he came in through the back door of the cathedral and walked across the transept to the chapel of the Blessed Virgin. He went into the first pew, knelt down, and spent about fifteen minutes in prayer. Some members of the Work were already there—they had come on their own to greet our Lady for a moment, as is customary in Saragossa—and they came up to join him. His presence was also noted by a canon of the cathedral. When he finished praying, the canon greeted him and asked him if he would like to kiss the image. Don Alvaro answered that he had thought this was no longer possible.

"It is for you, Father," the canon said, and then he made the appropriate preparations. He invited him into the sacristy to see the keepsakes left by Pope John Paul in 1982 (a skullcap and a rosary) and asked him to sign the visitors' book. Don Alvaro wrote in it, "Thank you, Mother, for all the help you gave our Father, the founder of Opus Dei, during his times in Saragossa and always! Blessed art thou! Alvaro del Portillo, Prelate of Opus Dei / 6.IX.83."

Near the end of 1983, a new horizon opened up for him in his devotion to our Lady. On November 27, in Rome, he told us about it quite simply. "When I have spoken of the Blessed Virgin," he said, "I have thought of her as the Mother of Jesus and as the Mother of all of us. But now it's dawned on me that when I'm speaking with Jesus Christ *a quattro occhi,* or 'alone together,' as they say in Italy, I can talk to Jesus about '*our* Mother,' because she's the Mother of both of us—him and me." This realization gave him a new closeness to Jesus Christ. "Now," he said, "it's as if two brothers are talking about their mother."

Naturally, Don Alvaro observed with a special intensity the Marian Year celebrated by the universal Church in 1987. From the moment it was announced by the Holy Father, he encouraged the faithful of the Prelature to prepare themselves well. Once again he recommended that they do everything with and for our Lady, in the conviction that this would result in abundant fruit. On May 31 he wrote a long letter to the centers of Opus Dei. Among other ideas, he proposed a very specific way to observe that Marian Year: namely, to carry out "a capillary apostolate of spreading among Catholic families the habit of praying the rosary." Through this substantial devotion, he hoped to obtain from our Lady much good for the Church and for all humanity.

Not surprisingly, he readily accepted the suggestion made by Father James Kelly, an American priest then working at the central headquarters of Opus Dei, that he visit once again Our Lady of Guadalupe when he traveled to the United States and Canada in 1988. He stayed in Mexico City from January 29 to February 2. And at the emotional moment of another farewell in the villa, he said in a loud voice, "It has given me great joy to take this big detour on my trip from Texas to California to come see you, Our Lady of Guadalupe! You know how much we in Opus Dei love you, and how much this sinner who is now talking with you loves you! We are, as our Father used to say, sinners who love Jesus Christ, and we love you, my Mother, with all the madness of which our hearts are capable!"

I don't think it is necessary to describe at great length Don Alvaro's ardent love for Saint Joseph. Like the founder of Opus Dei, Don Alvaro could not separate Saint Joseph from Holy Mary. He continued to practice the manly Catholic devotions that he had loved since 1935, among which was the ancient custom of dedicating to Saint Joseph the seven Sundays before his feast day, March 19.

He prayed a lot to the Holy Patriarch, often through Blessed Josemaría. He was sure that Saint Joseph would not fail to grant what was being asked for through the intercession of someone who had loved him so much on this earth. He also thought that a title sometimes given to the Blessed Virgin, "All-powerful Suppliant," could be applied to Saint Joseph as well, albeit on a different scale. This was how he explained it: "Saint Joseph did so much for Jesus. He was like a real father to him on this earth. He sacrificed himself for him to an incredible degree. Even before Jesus was born he suffered greatly, when he saw that Mary was pregnant. He must have undergone terrible sufferings. Not that he had any doubts about our Lady—I am sure that he had none— but because he thought he had to separate himself from her, since something had happened that was beyond his ken. He must have thought that here was a divine mystery of which he was not worthy. And later on, how much he suffered for the Child Jesus! And then he taught him his trade; he taught him the way by which he would make his living. So if Saint Joseph asks him for something, Jesus cannot deny it to him."

I especially noticed this loving conjoining of devotions during Don Alvaro's visits to Torreciudad. From the founder of Opus Dei he had learned to love the Blessed Virgin in all of her manifestations. With him he had made pilgrimages to countless shrines and chapels in Europe and Latin America. But, also along with Monsignor Escrivá, he felt it was like this: "Among the innumerable photos of loved ones that are kept in a family album, there are some which are especially cherished—perhaps because they are more beautiful, objectively speaking, or because they stir up deep feelings in one's heart, or because they awaken the memory of some past but very intense feelings. And so, among all these many family photos, each family member will have his or her favorites." This explanation was given by Don Alvaro in his introduction to a book on Torreciudad which was published in 1988. He gave it as a lead-up to his frank admission that Our Lady of the Angels of Torreciudad "awakens in me a string of experiences which makes me consider it one of my favorite portraits of my Mother in heaven."

He was especially happy to hear news of the apostolic work that took place at the shrine of Torreciudad. When he heard about people who publicly expressed their joy after going to confession there—people who had not approached the sacrament of Penance for years and years—he was thrilled. Among the many times when I myself witnessed this intense joy of his, I especially remember one evening near the beginning of September 1991. On that evening, he went to the old shrine to pray the rosary. Afterwards he prayed some more to the Blessed Virgin, and then he thanked the founder for all the many blessings which had come from heaven to the Work through his intercession. He thanked him also for his fidelity and particularly for his sense of gratitude, which was what had made possible Torreciudad and all the wonderful things now happening at that shrine. Then he asked our Lady to pray for the Church, for Pope John Paul and his coworkers, and for the Work and the fidelity of its members. He finished by saying a Memorare.

It was also with our Lady that he wanted to go through the final stage of the process of beatification of Monsignor Escrivá. On January 1, 1992, the feast of Mary, Mother of God, he reminded us that in Opus Dei, "every step we have ever taken has been preceded, accompanied, and followed by the protection of the Mother of God and our Mother." And with that in mind, he decided to start on January 9— the founder's birthday—another Marian Year, which would end on the same date in 1993. "Thus, led by the hand of Holy Mary," he said, "we will prepare for and experience the beatification of our Father with that yearning for renewal which our Lord expects from us—with a personal conversion, so that we can do Opus Dei by truly being Opus Dei."

He renewed these desires every day, but especially
during the visits that he made to Marian shrines in Europe
(starting with Fatima) to thank our Lady and to leave at her
feet the intentions which he thought that Blessed Josemaría,
from heaven, probably had for the Work. When doing this,
he made his own that confident request which the founder
had made to the Blessed Virgin from as far back as the
twenties: "Domina, ut sit!" (Lady, let it be!).

It was, perhaps, for such reasons that, a couple of months
before the beatification, Don Alvaro wrote to the Saragossa
city council to say that he would like to present the gift of a
mantle for the image. (Putting a mantle on an image is a
centuries-old tradition among the people of Aragon.) The city
council happily accepted his offer, and the official presentation
took place on June 23, in a celebration both simple and solemn.
Don Alvaro sent a message which the regional vicar of Opus
Dei in Spain, Monsignor Tomás Gutiérrez, read out loud.
On the mantle had been embroidered the aspiration which
Blessed Josemaría had prayed so often and had even etched
into the base of a carving of Our Lady of the Pillar on May
24, 1924: "Domina, ut sit!" The founder had been praying for
Opus Dei when he hadn't even thought of it yet! And now,
after all those years, Don Alvaro was saying to our Lady, "Once
again we place ourselves entirely in your hands, our Mother.
Treat us as your own and make us love your Son more every
day, with a fidelity to God and to the Church such as our
founder had."

Two days afterward the Mass of the new blessed was
celebrated on the main altar of the cathedral. The main
celebrant was the archbishop of Saragossa, the Most Reverend
Elías Yanes. In the chapel of the Blessed Virgin, as a sign of
Don Alvaro's gratitude and as a kind of summary of the life
of Blessed Josemaría, Our Lady of the Pillar wore the mantle
given her by his successor.

25

Gratitude to God

The last time that I lived near Don Alvaro was the summer of 1993, when he had a cataract operation. I later summed up my impressions with three phrases which he often used during this time: "Thanks be to God!"; "You offer it up, and that's that"; and "Well, what can you do about it?"

Actually, to a great extent, those three phrases well sum up what I had seen him become more and more with each passing year. Day by day, Don Alvaro visibly became more human and affectionate, because he looked at all events *sub specie aeternitatis,* from the standpoint of eternity. He thought only about God, about the glory of God, and—always in relation to God—about everyone's needs. His words and deeds were a window on what went deepest in his heart: his desire to be completely abandoned into the hands of the Lord while working hard in his presence. He was living proof of what Monsignor Escrivá had said in point no. 801 of *Furrow:* "There is no heart more human than that of a person overflowing with supernatural sense."

Don Alvaro had learned from the founder not to allow himself to be served. Inevitably, though, people would do him favors—perhaps not personal favors, strictly speaking, but favors nonetheless. And I'll never forget how deeply grateful he was. He would thank me just for doing some simple job, like serving his Mass, or helping him in his work, or giving one of the talks for a monthly day of recollection. He was always thanking somebody, and doing so in the tone of voice that one uses when one has received a really big favor.

At the same time, I was always hearing him say, "Thanks be to God!" From him this sounded very natural and never trite. He would often say it after Mass, after his private prayer, when he finished a job, after going for a walk or doing some other kind of exercise, or when he heard news that showed the spiritual fruitfulness of members of Opus Dei in all kinds of different places in the world.

I came to realize what a capacity he had for gratitude to God in August 1976, when people were telling him about an ordination which had taken place a few days before in Madrid. Don Alvaro punctuated their accounts with short exclamations made in a rather loud voice, such as "Thanks be to God!" and "It is our Father who is doing this!" and "Our Father is very active!" I'm sure he must have made such comments on previous occasions too, but this was the first time they caught my attention. From then on, I was always impressed by how easily and spontaneously words of thanksgiving sprang from his lips.

As he wrote in a letter in August 1977, Don Alvaro was convinced that in Opus Dei "absolutely everything is a motive and an occasion for raising our hearts to the Triune God in gratitude for the mercy with which he has always made our poor efforts fruitful." He concluded this letter by saying, "Be thankful, my children, and you will be faithful. And remember that serving others is one of the best ways to show gratitude."

In June 1985 he warmed to this theme as he recalled the gifts obtained for Opus Dei by its founder in the ten years since he went to heaven. "Really and truly," he said, "it is enough to make us prostrate ourselves face down on the ground, overwhelmed by God's generosity, and to spend the rest of our days giving thanks for these benefits and praising the thrice-holy God who has shown us so much mercy. *Gratias tibi, Deus, gratias tibi!*"

It was, in fact, with a canticle of thanksgiving that he began his homily in his last solemn Mass that I attended, which was at Torreciudad in 1993. "Thank you, Lord," he said, "for the faith which you have granted us and for the infinite generosity in all your gifts! Thank you for constantly being present among us and for prodding us to follow you closely and identify ourselves with you! Thank you for the great blessing which you are bestowing upon the Church with the ordination of these new priests!"

His gratitude was a sign of his contemplative spirit. Quite often he would get enraptured when he thought of the face of Jesus Christ—that face at once divine and sublimely human. He loved to ask people a specific question that he had often heard from Blessed Josemaría: "What would be the look on Jesus' face?" He found answers in the Gospel, where Christ constantly gives us examples of how to really *see* God in everything: "In creatures: 'Consider the lilies of the field, how God clothes them'; in the most diverse situations, including pain; and in the sickness or death of loved ones." (See Mt 6:29–30, Jn 9:1, and Jn 11:4–44.)

The look of the Lord "is always one of love for souls," Don Alvaro would say, and then he would ask another great question, this time addressing the Savior: "Lord, how would you look at the persons and the situation around me in my work, in my family, on the street?" And he would tell us to "ask him to let you always see things with his eyes, to make his sight work through yours."

At his side—I am not exaggerating—one could make out something of his ongoing internal conversation with the Lord. There were fleeting moments when he seemed far away, and when his eyes would turn upwards as if to get a right perspective on things. One could tell that he was still attentive to those around him, but at the same time immersed in God and in the things of God. He truly was, to borrow the words of the founder of Opus Dei, "in heaven and on earth." He lived a contemplative life in the midst of mundane activities.

And all of this happened by means of the normal action of the Holy Spirit in souls. Don Alvaro himself, using examples taken from Sacred Scripture, described it thus: "It is like the gentle rain which soaks into the earth and makes it produce fruit, or like the breeze that cools one's face, or like the fireplace that spreads warmth throughout the house, or like the air that we breathe almost without realizing it."

However, he never stopped using tangible devices to maintain or strengthen his awareness of God's presence. One day Don Javier Echevarría was teasing Don Florencio Sánchez Bella about the old-fashioned watch he was wearing, and Don Alvaro pointed to the face of his own watch, which showed not only the time and the date, but also the day of the week. This helped him keep in mind the traditional devotion for that day of the week. "Today," he said, "is Thursday: the Eucharist."

He placed great importance on the smallest details of piety, including the pace of vocal prayers and the attention paid to them. He once admitted publicly that at that time in his life he was making his particular examen more or less a vocal prayer (following the example of the founder), in order to do it well.

I think it was in about 1978 that he began to recommend strongly that the faithful of the Work—not as any kind of obligation, but in total freedom—develop their spirit of contemplation by choosing each day an aspiration to use like an army password. One day in February of that year, he told us that a few days before, his password had been "the consideration 'Tempus breve est!'—because the time for love is short. And my response was, 'Ecce adsum!' (Here I am,

Lord!). Because that's what passwords are—they're phrases used in the army, phrases to which the guards reply when they recognize them." And he went on to say, "In our case, the password can be a look full of love which we cast at an image of the Blessed Virgin, and the response can be an aspiration, a heartfelt compliment to our Mother in which we show our affection, our dedication... whatever you want. The important thing is that in all your activities, you increase your awareness of the presence of the Blessed Virgin."

Everything pointed him towards God, and towards God he pointed everything. He did this with no eccentricity or ostentation, but with palpable supernatural sense; he simply contemplated human realities from a divine perspective. I was impressed, for example, by a comment he made in connection with the death of a member of Opus Dei in Ireland on August 1, 1980. This man, whose name was John, died in a train accident on the same day that Don Alvaro arrived in Dublin. Don Alvaro was told that before leaving home, John had served his wife breakfast in bed, since she was recovering from the birth of a child, and had then gotten together some documents that he could work on in the train. "I think," said a priest of the Work, "that he died working." Seamus Timoney, who had been listening to the account, said, "Or praying—which is the same thing." Then Don Alvaro said, "Or resting. Whoever works has a right to rest, my children. Rest ought to be a consequence of and a preparation for work. Rest is something good and holy."

In March 1988, upon arriving in Toronto, Don Alvaro noticed the slogan on the cars' license plates: "Ontario. Yours to discover." Immediately he applied this to spiritual life. "In this city," he said, "there are many things to discover, but there are many more things to be found in God. Our Lord has many more reasons than this city has to say to each of us, 'Yours to discover.'"

In April 1989, during a visit to Kenya, he learned a

Kikuyu proverb which he would use for his own interior
life and also for the encouragement of others. I heard it in
Rome a few days later: "When a friend is at the top of the
mountain, it is easier to climb." Don Alvaro compared life,
with its maladies, shortcomings, and misunderstandings, to
a climb to the top of a mountain. "Waiting for us at the top
of the mountain," he said, "is Christ, our friend. He guides
us and shows us the easiest way to reach the peak. He is both
waiting for us and helping us."

In the summer of 1989, while taking a walk by the sea,
Don Alvaro and some companions crossed paths with a
fisherman who was heading for the rocks with his rods and
tackle. Alejandro Cantero asked this man if there were any
sea bass in the area, and he instantly replied, "There are;
sure, there are. The tricky thing is finding them." Much later,
at Christmas time in 1992, Don Alvaro reminded us of this
simple statement to encourage us in our apostolic endeavors.
He said, "There are many souls waiting for us—it's just hard
work finding them." The conclusion was obvious: "We have
to look for them."

He supernaturalized everything. One could not help
but feel the intensity and continuity of his dialogue with
the Lord. It was easy to tell that for him, personal prayer
truly was "the conversation of people in love: a conversation
in which there is no place for boredom or distraction; a heart-
to-heart talk to which we look forward impatiently, to which
we go with a hunger to get to know Jesus better and really
relate to him; a conversation that is conducted with the
delicacy of a soul in love, and which ends with a renewed
desire to live and work only for the Lord."

With the years, Don Alvaro found it increasingly
difficult to sleep well at night, though he would stay in bed
for the standard amount of time, as his doctors recommended.
I know (because I occasionally happened to witness this)
that he used his times of insomnia as opportunities for prayer.

He would start praying very early in the morning, even before he got up, and he would arrive early in the chapel for the half hour of meditation before Mass.

The intensity of his search for God could be observed in those external details: his arriving early in the chapel in the morning; his moving up a time of mental prayer when a trip, an errand, or some other business might keep him from doing it at the regular time; his not putting off the rosary, or his afternoon meditation, even for urgent tasks that had to be done by a certain time; his obvious ability to control his thoughts and feelings and concentrate on God without any distraction; the comments he would make throughout the day that showed preparation or that were obviously the fruit of personal contemplation; the familiarity with the life of Jesus Christ that was evident in his preaching; and, finally, his silence at night, from the very instant that he brought to a close the last family get-together of the day.

For me it was a wonder to behold how his inner spirit translated into action. Because of his supernatural outlook, he could always work very calmly and effectively and finish things on time. This was a reflection of the reality of a harmonious and attractive blend of prayer and action. It clearly showed that the sensibilities of a contemplative soul in no way lead to agitation or nervousness. Hardworking as he was, it was obvious that his overriding attitude was one of abandonment in the hands of God—that he looked to God for everything—and that this attitude overflowed into authentic priestly service. As Jess P. Stanislao summed it up in the 4/10/94 issue of *Manila Bulletin,* "The more immersed he was in the things of God, the larger grew the capacity of his heart to truly love and go all out for each person he was with."

Don Alvaro's conversation, too, flowed in a very natural way from his constant dialogue with God. For this reason he was able to preach very persuasively this truth that he had learned from Blessed Josemaría: that there is no opposition between prayer and action, not even in environments in which the dazzle of activism makes prayer seem archaic. "When it goes out of fashion for children to love their fathers, and to call them Daddy, and to talk with them with all the tenderness that small children have towards their parents," he said in Mexico in 1983, "then and only then will talking with our Father God go out of fashion."

This was summed up very well by Monsignor José Sebastián Laboa, then the papal nuncio of Paraguay, in an article published in the Asunción edition of *ABC* shortly after Don Alvaro's death. Monsignor Laboa, who had known and associated with Don Alvaro since 1954, remembered particularly the tone of voice in which Don Alvaro once quoted a text from Saint Paul. "I will never forget," he said, "this one time when he had some big problem, and suddenly, in a changed tone of voice and with a totally serene look on his face, he came out with this: 'Who shall separate us from the love of Christ? . . . For I am sure that neither death nor life . . . nor anything else in all creation will be able to separate us from the love of God in Christ Jesus our Lord'" (Rom 8:35, 38–39).

On March 23, 1994, a journalist asked Don Javier Echevarría what he thought had been Don Alvaro's most outstanding qualities. This was his answer: "His peacefulness, his naturalness, his supernatural outlook, his capacity for loving people, his readiness to serve everyone, his enormous capacity for work, and, above all, his determination always to be attentive to what God was asking of him, by means of prayer and mortification. He never refused mortification, which is another way of praying."

Besides the promptness with which he always fulfilled his duties (even on days when he was ill or worn out), I also saw him practice many small voluntary mortifications—though these were not easy to notice, since he did them with such grace and naturalness. A few examples: he would sit without crossing his legs, and would wait for a good while before leaning against the back of the chair; he would choose the worst seat for himself, always focused on making life more pleasant for others; on a hot day he would wait for a while before drinking a glass of water. One day towards the end of August 1976 I noticed that Don Alvaro, who so much loved the sea, was sitting with his back to it so that others could be the ones to enjoy the beautiful view.

As for other things, I didn't know what to say about his abstentions at mealtime until it occurred to me to borrow words that he himself used with reference to Blessed Josemaría in the book *Immersed in God*. Don Alvaro followed very strictly the diet prescribed by his doctors, but he made sure everyone else ate what they needed. "Whenever he did receive visitors . . . , he took care to hide his frugality so as not to make his fellow diners uneasy." Furthermore, he "sought to add to each dish the condiment of mortification." The women who worked in the kitchen and in the dining room put an incredible amount of professionalism and affection into the preparation and presentation of the food. But a plate of boiled greens with hardly any salt and with no tasty dressing loses its attractiveness as soon as the fork reaches the mouth. And more or less the same was true of his "meat or fish, usually grilled, with little garnishing." The desserts he ate looked marvelous, but their attractiveness was quite deceptive, since they lacked any tasty ingredients. Everything was, so to speak, decaffeinated. Usually he did not take wine; instead, in compliance with doctors' orders, he made himself drink more water than he wanted. And though he was, of course, served first, he would never start eating until all the rest of us had been served and the grace before meals had been said. (See Cavalleri 1996, 40.)

I myself heard him speak of a mortification which Blessed Josemaría observed at mealtime when his diabetes, or its complications, got worse. The founder and Don Alvaro, who at that time were in Rome, would eat by themselves so as not to oblige the younger ones to follow such a strict diet. (See Cavalleri 1996, 191–92.) When I first heard this, I thought it the most natural thing in the world. But now I realize that it must have been a big sacrifice for Don Alvaro to adapt himself so completely to the regime which the doctors had prescribed for the founder.

Juan Cabellos recalls the visit that Monsignor Escrivá and Don Alvaro made to the Portuguese city of Oporto around 1953. With the news that they were coming, they also gave him the menu—only greens, but lots of them, and always right on time, because Don Alvaro would have just given Monsignor Escrivá an injection of insulin, which would give the founder a huge appetite. Throughout that visit, they all ate the same thing. Don Xavier Ayala, who at that time was the regional vicar of Opus Dei in Portugal, suggested to Don Alvaro the possibility of his eating something different. But "he replied that it made no big difference to him, and that this way the Father wouldn't feel like an isolated case."

Dorotea Calvo tells a similar story about the day she arrived in Rome, from Chile, to attend a General Congress of Opus Dei—this must have been in about 1956. Monsignor Escrivá immediately invited her over. First, by way of welcome, he engaged her for a few minutes in a friendly chat, during which he mentioned the importance of praying for a lot of light from the Holy Spirit. Encarnación Ortega, who was then the Central Secretary of the Work, was also present. At the end of the conversation, Monsignor Escrivá said, "Encarnita, I'm going to be fasting during these days. Please ask them just to put out a glass of milk." Instantly Don Alvaro added, "And another one for me."

Many years later, after the death of Don Alvaro, Encarnación said, "No one knew what kinds of food he liked. He always adapted himself to the people with whom he was living, with a total detachment from his own likes and dislikes."

Don Alvaro tried always to keep alive in himself and to communicate to the faithful of the Prelature that deep love for the cross which the founder had communicated to him. In February 1990 he urged them to spread this spirit and thus achieve through strength a real *gaudium cum pace* (joy with peace). He considered this an important objective for spiritual formation programs. Among other things, he saw it as a good way to counteract the negative effects of modern mentalities which give pride of place to the search for one's own well-being—a well-being that is more or less hedonistic, or at least heavily tainted with egotism. That pure fortitude would make people "sowers of peace and joy" not only in their personal lives, but in civic life as well.

He promoted that key feature of the Christian life even among people who were opposed to some of the traditional means of living in a spirit of mortification. At the end of the eighties, in some Western countries, several superficial reports were published which depicted the faithful of Opus Dei as strange beings who were still wearing hair shirts and using scourges. One such article was published in Canada not long before Don Alvaro's visit there in February 1988. In the auditorium of the University of Montreal, a student from Kenya questioned him about that article, and he gave her this good-humored answer: "Not long ago, I happened to arrive in Washington at lunchtime, and many Marines were out there doing exercises—mainly running and jogging. And I thought of one time when I was talking with Cardinal Ratzinger, and we agreed that if the Church were to impose daily jogging as a mortification, almost everyone would disobey. They would say the Church was getting cult-like and fanatic. And yet you see so many people doing those exercises every day. They are real mortifications, done to keep one's figure or to keep fit..."

In September of that same year, in Zurich, he pointed out that such penances had been utilized for centuries by many people, both men and women, who wanted to get closer to God. He made it clear, of course, that they are not indispensable means for growing in holiness. "I am now thinking," he said, "of those many mothers and fathers in Christian families who have never used a scourge or worn a hair shirt, but who have known how to take with a great love for God, and with a joy full of faith, all the pains and frustrations of everyday life." Certainly one can acquire in that way a spirit of sacrifice which leads to holiness, without need of those traditional corporal mortifications. But Don Alvaro also made this clarification: "Neither are they masochistic anachronisms from the Middle Ages. Even today they are practiced by many contemplative souls, by many men and women all over the world."

More generally, Don Alvaro wanted everyone to turn their eyes and their hearts towards "Christ crucified, who gives himself without reserve for the salvation of the world, even to the shedding of his last drop of blood and the exhaling of his last breath."

I particularly noticed his devotion to the holy cross in August 1977, during a visit to the church of Saint Turibius of Liébana. He walked through the church, prayed before a relic of the True Cross, and then venerated and kissed the relic of Saint Turibius. As he was leaving, he mentioned that Bishop Carmelo Ballester, when he was bishop of León, had made a gift to Blessed Josemaría of a piece of that relic of the True Cross which is venerated in Liébana. Blessed Josemaría used to wear it on his chest, and now he himself did. He unbuttoned his cassock a bit and showed us the relic. Then, with a look of love on his face, he kissed it and invited the rest of us to do the same.

He encouraged people to learn to embrace the cross in the guise of their own difficulties and frustrations. God permits these, he said, as confirmation that one is on the right path. Again and again, with joy and gratitude, he reminded his listeners of this teaching of the founder: "God blesses us with the cross."

He recommended frequent meditation on the Passion of the Lord. Once I heard him mention in passing the Shroud of Turin. Without making any kind of prejudgment—for the Church has made no official pronouncement about the authenticity of this extraordinary relic—he expressed interest in the scientific research being done on it. In the Holy Year of 1983, when someone mentioned that the Shroud showed Jesus to have been about six feet tall, Don Alvaro said this in response: "He was a very tall man for his time. And he was a very fit man who could fast for forty days and forty nights and spend whole nights in prayer before making important decisions, such as the choice of his apostles. Well, now consider the fact that this man who was so strong was not able to carry his cross by himself. They loaded it on him, and he needed the help of the Cyrenean. And then, even with that help, he still fell three times to the ground, before dying on the cross..."

Truly immersed in God, Don Alvaro continually gave him thanks. His contemplative soul generously accepted discomfort, and surmounted in advance all possible problems, with a simple "You offer it up, and that's that." In painful times he would try every possible remedy, but while and after doing so he would cheerfully embrace the will of God, even if his heart was broken. From time to time he would quietly say, "Well, what can you do about it?" without giving the matter too much importance.

He was living proof of that reality expressed so vividly by Blessed Josemaría, "Joy has its roots in the form of a cross." And, like the founder, he would each year write on the first page of his ordo (a booklet listing the offices and feasts of the Church for each day of the year) this penitential and joyful aspiration: "In laetitia, nulla dies sine cruce!" (In joy, no day without the cross!). In 1993 he explained it this way: "'Ut iumentum, semper in laetitia'—we live like donkeys, but always with joy. If they beat us, so what? Forward we go, always in joy."

26

Meeting the Blessed Trinity

"He who does not think of himself deserves everything." These words spontaneously came to my lips when I toasted Don Alvaro on his eightieth birthday, March 11, 1994. I had no idea how soon he would be receiving, by God's fatherly providence, everything he deserved. Death came upon him at a time of deep joy—just after his long-awaited pilgrimage to the Holy Land. In Madrid we had received detailed news of his travels and his Masses in Nazareth, at Mount Tabor, in Jerusalem, and in Bethlehem. It was easy to accompany him in spirit, and to imagine how moved he must have been as he walked day after day over the landscapes that Jesus contemplated during his earthly walk. Nothing led us to suspect that upon his return to Rome, the Lord would call him to his presence.

On March 23, 1994, Don Javier Echevarría made this announcement: "Last night a heart attack ended the life of Bishop Alvaro del Portillo, Prelate of Opus Dei. A little before four in the morning, he called me to tell me he was feeling bad. While the doctor was tending to him, I myself gave him the last sacraments, in accord with his explicitly and often stated wish."

The present Bishop-Prelate of Opus Dei, despite his

obvious sorrow, said he was sure that "the circumstances which have accompanied his passage to heaven bear the seal of a final paternal caress from God." Don Alvaro's pilgrimage to the Holy Land had been, after all, "a week of intense prayer during which he was able to follow, in deep recollection, the footsteps of Jesus." Above all, Don Javier reflected on the fact that Don Alvaro had celebrated his last Mass in Jerusalem, in the Church of the Cenacle.

Don Alvaro had come back very happy. Shortly before returning to Rome, he had said, "I am so happy to have made this trip. It has felt to me like a caress from the Lord."

Don Javier has many times spoken of this pilgrimage, so deeply is it engraved in his heart. "In retrospect," he has often said, "it is obvious that the Holy Places were the best possible venue for the last stage of his life, which was just one long journey toward God."

As soon as the news of his death got out, an unending stream of people visited the prelatic church of Opus Dei to pray before Don Alvaro's mortal remains. Many eyewitnesses have spoken of the emotion that was reflected in all those faces—of how filled everyone was with affection and gratitude, and with the conviction that they were praying before the body of a holy man who would intercede before God with all the strength of his magnanimous heart.

As for the faithful of the Prelature, they had special reasons for gratitude, and also the certainty that Opus Dei would continue to move forward, following the track solidly marked out by Don Alvaro in the era of continuity, the era of fidelity to the legacy of the founder, which had begun in 1975.

It was certainly a great consolation to know that the Holy Father and bishops all over the world shared this grief. Pope John Paul went in person to pray in the funeral chapel, accompanied by Cardinal Angelo Sodano, the Vatican Secretary of State. And before and after that extraordinary visit, many cardinals and prelates of the Roman Curia and superiors of religious orders went to pay their last respects.

Pope John Paul was especially touched by the fact that the Lord had called Don Alvaro home upon his return from the Holy Land. He put a lot of emphasis on this in the audience that he gave to the participants of the 1994 UNIV Congress, which, as usual, took place in Holy Week. "At this time," he said, "the thought of the Holy Land is for you very tied in with the person of Bishop Alvaro del Portillo. Just before calling him to himself, God allowed him to make a pilgrimage to those places where Jesus spent his life on earth. Those were days of intense prayer which united him very closely to Christ and, in fact, prepared him for his final meeting with the Blessed Trinity."

On every continent, the Prelature received messages of nothing but communion and solidarity from Church officials. Innumerable bishops and pastors promised to say funeral Masses in their own dioceses for Don Alvaro. Monsignor Tomás Gutiérrez, the regional vicar of Opus Dei in Spain, mentioned this with great gratitude in a published interview. "I have been deeply touched," he said, "from those first hours on March 23, by the expressions of affection for the Bishop-Prelate of Opus Dei that I have received from so many Spanish bishops and archbishops."

At that time—in the prelatic church, in cathedrals and churches all over the world, and even outside them—one could clearly see how universally Don Alvaro was loved. Thousands and thousands of very different people expressed their great affection for him. Among the countless instances that followed in quick succession, I have chosen the one related by Rachel E. Khan at the beginning of her article in the 3/30/94 issue of Manila's *Business World*. "Last Saturday," she says, "I went with a friend of mine to a funeral Mass in Manila's cathedral. We were going by taxi, and she could not keep from bursting out in tears. It made me a little nervous, so finally I told the driver that my friend's father had died. It was my way of taking up for her in case the driver was taken aback. But it was I who ended up being taken aback. 'Did your father die in Manila?' the driver asked in Tagalog. 'No,' my friend said, 'he died in Rome.' 'Well, then,' said the driver, 'your father must be Bishop Alvaro del Portillo.' And then he added, 'He is my father too.'"

A newspaper reporter asked Don Javier Echevarría what thoughts Don Alvaro had expressed to him about the eventuality of his own death. Don Javier had to admit that Don Alvaro had never said anything on that subject specifically. "But he did talk about death," he said. "In Opus Dei we are used to looking upon death as life. We do not fear death; rather, we await it as our beloved sister. Don Alvaro was sure that this moment for him would come when, where, and as the Lord wanted it to, and that he would be happy about it. In short, he was very well prepared. I can say that he used to speak of death as a kind of family reality. To him it was like the return of a son to his father's home. There the Lord was waiting for him, waiting to give him an everlasting hug."

And that is surely the way it was. After I had time to reflect on my many memories of life with Don Alvaro, the vividness of them struck me as paradoxical in connection with the simplicity of his fidelity and the naturalness with which he always tried to go unnoticed. He did his best to avoid all unnecessary attention. The responsibility that he felt on account of the call he had received from God in 1935 just helped him grow in rectitude of intention. And his humility led him to say to God on his birthdays and on important anniversaries, "O Lord, thank you; forgive me; give me more help!"

His whole life—even, I repeat, the most ordinary aspects of it—revolved around God. At Solavieya, on August 6, 1977, he set aside a copy of the first edition of a Latin American missal to give to Justo Sabadell, whom he had invited over for dinner. But then he forgot about it until the last minute, when his guest was walking out the door. So, standing right there in the hall, leaning over the big table there, he wrote these words for a dedication: "Faciem tuam, Domine, requiram semper et in omnibus!" (Your face, Lord, I seek always and in everything). That day was the feast of the Transfiguration. "This is the agenda," he said as he handed him the missal, "that we must carry out each and every day. We must seek the face of Jesus in all the circumstances of our lives."

Later he commented that this was what the founder had always taught people: that we must look always and in all things to Jesus Christ in the midst of the world.

On the other hand, he truly felt—without any false humility—a great responsibility before the Lord because of all the time he had been privileged to spend with Blessed Josemaría. He expressed this with striking clarity, though always with a friendly smile and in a confident tone of voice. On his birthday in 1977, for instance, he said rather loudly, "I will be asked for a strict account of these years. Pray for me! Thanks be to God, I have always remained loyal to the Father, but he must already have had to forgive me many a time for my lack of dedication, for my meager work, for so many things!" Then he applied to himself the Gospel story of the sinful woman who washed the feet of Jesus, and he concluded with this: "Well, since our Father has had to forgive me more than he has all of you, I ought to love him more. And therefore he will look at me, as they say in Italy, with an *occhio di riguardo:* he will turn a blind eye to my weaknesses and will help me more, especially on a day like today."

On September 15, 1982, at Molinoviejo, he celebrated the seventh anniversary of his election as Monsignor Escrivá's successor. When he finished his thanksgiving after Mass, we congratulated him, and he commented very matter-of-factly that since he had now completed seven years—seven being the number of perfection, of plenitude—God might summon him, and therefore this was for him a day to do a thorough examination of conscience. "And I've already started doing it," he added. But even when it came to his own death, Don Alvaro did not think of himself. When he turned seventy, in 1984, he asked this: "Please pray for me that when I come to stand before the Lord—when he wants, whether today or twenty years from now—I will be able to offer him pearls, diamonds, emeralds, and amethysts; in other words, the fidelity of my daughters and sons, which I, with God's grace, will have helped to preserve. Be faithful for me; don't let me go to the Lord with empty hands."

Not long before, he had written this: "Following in the footsteps of our Father, I too want to be only seven years old, to be always little—more so every day—so that I can find me a good place in the arms of Mary and in the arms of Joseph, very close to our Jesus." In the end, all that mattered to him was to reach heaven and to help others do the same. "This," he said, "is the goal of all our strivings, the direction of all our steps, the light which ought always to illuminate our earthly journey."

In 1983, in Mexico, a woman asked him to talk about love for God and about the reward that God has prepared for those who persevere in loving him. Immediately he gave her this response: "You ask me to talk to you about heaven. Well, that is something I cannot do. If Saint Paul, who was snatched up there in a vision, says that there are no human words to describe it, then what can I say to you? 'No eye has seen, nor ear heard, nor the heart of man conceived, what God has prepared for those who love him.' When we make the great leap, God will be waiting for us, to give us a big hug and to let us look upon his face for ever and ever and ever. And since our God is infinitely wonderful, we will be discovering new marvels for all eternity. We will be satiated without satiation. Never will we get tired of tasting his infinite sweetness." Among those marvels, he mentioned the Blessed Virgin, who is also waiting for us in heaven. And this was his conclusion: "What a joy it is to struggle to arrive at that endless happiness! It's well worth it, my children; it's well worth it!" (See 1 Cor 2:9 and 2 Cor 12:2–4.)

On June 25, 1993, someone remarked that just one year later he would be celebrating his priestly golden jubilee. "That's still a year away," he said, "and in a year many things can happen. I ask the Lord to help me be faithful minute by minute, day by day. That's how I want to prepare for my golden jubilee, if it comes..." At that point Don Javier interjected a filial protest, but Don Alvaro went right on. "And if not," he said, "then I'll celebrate it in heaven. Wherever God wants. It's more comfortable to go—too comfortable. I want whatever the Lord wants." Then he spoke about the importance of faithfully fulfilling the duties of each present moment, of generously putting into practice the founder's advice "Age quod agis" (Do what you do).

Just before his eightieth birthday, in a letter written to the centers of the Prelature on February 1, 1994, Don Alvaro described himself as being, in relation to God, "like a poor little beggar with empty hands." He then made this request of his daughters and sons: "I beg you not to leave me without the charity of your daily prayer for me and for my intentions!"

At the same time, both for his eightieth birthday and for his priestly golden jubilee the following June, he expected from the faithful of the Prelature this meaningful gift: a rejuvenation of their desire for personal holiness and of their apostolic zeal.

In March he wrote to his daughters and sons these touching words: "I beg you that when you pray for me, you ask God to grant me more abundantly each day that wisdom of heart and mind which is the essence of a true zeal for

holiness. Ask him to grant that the desires to please him
which fill my heart, and which by his grace I try to renew
many times each day, may be sparks burning with his love—
a love which will burn away all my wretchedness, purify
me, and set me more and more aflame with the yearning to
become fully united to my God and to make him known to
all his creatures."

On March 11, 1994, his last birthday, he celebrated Mass
in the prelatic church of Our Lady of Peace. On this occasion
only his daughters were present, and he gave them a short
homily which was a summary of his life. I present it now, in
its entirety, as a summary of everything I have tried to
communicate in this book.

"My daughters, I shall say just a few words so that you
can help me give thanks to God.

"For some time now, I have been preparing myself for
this day. As always, I have tried to follow in the footsteps of
our Father. I feel the need to become ever more united with
our holy founder as I contemplate with ever greater depth his
lovable self and his dedication to his daughters and sons of all
times. And I want to respond to the many inspirations which
I have received from his life. I know that by loving our Father
and uniting myself with his intentions, I become more united
with the Blessed Trinity. I advise you to do the same.

"I remember as if it were happening right now how
our Father prepared himself to turn seventy. For several
months before, besides giving much thanks to God, he asked
our Lord to make him smaller inside so that he could take
shelter in the lap of Holy Mary, next to Jesus. Our Lord
amply heeded that request. We ourselves are witnesses of
how our Father kept making more and more progress along
the path of spiritual childhood, especially during the last
years of his life.

"On his seventieth birthday, January 9, 1972, with that
good humor which concealed the intimacy of his relationship

with God, he declared that he was only *seven* years old. He had told the zero to get lost, he said, and now there remained only the seven. He didn't want to get any older than that, he explained, because after the age of seven, children start losing their simplicity. Our Father wanted to be always a very small child in relation to God.

"By God's goodness, I today complete eighty years of life. I could not begin to name all the marvels I have seen in all these years. I have received countless gifts from God, and many, many caresses from my Mother the Blessed Virgin. It is only natural that today, in a very special way, my heart should be overflowing with gratitude and that I should ask all my daughters, and all my sons, to accompany me in my giving of thanks.

"I thank God for giving me the gift of life, and for having me be born into a Christian family in which I could learn to love the Blessed Virgin as my Mother and God as my Father. I thank him also for the upbringing which I received from my parents—an upbringing in true piety, not its caricature. This prepared me for that providential meeting with our dearly beloved founder which would set the course of my life. I was then twenty-one years old. From that day in July 1935, how many proofs of God's goodness I have received! My vocation to the Work, my getting my formation from our Father himself, and, later on, those months during the civil war (and very hard times they were!) in which, by a special divine plan, the Lord gave me the gift of living very close to the founder, of being a witness to his sanctity, to his union with God... Then, so much time—so much!—of being constantly at his side, like a shadow which never leaves the body. And my ordination as a priest, nearly fifty years ago...

"The good things I owe to God, my daughters, are incalculable. Eighty years are a lot. But they're also very few, because—I'm not trying to sound humble, I'm just telling you the simple truth—I stand here empty-handed, incapable of repaying my Lord and my Mother the Blessed Virgin for such generosity... Do you understand why I need your prayers, your acts of thanksgiving, your fidelity, your cheerfulness?

"Thank you, Lord! Forgive me for all the times I have failed to respond as I should, and help me more. And you, my daughters, pray that I may learn to fill up the gaps in my life by putting a lot of love into everything. Today, in addition to working up in myself a sincere and joyful contrition, I resolve to say with more zest than ever, 'Nunc coepi!' (I begin now!), which was our Father's motto. Yes, right now I shall begin again, with God's help, to travel along the path of holiness, the path which leads to Love, with a new litheness—a litheness which your prayers will gain for me. Don't leave me alone! I need you all, each and every one of you! I need your loyalty, your fidelity to your vocation. I need your constant prayer. I need your work, well completed and done with love. I need you to bring me more daughters and more sons—more vocations, and more perseverance!— as a result of your ceaseless apostolate.

"In conclusion, I will say this. In my heart, thanks to God and to the intercession of our Father, the fire of love is burning vigorously. For this reason I feel very young, and I really am. Also I feel, with a holy pride, very much a child of our founder—and I want all of you to feel the same. A youthfulness in terms of years is something merely physiological, and it has no more importance than that. What really matters is interior youthfulness. That's what all daughters and sons of God in Opus Dei have and always must have: the youthfulness of someone who is in love—in love with God—and who makes an ongoing effort to grow in that love.

"*Ad Deum qui laetificat iuventutem meam!* To God, who gives joy to my youth! So that we can grow every day in that youthfulness of spirit and heart, let us go to the altar of God, to the Blessed Eucharist, very well disposed. Led by the hand by the Blessed Virgin and Saint Joseph, and wholeheartedly having recourse to the intercession of our dearly beloved and holy founder, Blessed Josemaría, let us seek intimacy and union with that God who is our Good and our Love. Let me make a suggestion to you, using words that our Father spoke in this very same place at the end of Mass on one of his birthdays. 'Receive Communion hungrily, every day, even if you do not feel like it, even if you can't feel anything. Tell Jesus that you want to show him your love and your faith, since he is truly present—body and blood, soul and divinity—in the host.' Our founder said we should confide to Jesus 'that we love him truly, and that we are grateful to him for staying with us.' He then gave this advice: 'Tell him all this with a youthful heart—a heart full of enthusiasm, a heart full of love.'

"My daughters, may God bless you."